# STEINBECK'S UNEASY AMERICA

# STEINBECK'S UNEASY AMERICA

## REREADING *TRAVELS WITH CHARLEY*

EDITED BY
**BARBARA A. HEAVILIN** AND
**SUSAN SHILLINGLAW**

THE UNIVERSITY OF ALABAMA PRESS
TUSCALOOSA

The University of Alabama Press
Tuscaloosa, Alabama 35487-0380
uapress.ua.edu

Copyright © 2025 by the University of Alabama Press
All rights reserved.

Inquiries about reproducing material from this work should be addressed to the University of Alabama Press.

Typeface: Adobe Caslon Pro

Cover image: John Steinbeck and Charley; courtesy of the Martha Heasley Cox Center for Steinbeck Studies, San Jose State University
Cover design: Sandy Turner Jr.

Permission to quote from the *Travels with Charley* autograph manuscript (1961) is granted by the Steinbeck estate and the Morgan Library and Museum, MA 2199. Gift; John Steinbeck; 1962. (Autograph manuscript in pen and pencil, written on yellow pad paper, loose ledger leaves, and in a bound ledger, ca. 1961, complete manuscript.)

Permission to quote from the *Travels with Charley* typescript (1961) is granted by the Steinbeck estate and the Morgan Library and Museum, MA 2470. Gift of Mr. Steinbeck, 1965. (Corrected typescript, [1961], complete manuscript.)

"Steinbeck Laughing: *Travels with Charley* as American Picaresque" by Carter Davis Johnson was originally published in *Steinbeck Review* 18, no. 2 (Fall 2021): 149–61. Used with permission from Penn State University Press.

Cataloging-in-Publication data is available from the Library of Congress.
ISBN: 978-0-8173-2219-9 (cloth)
ISBN: 978-0-8173-6181-5 (paper)
E-ISBN: 978-0-8173-9539-1

Frontispiece: Artist and illustrator Don Freeman created this map for the first edition of *Travels with Charley in Search of America*, Viking Press, 1962. Used with permission from Roy Freeman.

To the Charleys of the world, who help keep us sane.

And to Jack Benson (1930–2023) who navigated highways that many of us have followed, doggedly.

# Contents

List of Figures  xi

Foreword: About This Volume
    Robert DeMott  xiii

Acknowledgments  xxi

### PART I. A QUESTION OF GENRE

1. *Travels with Charley* as Autofiction
    Jay Parini  3

2. Histories of the Future: *Travels with Charley* and the Culture of the Cold War
    Gavin Jones  9

3. "Travels with Charley": A Mongrel Manuscript
    Susan Shillinglaw  28

4. Myth and Observation: The Dual Axes of *Travels with Charley*
    Charles Etheridge  50

5. Steinbeck Laughing: *Travels with Charley* as American Picaresque
    Carter Davis Johnson  65

6. Operation Windmills: *Travels with Charley* and *Don Quixote*
    William P. Childers  76

### PART II. *TRAVELS WITH CHARLEY* AS JEREMIAD: 1960S AMERICA AND TODAY

7. Steinbeck and the "Longue Durée" of Deep Time in *Travels with Charley*
    Barbara A. Heavilin  107

8. Of Hurricanes and Hope: *Travels with Charley* and the Crises of Our Times
    Kathleen Hicks  123

9. Travels with John Steinbeck in Search of "True Things"
   BRIAN RAILSBACK   138

10. *Travels with Charley* as a Space for Cross-Cultural Relationality
    DANICA ČERČE   154

## PART III. CONTEMPLATING AMERICA: *TRAVELS WITH CHARLEY* AS ROAD TEXT

11. John Steinbeck and R. K. Narayan in Search of America
    NICHOLAS P. TAYLOR   165

12. Inspiring *Travels with Charley*: John Steinbeck and the Millennial Multitiered Quest
    CECILIA DONOHUE   178

13. "Takin' on Texas" in *Travels with Charley*
    MIMI R. GLADSTEIN   193

14. Texas Tales and Beyond: A Niece Recalls
    DONALD V. COERS INTERVIEWING SALLY S. KLEBERG; SUSAN SHILLINGLAW, EDITOR   201

Works Cited   223

Contributors   233

Index   237

# Figures

Frontispiece  v

1. Steinbeck in Navy hat  xiii

2. Steinbeck's hexagonal writing house in Sag Harbor  8

3. Steinbeck and Bob Berry at the Sag Harbor Old Whalers Festival, 1964  20

4. Charley in Sag Harbor  41

5. Postcard Steinbeck wrote to Jack Ramsey from Chicago, postmarked October 6, 1960  54

6. Steinbeck laughing  66

7. Steinbeck in Joyous Garde  125

8. Jack Ramsey and Steinbeck looking at Rocinante  167

9. Elaine and John Steinbeck  201

# Foreword

## About This Volume

ROBERT DeMOTT

Figure 1: Steinbeck in Navy hat. Brad Bennett collection (grandson of Jack and Daga Ramsey, Steinbeck's Sag Harbor neighbors), Courtesy of the Martha Heasley Cox Center for Steinbeck Studies at San Jose State University.

Here at last, after sixty years, thanks to the determined efforts of coeditors Barbara Heavilin and Susan Shillinglaw, we have an individual critical anthology devoted solely to John Steinbeck's wildly popular *Travels with Charley in Search of America* (1962).[1] Judging from the impressive range and depth of the critical essays in this collection, the contributing scholars have found a level of intellectual kinship with Steinbeck's book that not only bodes well for future Steinbeck studies but also hits an entirely new level of engagement. *Travels with Charley* has never been so well served.

This new scholarly attention has a great deal to do with the fact that *Travels with Charley* is written in a more personal narrative register than many of Steinbeck's earlier books and invites a wide range of contemporary critical methods to understand its many levels of achievement. The text is marked by a pliable, ad hoc form; an inviting but somewhat anxious personal voice; and an insightful and often unflinching commentary on a wide range of topics of interest to Americans then and now, from society to environment to race. It is a book that sums up a past American era but speaks loudly to our own age as well. All of which, taken together, is especially appealing to contemporary scholars in these genre-bending times and raises deliciously complicated questions about Steinbeck's self-conscious employment of expressive writing and his melding of nonfictional and fictional techniques.

In fact, Penguin Random House no longer markets *Travels with Charley* as nonfiction, as it once did. We should not be surprised; anyone who pays attention to Steinbeck's career in letters would probably have already noticed that *Travels* was only partly nonfiction in the first place. Steinbeck always had a contested relationship with realistic representation, and his road letters to his wife Elaine from that period and the excised portions of the *Travels* manuscript show numerous authorial inner debates about the fraught task of writing realistic truth. "A writer must so rearrange reality so that it will seem reasonably real to the reader," he muses in the manuscript. "There's a sentence for you—reasonably real to the reader. . . . A thing's happening doesn't make it seem real, sometimes quite opposite" (Steinbeck 1961, 145). *Travels with Charley* was never strictly documentary journalism; rather, it benefited from elements of both nonfiction and fiction, mixed portions of reality and imagination, conjoined strains of objective experience and poetic truth. Better to call it something else, something in between: fictive travelogue is one possibility. Where Steinbeck is concerned, paradox and irony frequently offer the most accommodating views of his work.

Which is to say that the line between fact and fiction is always blurry and becomes a contested ground the moment pen is set to paper. Language, David Shields reminds us in *Reality Hunger: A Manifesto*, is a writer's true realistic determinant (2010, 65–66). Language takes us in directions that experience and memory (the latter is inherently flawed and partial) by themselves cannot, at which point the best one can do is hold on for the ride and follow the dictates of words wherever they lead. Vibrant tension is evident in most belated, retrospective accounts of experience, including Steinbeck's.

*Travels with Charley* is an ambitious tale about a harried, tired, reclusive, and somewhat cranky and disillusioned writer out to rediscover his lost sense of America and redeem his receding, aged manhood. It proved to be a more difficult and perplexing project than he initially realized. Achieving the "reasonably real" came not on the road but after the journey was done. The shifting tension among reality, desire, memory, and imagination suggests that literal facticity—which sometimes occludes density and texture and nuance—is a starting point rather than an end result. "Surely," Steinbeck told Carlton Sheffield in 1964, "the fictionalizing and day dreaming and self aggrandizement as well as the self attacks are as much a part of reality as far as the writing is concerned as the facts are. And even the facts have a chameleon tendency after a passage of time" (Steinbeck 1975, 798). It is possible to have all the facts in hand and still miss the point, still shoot wide of the story mark. For Steinbeck, the retrospective story—not a verifiable collection of indisputable facts—*was* the goal in his creation of "something entirely new," as biographer Jackson J. Benson (1984, 864) describes the work.

The lively, informed essays collected here open up a critical conversation on *Travels with Charley* in legitimate, diverse, and illuminating ways. At every turn, the contributors to this volume bring fresh insights, inspired critical methods, and plain common sense to bear. The essays constellate themselves around three major topics: genre, jeremiad, and road text. There is unavoidable overlap and cross referentiality in these pieces, but as a whole the result is a long overdue assessment of one of John Steinbeck's signature texts that promises to carry us well beyond the proliferating one-sided, reductive views of the writer and his work.

In the opening section devoted to discussions of genre and form, six scholars address the related, all-important distinctions between nonfiction and fiction, the performative elements of Steinbeck's authorial stance, and the epistemological tenor of his interior self-reflexive musings, all of which reveal his tendency toward experimental postmodernist strategies. Coeditor Susan Shillinglaw sets the tone of engagement when she lifts the veil on Steinbeck's creativity and offers the first-ever extended account of his elusive original manuscript version of *Travels*. In doing so Shillinglaw provides an invaluable baseline introduction to and textual map of his "exploratory manuscript," which she claims, proves more powerful in some aspects than the published version. Her essay is a stark reminder of the value to be found in Steinbeck's archival manuscripts, which have often been too cavalierly dismissed, ignored, or neglected. In the search for truth, Steinbeck, it seems, can always teach us something of value.

Jay Parini, Gavin Jones, and Carter Johnson address the central, contested questions of form and genre head-on. Each brings a wealth of critical insight and heightened contextual awareness to Steinbeck's mixing of nonfictional form and fictional strategies. Jones's richly inflected comments on Steinbeck's attunement to "the fictionality of the real" are especially relevant and take us seamlessly into the dense Cold War cultural and sociological background behind *Travels*, illuminating how Steinbeck responded to historical and cultural determinants of his era. Jones's skillful reading of a number of contemporary tropes and images Steinbeck employs in *Travels* is especially nuanced and rewarding and reminds us he was a writer in and of his times in multiple ways. Among "Steinbeck's great talents," Jones says, "was his ability to intuit the emergent, to serve as historian of events and processes just beginning to take shape, before they have fully jelled."

Equally instructive is Parini's belief that Steinbeck was a pioneer in writing "autofiction," a type of personally inflected blend of autobiography, memory, and fiction that Steinbeck found congenial to his artistic temperament in his later years. "Much of the emotional travel in the book," Parini claims, "took place in Steinbeck's hexagonal study in Sag Harbor, where he soon enough returned to his desk to write his account, basing the story partly on notes and letters but hugely on what he could recall." Johnson reads *Travels* from the thematic perspective of the picaresque, the archetypal episodic comic narrative pattern, and finds intriguing parallels with Royall Tyler's early nineteenth-century novel, *The Algernine Captive*. The "convergence of fact and fiction is a fundamental attribute of the picaresque," he suggests, just as "social commentary is a fundamental purpose of the picaresque"—two interlocking strains that help explain Steinbeck's efforts in *Travels with Charley*.

Similarly, two other contributors delve into aspects of intellectual and creative background as pathways into treating matters of form, style, and genre. Charles Etheridge and William Childers explore the presence of influential writers and texts on the literary fabric of *Travels*. Steinbeck—a self-admitted "shameless magpie . . . picking up anything shiny that comes my way" (Steinbeck 1975, 95)—rarely wrote in a vacuum, and so it should come as no surprise that he sometimes left clues as to who his favored predecessors were. With scholarly gusto and impeccable precision, Childers traces Steinbeck's considerable and often remarked-upon attention to Spanish novelist Miguel de Cervantes Saavedra's *Don Quixote*, not only in *Travels* but in other published and unpublished Steinbeck texts, especially the unfinished "Don Keehan, the Marshall of Manchon." "Since the mid-1940's," Childers writes, "*Don Quixote* has been a constant presence in Steinbeck's reading and writing life." His essay is a reminder that, like Herman Melville, Steinbeck often read to write. Etheridge understands that dynamic, too. He unpacks some mythic underpinnings of questing in the making of *Travels* and astutely calls attention to the presence of Cervantes, as well as to English essayist Joseph Addison, for whom Steinbeck expressed significant admiration. Etheridge does not stop there, however, but carries his discussion into the realm of popular twentieth-century nonprint media current in Steinbeck's time. Steinbeck's recognition "that nonprint media are in the process of changing the way observation and reportage are transmitted and recorded is an underappreciated aspect of *Travels with Charley*," Ethridge notes. His attention to these elements helps contextualize the dissonant strain of the travelogue's closing section.

Part 2 of this valuable collection shifts gears to focus on the nature of the jeremiad, an age-old mournful complaint or lamentation regarding social conditions of a given era. The further Steinbeck journeys, the more *Travels with Charley* builds on a long list of related contemporary woes to be addressed, acknowledged, and heeded, if not rectified. In one of the most poignant, searching pieces here, coeditor Barbara A. Heavilin applies sophisticated critical concepts of "deep time" and "long duration" to *Travels* and finds remarkable resonances in its global temporality and spatiality. Steinbeck, she believes, creates "a layered perspective that helps readers understand not only Steinbeck's era but our own." In other words, Steinbeck, sage-like, prophesies across time as we seek an equitable global civic order in which hopefulness (and more) might still be attainable. Such a "temporal and spatial perspective provides a different way of seeing ourselves in the light of other ages, other countries, other backgrounds," she writes. Kathleen Hicks, too, muses on the concept of hope throughout her sobering essay. She puts her finger on the pronounced strain of pensive interiority in *Travels* when she says it "is a book about thinking." Thinking, musing, reflecting, contemplating, criticizing, and lamenting were all ways Steinbeck dealt with the hurricane storm of changes in midcentury America. His era's "nuclear threats, unbridled consumption, environmental destruction, divisive politics, and racism" have morphed, Hicks states, into "the most critical problems facing America, and the world, today."

Several chapters address the slippery, topsy-turvy nature of truth, an especially relevant topic in our current fractious, divisive political climate. Brian Railsback sets the tone when he avers that *Travels* and Steinbeck's later essays in *America and Americans* "are as relevant and essential to understanding Post-Truth USA as any he ever wrote." Railsback finds *Travels* is "the physical manifestation—the book-length metaphor—of his quest for what is true and his realization that one cannot find it: as it emerges from this travelogue, truth for the individual is a process, never a conclusion." Slovenian scholar

Danica Čerče, writing from an international point of view, reminds us that Steinbeck "may not reach firm conclusions, but nevertheless he compels us to face up to and confront the actions that have institutionalized group identity" and repressive social structures in America. *Travels* "never ceased to denounce any kind of injustice and tyranny," she adds. Steinbeck's speaking truth to power is, was, and always will be one of the chief reasons we keep reading him.

The final section of this collection considers *Travels with Charley* as a road text, a travel adventure, and a literary influencer. One essay takes us down the highway in directions that look beyond Steinbeck's iconic book. Veteran Steinbeck commentator Mimi Reisel Gladstein interrogates the author's portrayal of Texas, her home state, and, as with so many other contributors to this volume, finds much to comment upon in *Travels* that has escaped prior critical notice or escaped deep analysis.

Other scholars pay attention to works that might have been influenced by or share similarities with Steinbeck's book. Cecelia Donohue establishes that for decades, *Travels* "has inspired a host of writers who have published narratives of their pet-accompanied trips" around the United States. She nimbly focuses on Jessica Bruder's book *Nomadland* as a cross between *Travels with Charley* and *The Harvest Gypsies* (1988), Steinbeck's Depression-era journalism about the plight of migrant workers in California. "Bruder adds a new dimension to the Steinbeck travel template," she concludes. Novelist and former San Jose State University Steinbeck Center director Nick Taylor creates some needful sparks by comparing *Travels* with Indian writer R. K. Narayan's contemporaneous *My Dateless Diary: An American Journey* and asks, "Were a foreigner's 'stored pictures' of the *Travels with Charley* route different from Steinbeck's? If so, how were they different and how should we explain the difference?" Take a deep dive into this stellar collection to find answers to those questions and to many other related issues and concerns.

Despite the work's appealing, easygoing conversational style, John Steinbeck struggled with the writing of *Travels with Charley* and found it a more difficult task than he had originally hoped. Under what he called the "whip of duty" (Steinbeck 1975, 700) caused by commercial publishing expectations, pressures, and demands, he never found the sure-handed narrative line that we associate with his best work. The jangly, stop-and-start nature of the book, its alternately joyous and disillusioned voice, and its somber summary belief that a journey may be over and completed before the traveler returns home all underscore his graphic mid-1961 admission to Viking Press editor Pascal Covici that his "little book of ambulatory memoirs staggers along"

and that it is "a formless, shapeless, aimless thing and it is even pointless" (Steinbeck 1975, 702). But Steinbeck was often his own harshest critic and frequently doubted his own talent, whether he was talking about *The Grapes of Wrath*, *The Wayward Bus*, or *Travels with Charley*. Steinbeck's despairing sense of America's "haunting decay" overrode other technical concerns and fueled his confession to Covici that *Travels* was "haphazard," and "pointless—ant hill activity" (Steinbeck 1975, 702–3).

Now, six decades later in a more forgiving and tolerant literary climate, we find in *Travels with Charley*'s hybrid, loose-limbed form, candid back-and-forth cultural commentary, and humorous interspecies dialogue between a man and his beloved dog a kind of forward-looking contemporary attitude of "sharpest realism" that speaks pointedly to our times (Steinbeck 1975, 702). Which is to say that the pointlessness John Steinbeck decried is exactly the point; the aimlessness, too, is a fitting perceptual trope for our beleaguered, chaotic times. Steinbeck's uncertainty and hesitation about being able to express the whole truth about America is precisely the bone-honest, sharply realistic lesson to be learned and has a hard, fierce beauty of its own. Gilding the lily was not his habit.

These lively essays demonstrate the multilayered dimensionality and powerful, prophetic, and still relevant, messaging of *Travels with Charley* and prove, I suspect, that we turn to Steinbeck's book for more reasons than we can probably count: information, enlightenment, pleasure, engagement, knowledge, insight, curiosity, inspiration. "We find after years of struggle that we do not take a trip; a trip takes us," Steinbeck announces (1997, 3). There are as many versions of Steinbeck's trip represented in this collection as there are contributors. The struggles never cease, the road still winds, but the trips go on, leading us where they will. We take from *Travels* as much as we are able to bring to bear from our own lives, perspectives, and warps. As Steinbeck wrote to his friend Peter Benchley, "The story goes on and leaves the writer behind, for no story is ever done" (Steinbeck 1975, 529). That is a good—perhaps even blessed—thing, I believe, and as much as we can ask of any book that touches us deeply. In the end, the traveler always comes home.[1]

## Note

1. Over the years Steinbeck's book has been published under several versions of the title, including ones that treat *In Search of America* as a separate subtitle or omit it altogether. The work is generally known as *Travels with Charley*, which is how most of the chapters in this book refer to it most of the time.

# Acknowledgments

*Steinbeck's Uneasy America: Rereading "Travels with Charley"* was inspired by a passage in Jackson J. Benson's definitive biography, *The True Adventures of John Steinbeck, Writer*. About the inception of *Travels with Charley*, Benson writes, "This period of thought and self-examination, constant self-questioning, did, as subsequent events were to show, mark a dramatic turn in his career. He was able to turn aside from the indecision, constant self-questioning, and lack of direction of the previous decade. His determination was not so much to reach out for something entirely new—although with both *Winter* and *Charley* he did achieve precisely that—but to write, to produce and not torture himself so much with possible consequences." (864)

Benson's astute assertion that in *Winter* and *Charley* Steinbeck did indeed create "something entirely new" was intriguing. Following through on his observation, I found several top Steinbeck scholars interested in this topic who agreed to submit a chapter to a book; invited Susan Shillinglaw to serve as coeditor (a most fortunate choice); and subsequently presented a book proposal to the University of Alabama Press.
—Barbara A. Heavilin

This project has been a joy, from start to finish—and not often can one say that about editing. Thank you, contributors, for your patience and assistance. My own contribution to this project would not have been possible without the incredible assistance of Philip S. Palmer, the Robert H. Taylor Curator and Department Head, Literary and Historical Manuscripts and Archives, at the Morgan Library and Museum. During COVID, travel to New York City and the rich archives at the Morgan wasn't possible. Philip photographed pages of the "Charley" manuscript and emailed them to me, chunk by chunk, so I could write my essay. His steadiness of purpose and generosity of spirit made my work possible. Archivists are indispensable for scholars, of course—heroic in this instance.
—Susan Shillinglaw

# STEINBECK'S UNEASY AMERICA

# Part I

# A QUESTION OF GENRE

# 1

## *Travels with Charley* as Autofiction

### Jay Parini

I've admired *Travels with Charley in Search of America* for many decades, mostly because of its tone, which is suffused with irony and charm. Steinbeck takes a nostalgic and sometimes harsh look at America, conjuring a whole continent and its many contradictions in a narrative that is as much a waking dream as a travelogue, not unlike the sleeping dog Charley, who once "had a dream so violent that he awakened me," the author tells us. "His legs jerked in the motions of running and he made little yipping cries. Perhaps he dreamed he chased some gigantic rabbit and couldn't quite catch it. Or maybe in his dream something chased him" (Steinbeck 1997, 112–13). This note of whimsicality is never far from the pages of the story.

Steinbeck had a clear sense of what he hoped to accomplish on this highly plotted journey. As he wrote to a friend before taking off, he hoped to learn about his country once again: "I've lost the flavor and taste and sound of it." So he set out to taste and listen. He also noted to his friend that "Elaine will join me occasionally," referring to his wife, Elaine Steinbeck; he added that he had hoped he could go alone, so he could "look and listen" without disturbance (Steinbeck 1975, 666–67).

Elaine, who tended to hover over her husband in his later years when his health began to fade, naturally worried about his going on such a long trip. She would not have let her beloved husband die on the road by himself; indeed, she determined to drop in as often as she could. Owing to research by Bill Steigerwald (2013), we now understand the extent to which Elaine stuck invisibly by her husband's side. "Steinbeck was gone from New York for a total of about 75 days," he writes. "On about 45 days he traveled with, stayed with and slept with his beloved wife, Elaine, in the finest hotels, motels and resorts in America, in family homes, and at a Texas millionaire's cattle ranch near Amarillo." The question is: Does this matter?

I doubt it does. *Travels* fits more comfortably into the genre of fiction or "autofiction" than reportage, and Steigerwald himself notes that Steinbeck admits that "he wasn't trying to write a travelogue here or do real journalism." I would argue, in fact, that Steinbeck was a pioneer, plunging into the world of autofiction with abandon, sensing instinctively the genre's parameters. In his own way, he was anticipating a type of writing that would emerge explicitly as a genre only in the seventies, in France, where writers like Serge Dubrowsky and Margarite Duras "wrote fiction in which characters share names and characteristics with their authors," as Rebecca van Laer notes in "How We Read Autofiction"—a fine survey of contemporary thinking about this hybrid genre (2018), which has become one of the go-to places for experimental writing in recent years, with important works by such writers as Rachel Cusk and Karl Ove Knausgård.

Autofiction, generally speaking, refers to texts that blur the lines between autobiography and fiction. One has often seen novels that refer explicitly to the author's life experience. How else could one read James Joyce's *A Portrait of an Artist as a Young Man*, for example, or *Invisible Man* by Ralph Ellison? But autofiction comes at this from the opposite direction, by seeming to be nonfiction, using the author's real name, referring to obviously "real" events, presenting dialogue that looks and sounds like something that has emerged from the author's notes. Again, we're thrown back to having to distinguish between fact and fiction.

So what is a fact? "The English are always degrading truths into facts," quipped Oscar Wilde in "A Few Maxims for the Instruction of the Over-Educated" (1894). The term goes back to *factum*, a Latin word meaning "an event, an occurrence." The connotation of the term as something that has a strict and immoveable presence in the world is fairly modern. One thinks, for example, of Thomas Gradgrind, the headmaster in Charles Dickens's *Hard Times*, who regarded his pupils as pitchers, each of whom must be filled with facts. "Fact, facts, facts!" he shouted. Nevertheless, facts, even lifeless ones, may be difficult to access. Alternatively, they can possess a mysterious reality of their own. Arthur Conan Doyle's Sherlock Holmes notes in "The Boscombe Valley Mystery" that "there is nothing more deceptive than an obvious fact." That is, one can know every external fact about a person or a place and not understand the soul of that person or the spirit of that place. Names and dates alone tell us very little. It takes a great deal of imaginative work—often the work of "fiction"—to bring facts to life.

It's probably worth noting that fiction is, as much as anything, a method used in the excavation of reality. The word itself comes from the Latin *fingere* or *fictio*—meaning "to shape." That is, one gathers the known or "agreed up" facts and arranges them in a particular order. This means, in effect, that one suppresses certain things and amplifies others. In many languages—Hebrew, for instance—few distinctions are made between fictional and nonfictional narratives that fall into the category of nonfiction and narratives that fall into the category of fiction. In Israel, novels and historical works will be found on the same bookshelf of any Israeli bookseller, under a category called *siporet*. What matters is that both styles of book are telling stories.

Steinbeck was, in the thirties, the creator of famously realistic fictions. His great California stories and novels written during and just after the Great Depression offer a seemingly "true" picture of life in that part of the world, which the author knew so well, invoking its flora and fauna with astonishing fidelity to place, creating speech patterns that sound, at least to the outsider, accurate. But a mythic element underlies most of Steinbeck's best fiction, giving it shape and meaning, as in *The Grapes of Wrath*, where the journey—perhaps the most classic myth—elevates members of the Joad family to an allegorical level, creating a sense of timelessness, although the actual story itself is both road- and time-bound. The brilliance of Steinbeck in this novel lies in the writer's careful manipulation of the realistic and mythic elements, which blend in so many ways that this distinction seems to fall away.

*Travels with Charley* invites us to think about the realistic frame of the story, which takes place in "real" historical time, in 1960, on the eve of an important national election. What better time to take the pulse of the nation by taking the road in a van named after Rocinante, the lazy horse in *Don Quixote*. The mere act of naming it in this fashion shows that Steinbeck was fully aware of the many levels on which he hoped to write, creating a kind of road novel in the tradition of Cervantes. And from the outset we get the animated storm of Hurricane Donna: "The wind struck on the moment we were told it would, and ripped the water like a black sheet. It hammered like a fist. The whole top of an oak tree crashed down, grazing the cottage where we watched" (11). One can't know, or care, whether or not this oak tree—the symbol of stability and home (as in *The Odyssey*, for instance)—really existed. Steinbeck is working in his mythic vein here, as a novelist, setting the scene, creating an obstacle that must be overcome. As a novelist, he did so instinctively, not having to pause to think about it any more than world-class tennis players have to pause to think about the position of their feet or elbows before hitting a hard backhand over the net.

In a similar vein, Steinbeck presents himself as racing toward the bay to rescue his boat, which is tied offshore; he struggles all the while to keep his balance in the wind. Could anything be more symbolic—a man at odds with nature, with the concrete physical world, even the world of his body? The elements crush against him, as his wife calls helplessly after him: "Stop, John!" But, as Steinbeck describes it, he barrels forward, leaps into the water, fights his way through waves to the boat. He cuts it loose and climbs aboard. The motor starts at a touch, and the author pilots the craft some hundred yards into the bay, where he drops anchor in safer waters. "Well, there I was," he writes, "a hundred yards offshore with Donna baying over me like a pack of white-whiskered hounds" (Steinbeck 1997, 13). In an even more unlikely act, he leaps into the sea again, hanging onto a branch, getting himself washed back up on shore, where Elaine and a neighbor wait in terror. Soon he's sitting at his kitchen table, whiskey in hand.

Who cares if this "really" happened? Fiction-makers work by allegory, by symbolic little nuggets of narrative that undergird and reinforce a larger story. And so Steinbeck, about to set off on this classic journey, which he calls "Operation Windmills," begins the work of tilting at windmills early in the tale. He signals to alert readers that he has entered the world of autofiction, where the actual facts of the case don't matter as much as the mythic import. The tone—the attitude of the writer toward the material—trumps the actual content. Steinbeck is getting himself into his "once upon a time" mode. He invites the reader to approach the material in a certain way, as any good novelist would do.

The journey west, what Mark Twain famously called "lighting out for the territory," is among the great American tropes. As Robert Frost says in "The Gift Outright," America is "a land vaguely realizing westward / But still unstoried, artless, unenhanced." And so one of the functions of Steinbeck's account is to enhance the nation's story through the artfulness of his writing. He seeks to associate himself with those who go into the wilderness by themselves to find meaning: Thoreau's time at Walden Pond might seem an obvious starting point. At least in the narrative of *Travels with Charley* (not so much in "reality," it seems), Steinbeck avoids population centers and national parks, preferring places that radiate a private sense of meaning.

He listens to strangers as he moves, ignoring his wife, who sits (perhaps) invisibly beside him. It's in the tradition of travel writers from Alexis de Tocqueville to Barry Lopez or V. S. Naipaul for the speaker/author to have a solitary aspect, allowing the journey into the interior to become a metaphor for diving into the self. It would have ruined Steinbeck's narrative to have Elaine talking about what happened or questioning what was said. Better to put her, as he does, on the telephone, or in letters home that he imagines will become the matter of his book.

One of the wonderful ironies of the text is that Steinbeck himself is returning home on the westward phase of his journey. California looms as the

Promised Land, much as it did for the Joad family in *The Grapes of Wrath*. Yet Steinbeck had by now become a kind of begrudging New Yorker. (Elaine worked on Broadway as a stage manager, and their social life reflected this: Steinbeck hung out with famous figures from musical theater, including Frank Loesser, Richard Rogers, and Oscar Hammerstein II.) He must have felt in his bones that, once he left California in the forties, he had abandoned a place of deep imaginative value for him. The sad truth is that none of his later writing quite matches the transfixing power of the early novels and stories. As he describes the scene in *Travels with Charley*, the return to Monterey was nothing less than melancholy. Near Cannery Row, the site of one of his memorable fictions, he discovers the John Steinbeck Theater. The past returns as parody.

The return journey moves through Texas, Elaine's home, and these scenes seem both relevant and terrifying to this day. Some of the best writing in the story are found here, even in the overall descriptions of Texas, a state that (Steinbeck says with coy irony) "has its own private history based on, but not limited by, facts" (229). There follows a stinging critique of the myth of the Alamo—still taken by many Texans as a story of heroism against all odds, as conveyed by the words "freedom" and "liberty." Steinbeck keeps the quotation marks there, well aware that in fact "Mexico had abolished slavery in 1829." The irony is obvious: these "brave" Texans were fighting to keep their slaves. Texas would have to be "liberated" from Mexico for non-Mexicans on the land to keep their slaves.

It's also in this latter part of the journey that we encounter the scene of white mothers jeering and spitting at a Black child and a white child who seek to integrate a school. Steinbeck notes, with a sharp twang, that these women were known in the popular press as the Cheerleaders, and the sight of their naked racism leaves the narrator with a feeling of "weary nausea" (195). When someone asks if he travels for pleasure, he says, "I was until today" (198). Picking up a weary Black hitchhiker on the road in Alabama, a few days later, he hears the deep frustration in the young man, who says of American progress toward equality, "It's too slow. It will take too long" (206).

Steinbeck knew, of course, that progress always comes slow, and it rarely occurs in a linear fashion. On the other hand, he would be quite astonished by how many setbacks there have been since he wrote *Travels*, and how racial tensions continue to pose a major obstacle in the way of realizing the American dream of equality for all. Needless to say, this autofictional account of a journey through the American landscape in the mid-twentieth century continues to challenge us, as does any useful mythic tale.

A myth is, of course, a story with deep contours of symbolic meaning, and Steinbeck's *Travels with Charley* benefits hugely from participating, however tangentially, in the genre of autofiction, which derives strength from the ability of the author to bend reality, to find the sources of meaning, to make a literal journey into a figurative one that spirals inward as it unravels outward. This is hardly journalism. It's just too well-shaped for that, hence its fictive element. The facts don't matter so much as their arrangement, their flow. And indeed, Steinbeck's ten-week journey has its own distinct timbre, its motion, its allegiances to truths that can't be found in reportage.

Much of the emotional travel in the book took place in Steinbeck's hexagonal study in Sag Harbor, where he soon enough returned to his desk to write his account, basing the story partly on notes and letters but largely on what he could recall. The work of memory is crucial here. As in most good autofictional narratives, invention creates memory: a fictive tapestry is assembled, one that of course draws on the hard reality of an actual journey—the names and dates, the places, the route numbers and concrete situations—but works beyond it, finding meaning in the narrative fringes, in the cloth of the tale itself, which the author cuts to suit his own purposes.

Figure 2: Steinbeck's hexagonal writing house in Sag Harbor. Photo by Susan Shillinglaw.

# 2

## Histories of the Future

### *Travels with Charley* and the Culture of the Cold War

GAVIN JONES

When Steinbeck virtually surfs ashore at the beginning of *Travels with Charley in Search of America* (1962), having rescued his boat from the might of Hurricane Donna, he begins his travelogue with a moment of emergence, of mastering the moment, of going with the flow. Steinbeck's subsequent trip across country in his camper van Rocinante is likewise a process of onward movement, in which "we do not take a trip, a trip takes us" (Steinbeck 1997, 3). To describe his journey, in which being lost is frequently preferred to mapped direction, Steinbeck self-consciously places it in a number of traditions, both fictional and historical. These range from Don Quixote's episodic travels in Miguel de Cervantes's 1605 novel, to the 1803–6 expedition of William Clark and Meriwether Lewis to the Northwest territory, to Alexis de Tocqueville's journey to and around the United States in the early 1830s, to the various travelers who, in their subsequent memoirs, sought to capture the "real" America during the ideological confusion of the Great Depression. Steinbeck's journey, with its central ethic of *vacilando*—going somewhere without caring if one gets there (50)—is continuous too with contemporary works from the decades following World War II, works in which travel offers the possibility of self-transformation and an escape from the mainstream, even as they echo the broader impact of automotive transport on society at large. Examples include Jack Kerouac's Beat classic, *On the Road* (1957), or Ken Kesey's journey with his Merry Pranksters—just a few years after Steinbeck's trip—to "turn on" a decrepit culture. With its emphasis on the details of travel as a process of self-discovery, and its ethic of care for the mechanical mode of transportation itself, *Travels with Charley* perhaps even lays the groundwork for Robert Pirsig's *Zen and the Art of Motorcycle Maintenance* (1974). Like Pirsig, Steinbeck was well-versed in Buddhist thinking due to his early friendship with Edward F. Ricketts, though the parallels are of a more general kind. But let us return to questions implied by all of these journeys. Where are we heading as a society and a culture? And how does our means of travel define our identity and our destiny?

As I have shown elsewhere (Jones 2021), one of Steinbeck's great talents was his ability to intuit the emergent, to serve as a historian of events and processes just beginning to take shape, before they have fully jelled. This essay proposes that *Travels with Charley* is a remarkable cultural document that both records and theorizes dominant patterns forming in American society during the early phases of the Cold War. Claims that much of *Travels with Charley* is "untrue" (Steigerwald 2012) not only state the obvious—the work is clearly a fictionalized autobiography—but they also miss the point: one of Steinbeck's major drives is to explore the fictionality of the real and to theorize the profound ways that media was determining the "truth" of cultural messages. Moreover, this interest in fictionality is merely one aspect of the society and culture that Steinbeck charts during a period that scholars term postmodernity. As we will see, *Travels with Charley* offers profound insights into the mindset of the Cold War; the rise of consumer culture; the spread of suburbanization; and the new personality of the white collar, corporate employee who rose to prominence in the 1950s. Steinbeck's travelogue is something of a primer in concepts central to postmodernism itself, concepts such as the "death of the author," the instability of signs, and the idea that all aspects of social life are constructed through performance. And finally, *Travels with Charley* provides significant insights into the nature of the human species and its interrelationship with nonhuman animals, even as it suggests some apocalyptic conclusions about the problem of race relations in the American South.

## Feeling the Cold War

Steinbeck's first encounter after his journey begins, with the submarine and the submariner he meets while crossing the Long Island Sound, sets the mood of the Cold War that reverberates throughout *Travels*. Unlike the German submarine that Steinbeck remembers from World War II, the American submarine embodies a threat that is now internal and unlocalized. Quite literally the submarine represents a submerged form of worry, an uncontrolled anxiety always present beneath the surface of consciousness. This feeling of paranoia—of unknown, unseen, and perhaps nonexistent threats crowding in on him (48)—surfaces periodically throughout the book, for example in the writer's "Twilight Zone" encounter with a deserted motel in New Hampshire (59). An apocalyptic mood of dislocation and radical doubt prevails. Yet the submariner, who comes from a "submarine family," sees matters differently. "Do you like to serve on them?" Steinbeck asks the young man about the submarine, to which he responds:

> "Sure I do. The pay's good and there's all kinds of—future."
> "Would you like to be down three months?"
> "You'd get used to it. The food's good and there's movies and—I'd like to go under the Pole, wouldn't you?"
> "I guess I would."
> "And there's movies and all kinds of—future." (19)

How does a person survive psychologically in the face of impending nuclear apocalypse? This simple and halting conversation between Steinbeck and the submariner embodies a new psychological paradigm that finds the answer in economic security ("pay's good"), mass culture ("there's movies"), and a vague sense of a future that's "not bad" (20). Rather than an enthusiastic idea of progress, the submariner possesses a feeling of hope that is just strong enough to sustain him, preventing a slip into the nihilism that Joseph Dewey (1990) associates with the "apocalyptic temper" found in the American novel of the nuclear age. Steinbeck feels "better and surer" (20) on witnessing this protective ideology forming to counter the paranoia of the nuclear age.

The second direct encounter with the culture of the Cold War occurs in Steinbeck's conversation with a New Hampshire farmer on whose land he camps for the night. When Steinbeck asks the farmer whether he had listened to the radio today, their talk turns to Nikita Khrushchev's presence at the United Nations. "About all the news talked about," says the farmer (25), was the moment when the Soviet leader allegedly removed his shoe and banged it on the table, in protest at allegations of Soviet civil rights abuses in Eastern Europe, made by a member of the Filipino delegation and dismissed by Khrushchev as accusations motivated by "American imperialism." It remains doubtful whether Khrushchev really did bang his shoe—the single photograph of the incident is a fake—and this is the point of the conversation with the farmer in *Travels*. The public sphere, comprising informed opinion and political discussion, has collapsed because knowledge itself has become entirely shaped by its containing media—for example, the potential for fakery in a photograph or the way the radio news fixates on the sensational moment. Marshall McLuhan was beginning to formulate his theories of media in the early 1960s, arguing that the technology of the media itself has primary importance in determining the meaning of the message it contains. This point is already implicit in Steinbeck's encounter with the farmer. In other words, it remains irrelevant whether Khrushchev banged his shoe or not: the media itself formed the message of Soviet strength and aggression.

Steinbeck's conversation with the farmer further explores the reason for this situation. If his grandfather knew things with certainty, then the farmer does not "even understand the formula that says nobody knows. We've got nothing to go on—got no way to think about things" beyond what we are told (26). The speed of technological change, the pace and pervasiveness of mass media has outstripped an ability to think critically, leading to an age of radical uncertainty and anxiety. Hence local speech-ways are disappearing because of the existence of new forms of communication: radio, TV, the interstate highways, the "high-tension line" (82–83). In *Understanding Media* (1964), McLuhan argues that media represent extensions of our humanness, remaking our senses and bodies, and that they possess the power to place us in a state of "narcissistic hypnosis" that prevents us from seeing the real nature of the medium itself. Accordingly, many of the conversations that Steinbeck overhears in New England diners early in his journey comprise "a series of laconic grunts" (28), not least because people seem hypnotized into emptiness by the monotonous songs played repeatedly on the radio, a medium that "takes the place of the old local newspaper" (28). The richness of the public sphere has been destroyed by a medium awash with the culture of advertising that is almost contentless in its claims. Advertisements for Florida real estate may verge on the postfactual. "But that didn't matter," writes Steinbeck, "the very name Florida carried the message of warmth and ease and comfort. It was irresistible" (29). The capacity for repetition built into the medium can convince listeners without the content of an actual message.

## Consumer Culture

As it progresses, Steinbeck's continuing journey moves us deeper into the consumer culture dominating Cold War American society. Returning to the ecological themes of earlier works such as *Sea of Cortez* (1941), Steinbeck describes a culture dominated by waste in an era of planned obsolescence: "American cities are like badger holes, ringed with trash—all of them—surrounded by piles of wrecked and rusting automobiles, and almost covered with rubbish. . . . I do wonder whether there will come a time when we can no longer afford our wastefulness—chemical wastes in the rivers, metal wastes everywhere, and atomic wastes buried deep in the earth or sunk at sea" (22). To oppose this narrative of entropy, Steinbeck invents an ingenious method of processing his own dirt that implicitly invokes the Cold War once more. Steinbeck creates his own washing machine from a large plastic garbage bucket that is loosely secured in Rocinante so that it jiggles and automatically washes his laundry as the vehicle moves along. The subtext here may be the famous "kitchen debate" between Nikita Khrushchev and Richard Nixon at the American National Exhibition in Moscow in 1959, the impromptu discussion between two leaders (Nixon was vice president at the time) about the relative virtues of capitalism and communism. A built-in washing machine in a model kitchen at the exhibition became a flashpoint for Nixon's claims about the affordability of American labor-saving devices and the dangers of competition between the two superpowers (Saffire 2009). Steinbeck's washing machine riffs on this idea. It may oppose consumerism in its homemade quality, yet still it celebrates American ingenuity, just as it is made out of *plastic* and hence is dependent on the forces it critiques. This was the era of plastic. The easily moldable, reproducible, expandable material enabled the rise of the superficial, plastic, consumer culture of the 1950s, even as it inspired the mass-produced Pop Art works of Andy Warhol and others.

*Travels* features extensive descriptions of this new society in which plastic pervades. This was the era of *containment*—the containment of communism on the one hand, but also the containment provided by Tupperware and other plastics that seem to coat everything Steinbeck encounters. When Steinbeck meets a waitress in Bangor, Maine, he finds that more than her apron is sponge-off plastic. "This vacant eye, listless hand, this damask cheek" were also "dusted like a doughnut with plastic powder" (46). Problematically, the female body comes to symbolize—like a plastic Barbie Doll, one of the first toys to be based around a TV advertising campaign in 1959—the vacuity of consumer culture embodied in the waitress's alleged emptiness. Steinbeck's motel room is likewise completely "done in plastics—the floors, the curtain, table tops of stainless burnless plastic, lamp shades of plastic," just as the restaurant was "all plastic too" (37). Returning to his room with a bottle of vodka, only to confront glasses sterilized and sealed in cellophane sacks, Steinbeck finds a way to escape through memories of a very different kind of experience: "I remember an old Arab in North Africa, a man whose hands had never felt water. He gave me mint tea in a glass so coated with use that it was opaque, but he handed me companionship . . . without any protection" (38). Echoing the contemporaneous thesis of the American critic Leslie Fiedler in *Love and Death in the American Novel* (1960), Steinbeck flees the despondency of a plasticized, feminized world of containment and protection to find an authentic interracial male bond far from American civilization. A little later in the narrative, when he meets a young but lonely "guardian of the lake" in northern Michigan, the figure of the female comes to embody the plasticity and the emptiness of consumer society once more. The young man shows Steinbeck a photograph of his wife "in a plastic shield in his wallet," a wife who looks like "the pictures in the magazines, a girl of products, home permanents, shampoos, rinses, skin conditioners" (86–87).

Echoing his earlier thoughts about the unplasticized "old Arab," Steinbeck reacts to this vision of superficiality by fishing with his male companion in an episode that ironically suggests the barriers to any easy escape from a media-saturated modernity. They fail to get a "message" to the fish below the surface (87), and Steinbeck flees this scene of failure as his mind wanders immediately to other kinds of messages—to telegrams and the now ubiquitous telephone, which has become more than a means of communication. His periodic telephone calls back to his wife in New York, Steinbeck observes, "reestablished my identity in time and space" (88). The means of communication does not merely dominate the message but creates identity itself. Steinbeck immediately follows this observation with the recognition that "the nature of the road describes the nature of the travel" (88), tying together roads and telephones as communication media with the power to determine what they contain, creating its meaning. In fact, Steinbeck's observations of media and containers of information in general—whether roads, telephones, novels, radio broadcasts, or plastic shields—are so numerous that they seem less like "extensions of man" (to use McLuhan's terminology) than endpoints in themselves, as if the plastic that coats everything has become so thick and opaque that we see only it, and not the reality or meaning it contains.

Steinbeck's description of the road, particularly the new interstate highway system that would bind the nation together into a network, is thus hardly the vision of freedom that it seemed to countercultural travelers in the 1950s and 1960s (the interstate system was first funded in 1956). Instead, it creates the feeling of being locked into a system, a grid with minimum as well as maximum speed limits. The road controls the attention of the drivers, determining their acts of reading, and it dominates the entire body with its demands of constant surveillance and tiny, unconscious movements that represent an enormous "output of energy, nervous and muscular" (73). Truckers are no longer the big-hearted heroes they were in *The Grapes of Wrath* (1939). Rather, they are a separate tribe of technocrats who possess a specialized language, cruising over the surface of a nation to which they do not belong (71–72). If driving is akin to automation, then the road is dependent on "no-places," on service stations and vending machines that reinforce the road as a self-referential and self-sufficient space rather than a means to travel to a specific place. Again, the medium is the message. Even when Steinbeck recognizes that the automatic nature of driving leaves a space for thought, his mind turns only to questions of land reclamation, building, and converting nature into products, as if he cannot escape the processes that led to roads in the first place (73).

## Suburbanization and the White-Collar Worker

The large-scale construction of a national road network that began in the late 1950s exacerbated other sociocultural changes, not least the rise of suburbia. Planned suburban developments increased rapidly, with prefabricated Levittowns bringing techniques of mass production into the home. As Kenneth T. Jackson (1985) puts it in his history of suburbanization, *Crabgrass Frontier*, suburbia "is a manifestation of such fundamental characteristics of American society as conspicuous consumption, a reliance upon the private automobile, upward mobility, the separation of the family nuclear units, the widening division between work and leisure, and the tendency toward racial and economic exclusiveness" (4). Early in *Travels*, when Steinbeck is still in Maine, we already sense that the countryside is emptying out. The existing locales of democratic culture—for example the cracker-barrel store in which an informed rural population gathered to express opinions and to form a national character—are being replaced by forms of mass culture located in the sprawling suburbs. As he follows US Route 90 into Michigan, Steinbeck's attention turns to an extreme form of suburban, mass-produced living: mobile homes, the "new things under the sun" that were springing up all across the nation (74). Steinbeck's long description of the world of mobile homes amounts to a mini-ethnography of a "whole way of life" (75), with its own lifestyle magazines selling gadgets and appliances that wire these homes directly into the capitalist economy. Centered on the television and enabled by the air conditioner, the mobile home brings comfort to the masses. These homes enable flexibility in a world of uncertainty, an "uneasy permanence" that allows for upward mobility and the acquisition of status through the purchasing of new models. Steinbeck dedicates a significant amount of narrative space to the young owner of a mobile home (in one of a number of somewhat stagey dialogues in *Travels*, whereby Steinbeck implicitly develops his theories), who attacks the oppressive idea of "roots." Steinbeck's deep sympathy for this new way of living—"I've never had a better nor more comfortable meal," as he puts it (78)—flies directly in the face of contemporaneous critiques of suburbanization, most famously Jane Jacobs's 1961 *The Death and Life of Great American Cities*. Jacobs idealized the vitality of city neighborhoods, with their sidewalks, neighborhoods where people can put down roots and participate in communal life: precisely the living in tenement blocks that our young mobile-homeowner wants to escape.

Here we might place Steinbeck's work in conversation with an earlier journey to which it implicitly refers, Alexis de Tocqueville's travels through the young United States that would become the basis for his study of the national character, *Democracy in America* (1835). Tocqueville discovered an all-pervasive and active restlessness in the America he confronted, a superabundant force that Steinbeck again glimpses in the energetic Midwest. For Tocqueville, however, this "restlessness of heart" bred discontent because the failure to place a limit on the idea of success created an endless spiral of anxious striving that thwarted the achievement of a happy home:

> In the United States a man builds a house to spend his later years in it, and he sells it before the roof is on: he plants a garden, and lets it just as the trees are coming into bearing: he brings a field into tillage, and leaves other men to gather the crops: he embraces a profession, and gives it up: he settles in a place, which he soon afterwards leaves, to carry his changeable longings elsewhere. If his private affairs leave him any leisure, he instantly plunges into the vortex of politics; and if at the end of a year of unremitting labor he finds he has a few days' vacation, his eager curiosity whirls him over the vast extent of the United States, and he will travel fifteen hundred miles in a few days, to shake off his happiness. Death at length overtakes him, but it is before he is weary of his bootless chase of that complete felicity which is forever on the wing. (622)

Like Tocqueville, Steinbeck describes the antagonism to roots as a function of democracy and equality, not least because rootedness implies ownership and hence creates structures of inequality. But in this Cold War trailer-park culture, Steinbeck discovers a new ideology taking shape, a new dream becoming real—a form of restlessness that is *in synch with* rather than antagonistic to personal happiness. Steinbeck may bemoan much of what is being lost in the face of new national forces of standardization. But the mass-produced patterns of the mobile home have revolutionary implications because they tune American mobility and restlessness to new frequencies, combining them with the desire for privacy and a space for the family, thus allowing for comfort and happiness that survive not despite but because of the uncertainty surrounding them.

The end of part 2 of *Travels* moves from the ideal of the mobile home to a hotel room in Chicago, where our narrator expects to meet his wife for a break from his road trip. Allowed to enter an unmade room while his own is being prepared, Steinbeck has an opportunity to conclude his investigation into commercialized American culture and the white-collar worker. Quite literally, Steinbeck undertakes an investigation when he confronts the remains of the room's former occupant: "As I sat in this unmade room, Lonesome Harry began to take shape and dimension. I could feel that recently departed guest in the bits and pieces of himself he had left behind" (90). Steinbeck's investigation of Harry becomes an "investigation of America" as he attempts to understand the personality and behavior of a member of the white-collar, traveling businessman class. If the literary detective figure is traditionally understood as a normalizing force that makes individual behavior readable, decoding signs to discover meaning, then Steinbeck also makes knowable a series of psychosocial conditions just becoming visible in sociological studies of the American character from the era. In 1950 David Riesman published *The Lonely Crowd*, in which he charted a shift from "inner-directed" people to "other-directed" people in the context of the postwar abundance and consumerism that were loosening the hold of traditional institutions. Other-directed people, Riesman posited, were driven by attention to the behaviors and consumption-patterns of others and by the desire to gain approval, which made them flexible and relational in ways preferred by modern business organizations. In the following year, C. Wright Mills's *White Collar* turned attention to the influence of institutions on the self. Mills described the power of business bureaucracy to dominate personality and human relations by imposing a marketing mentality on the individual, which inevitably led to a self-alienation and estrangement from others. Lonesome Harry is an example of this emerging personality type, the "man in the gray flannel suit" (to reference the title of Sloan Wilson's 1955 novel).

In this scene, Steinbeck acts as a detective attempting to solve a "crime"—the earlier hotel-room rendezvous between Harry and a heavily perfumed brunette he calls Lucille—by reading a series of minute details in the evidence left behind. He reads various "texts" and signs—actual letters, shirts, cigarette butts, bottles of liquor and medicines—and connects these signifiers to what they signify to flesh out a portrait of the rendezvous and a portrait of a character whose name he knows "because he signed it a number of times on hotel stationary, each signature with a slightly different slant. This seems to indicate that he is not entirely sure of himself in the business world, but there were other signs of that" (90). Those signs reveal the lonely personality of the white-collar worker (even Lucille is a professional type; Steinbeck notices that she has poured her drink into a potted plant, presumably because she is "at work"), someone obsessed with gaining self-assurance and power in an uncertain commercial world. Harry is a person surrounded by commercial brands (Marshall Field, Jack Daniels, Tums, Bromo Seltzer), as if his very self has become a commercial product. In contrast to the happy-go-lucky trailer park culture of transience that Steinbeck has just encountered, Harry is trapped in his life; he is lonely, his nervous stomach "isn't up to it," and he is ultimately controlled by social forces that surround him: "He didn't do a single thing that couldn't be predicted—didn't break a glass or a mirror, committed no outrages, left no physical evidence of joy. . . . He hadn't even forgotten a tie" (91–92). The badge of the businessman, Harry's tie, ties him to a business world in which he is powerless, insecure, and dominated by a fear of failing and doing something wrong. This scene may be comic in tone, as Steinbeck is finally left hobbling around the room wearing one boot, looking for clues under the bed. But like this section as a whole, the episode's careful patterning of detail offers an implicit theory of emerging changes in the culture and society of the Cold War.

## The Death of the Author

Steinbeck's self-consciousness at the end of the Lonesome Harry episode is merely one part of a self-reflexive awareness that again links *Travels* to a series of postmodernist ideas that punctuate and complicate Steinbeck's travel narrative. The critique that much of *Travels* is fictionalized again becomes moot when we realize the book's fundamental assault on notions of "fact" and "truth." Even the understanding of Steinbeck as the *author* of the book becomes contested from an early point in the narrative. Of all the books Steinbeck takes with him on his trip, the only one he reads is an 1883 edition of Joseph Addison's *Addison's Spectator*, edited by Henry Morley. Sitting in the White Mountains, Steinbeck reads and quotes from the first number of the *Spectator* from March 1, 1711, in which the Spectator gives an account of himself: "I have observed that a Reader seldom peruses a Book with Pleasure, 'till he knows whether the Writer of it be a black or a fair Man, of a mild or cholerick Disposition, Married or a Bachelor, with other Particulars of the like Nature, that conduce very much to the right Understanding of an Author. To gratify this Curiosity, which is so natural to a Reader, I design this Paper and my next as Prefatory Discourses to my following Writings, and shall give some Account in them of the several persons that are engaged in this Work. As the chief trouble of Compiling, Digesting and Correcting will fall to my Share, I must do myself the Justice to open the Work with my own History" (*Spectator*, quoted in *Travels* 31).

This concept of the author, as the agent of responsibility for and intention in a text, solidifies in the eighteenth century in response to strengthening ideas of ownership and property. As Addison phrases it, the author does all of the "Compiling, Digesting and Correcting," thus shaping the free flow of discourse, solidifying its various strands, and giving a center to the many parts of the text, thus taking ownership of what was once circulating, and in the process becoming a patriarchal figure of authority who delimits the text's reception by the reader. Such ideas of authorial power and control were beginning to crumble by the time Steinbeck was writing in the 1960s (indeed, for Steinbeck the concept of sole authorship has already crumbled in *Sea of Cortez*, coauthored with Ricketts and written in the first person plural). Roland Barthes's famous essay on "The Death of the Author" (1967) assaulted such ideas in an attempt to liberate criticism from this intentional fallacy and to free readers to produce the text themselves as a multilayered discourse that has significance in the present, beyond the limits implied by its point of origin. Steinbeck's response to Addison, from the vantage point of January 29, 1961, resonates with these ideas: "Yes, Joseph Addison, I hear and I will obey within Reason, for it appears that the Curiosity you speak of has in no Way abated. I have found many Readers more interested in what I wear than in what I think, more avid to know how I do it than in what I do. In regarding my Work, some Readers profess greater Feeling for what it makes than for what it says. Since the Suggestion from the Master is a Command not unlike Holy Writ, I shall digress and comply at the same Time" (31).

Here we see two forces in operation to determine the meaning of the text. The ideas of *thinking* and *saying* suggest the free flow of discourse, whereas the reader's desire for an authorial figure responsible for the *making*—or the "how"—of the text embodies the need for authorial intention and containment as part of the meaning-making process. Steinbeck's response to this readerly fascination with his authorial self is to "digress and comply at the same Time"—that is, he recognizes how any authorial selfhood is a construction of the text rather than an entity that preexists (and therefore controls) it, while simultaneously working to construct his own identity from materials at hand.

The authorial identity that Steinbeck proceeds to construct is both resiliently masculine—he dwells on his beard as "the one thing a woman cannot do better than a man" (32)—while also being a self-conscious performance that requires a "costume" acquired from an army-surplus store. He even wears someone else's hat, a naval cap given to him during World War II, and he switches headgear to a Stetson when the context requires (32), as a shifting part of his performance. Steinbeck both establishes and destabilizes his authorial identity and seems to be verging on an idea of authorship as a manifold, free play of mind beyond conscious intention. He sits there "fingering the first volume of *The Spectator* and considering how the mind usually does two things at once that it knows about and probably several it doesn't," until he and Charley are confronted by "a rather stout and bedizened woman" and her female Pomeranian (33). The tension created between the two dogs, and between Steinbeck and the woman, whom he assaults with sexist language as he attempts to reestablish his power and control against the threat of chaos, suggests Steinbeck's authority is a fragile concept: "Addison had crashed in flames" (33). Such fragile identity necessitates aggressive reassertion when its tranquility is threatened, as Steinbeck's was during this period of shaky health that was reflected in the vacillation of his journey and the precarious state of the nation itself.

Figure 3: John Steinbeck and Bob Berry at the Sag Harbor Old Whalers Festival, 1964. Courtesy of the Martha Heasley Cox Center for Steinbeck Studies at San Jose State University.

Steinbeck's authorial self-consciousness in *Travels* fluctuates between sexist assertion and a postmodern distrust of fixed essences, one that posits authorship as the free play of performance or, even more radically, questions the integrity and persistence of the individual self. The latter idea predominates when Steinbeck contemplates the American writer Sinclair Lewis when passing through Lewis's birthplace of Sauk Center, Minnesota. Steinbeck thinks back to his lunches in New York with Lewis, the archetypal modernist author known for his debunking of the pretentions and hollow quality of middle-class life and small-town living. When Steinbeck drives through Sauk Center, he discovers the degree to which Lewis has been absorbed by the culture he rejected when he confronts the sign "Birthplace of Sinclair Lewis" (103). Just as the death of Lewis signifies the death of a particular kind of writer, the high modernist enfant terrible, the moment fails to shape itself into a coherent episode. Steinbeck simply drives on through, leaving the "Center" absent and avoiding any confrontation with authorial origins or grand narratives.

Indeed, the middle part of *Travels* is dominated by this sense of absence. Fargo, North Dakota—the middle point on Steinbeck's map of the country—is not the mythic town he had anticipated but an alienating place just like anywhere else. Similarly, when Steinbeck enters the land where east meets west, he is unable to write about it (118). In general, Steinbeck's encounter with the complicated hugeness of the Midwest does not reveal the heart of the nation; instead, it "resembles chaos" (83). In its very form—a westward journey by road through the nation—*Travels* might recall for the reader the central moment of Steinbeck's entire career: the migration of the Joad family in *The Grapes of Wrath*. But it does so with a postmodernist twist. The Joads, for example, do not confront traffic congestion, as Steinbeck does when he experiences the river of trucks in the Twin Cities (99–100). The Joads just *do* something, whereas Steinbeck is forced to confront what his own doing does, in an ultimate moment of autoreflexivity. And directly following this moment, when he is lost in Minneapolis, Steinbeck revisits the famous truck stop scene in *The Grapes of Wrath* when he converses with a cook and a waitress. Rather than providing a moment of sentimental drama and ethical clarity, as does the scene from *Grapes*, the encounter in *Travels* is meaningless and banal. Returning to the topic of Sinclair Lewis's birthplace, the waitress can only focus on the sign rather than on the presence of the writer himself. Surfaces and signs oust the aura of the individual in this new, empty reality.

## The Performance of Self

If the characters in *Travels* seem incapable of the sentimental performances that we glimpse in *Grapes*, perhaps it is because performance is everywhere in Steinbeck's travel narrative. The sociologist Erving Goffman published *The Presentation of Self in Everyday Life* in 1956, and Steinbeck's work follows in the wake of Goffman's influential understanding of the essential theatricality characteristic of all aspects of social life. Goffman argued that individuals are always playing a part in face-to-face interactions as they attempt to control others' impressions of a self that is marked by fragility. Hence, social acts take place in what Goffman describes as a "front region," in which the performance is given and received by the audience attempting to gain information about the performer, compared with a "back region" in which the performer can step out of the role and prepare for self-presentation. Goffman's ideas about human interaction, which blossomed into the discipline of performance studies, describe a postmodern idea of the self as anti-essentialist, unfixed, and precarious. We might find an illustration of these ideas in Steinbeck's interaction with the actor figure he meets while camping in North Dakota. "He did not give me a sweeping bow," notes Steinbeck on their face-to-face meeting, "but I had the impression that he might have" (112). Impressions are exactly what the old actor is attempting to control. He broadens the pronunciation of the letter A, Steinbeck observes, when he notices Steinbeck's British naval cap (a sign of Steinbeck's own performative costume), which leads to Steinbeck's closer reading of the impressions he receives: "His movements were pure youth but there was that about his skin texture and the edges of his lips that was middle-aged or past it. And his eyes, large warm brown irises set on whites that were turning yellow, corroborated this" (113).

Steinbeck reads the edges of the performance, the moments when the backstage truth leaks out (Goffman made the crucial distinction between the impressions performers "give" and the impressions they "give off" unintentionally). The actor describes the process in front of an audience in which he is transformed from a "harmless freak" (114) through his sincere engagement with material that normalizes the fragile nature of his personality. Yet this explanation of performance is also itself a performance—one that Steinbeck watches with pleasure—which becomes even more layered when we learn that the actor is not performing a conventional "part" but is performing a version of John Gielgud's *Ages of Man*: a compendium of Shakespeare's great speeches, performed on Broadway in 1959. Its title is taken from Jaques's "The Ages of Man" speech from *As You Like It*, which contains Goffman's ideas in a nutshell: "All the world's a stage and all the men and women merely players." Through his impression of Gielgud's *Ages of Man*, the actor becomes a performer giving a version of another performer's performances: a sign of how, in this interaction, there is no "backstage" space where we can see the actor's "real" self, which is why the episode leaves Steinbeck with more questions than answers: "But how did he live? Who were his companions? What was his hidden life? He was right. His exit whetted the questions" (116). The presence of Gielgud—the traveling actor possesses a personal letter from Gielgud—may help to explain why the actor's self is so precarious and why he lives (again following Goffman's ideas about the self) in fear of ridicule. Gielgud was arrested in 1953 for allegedly propositioning men for sex in a public restroom in Chelsea, a famous scandal that may suggest something about the hidden life of the actor that Steinbeck cannot access—the reason why he appears to be on the run from mainstream society.

Again, we can only read the impressions that the actor "gives off" rather than "gives" to understand what might be behind his fragility.

The performative nature of the self is a dominant idea that runs throughout the book. Not for nothing is the young man who Steinbeck encounters in an Idaho motel—the son of the hotel proprietor who, like F. Scott Fitzgerald's Jay Gatsby, is planning to break out of his cultural stagnation to become a success in New York—training to be a woman's hairdresser and is mastering the art of psychology so central to that profession (133). The interlude in Texas at the beginning of part 4 of *Travels*, when Steinbeck is joined by Elaine and attends Thanksgiving at the home of some wealthy friends, becomes an enormous space of performance. Steinbeck describes Texas as a land where the personal and the subjective are dominant, a space in which symbolism dictates reality, and where unity exists only in the mind (177). Steinbeck describes the idea of Texas as emerging since the "death of Hollywood" (179)—presumably since the end of the golden age of Hollywood that reached its height in the 1930s—to provide a new stage for the enactment and projection of national dreams. As guests arrive at the ranch, Steinbeck observes events as a sociologist or an anthropologist would: "But the studied detail did not stop there. Boots were scuffed on the inside and salted with horse sweat, and the heels run over. The open collars of the men's shirts showed dark lines of sunburn on their throats, and one guest had gone to the trouble and expense of breaking his forefinger, which was splinted and covered with laced leather cut from a glove" (180). Steinbeck has entered a state that theorists such as Jean Baudrillard and Umberto Eco would call *hyperreality*: a simulation of reality that is consumed as if it were real. Or rather, there is simply no distinction in this world between reality and performance. Everything is fake; yet everything is dazzlingly authentic. Hence the quail-hunting scene that ends the episode involves no actual quail: it is all a ritual for its own sake, yet it is a real experience, nevertheless.

Returning to the biological concerns on display in earlier works such as *Sea of Cortez*, Steinbeck's ultimate understanding of performativity turns to the human species itself. Steinbeck's sense of his identity as a human is relativistic and comparative because it emerges in relation to Charley, the French poodle who accompanies him on his journey. Charley is what Donna Haraway (2007), the theorist of postmodernity, would call Steinbeck's "companion species." "Species reeks of race and sex," writes Haraway in *When Species Meet*, "and where and when species meet, that heritage must be untied and better knots of companion species attempted within and across differences. Loosening the grip of analogies that issue in the collapse of all of man's others into one another, companion species must instead learn to live intersectionally" (18). Charley's presence in *Travels* works to decenter Steinbeck's humanness. Charley has as much "character"—as much space of behavior and interiority—as any of the humans that feature in the book. He possesses a kind of speech (21), or at least a body language that can readily be interpreted, which blossoms into actual dialogue (168). We learn that Charley's personality is itself a kind of performance that resonates with Goffman's understanding of a self driven by fundamental inadequacy. His manners and grooming mask "deep-down inadequacy" (95), and he is plagued by embarrassment (128)—a key concept in Goffman's theory. By possessing qualities similar to and at times in excess of humans, Charley qualifies any human sense of exceptionalism. Yet all the while, Charley remains resolutely different: "For Charley is not a human; he's a dog, and he likes it that way. He feels that he is a first-rate dog and has no wish to be a second-rate human" (137). Moments of interest and speculation emerge precisely because Charley does *not* see like "us": for example, he cannot recognize the majesty of the tremendous size and age of the giant sequoias and redwoods they encounter in the West (143–45), in a scene that leads Steinbeck to contemplate deep time and the inevitability of human extinction (147).

One of Charley's most important roles in *Travels* is thus as an agent of intersectionality defined by his simultaneous similarity to and difference from humans. Through him, we come to realize how our own species-identity is relative, constructed, and without fixed essence. We perform our identities just as Charley performs his. This performative idea of the self is resonant with ideas emerging in the 1950s and reaching their fullest expression in performance studies in the 1980s and 1990s, when such thinking deconstructed fixed essences and allowed for a liberational model of identity—particularly pertaining to gender—in which we are free as individuals to be what we want. If *Travels* at times approaches such recognitions, then the mood shifts considerably when Steinbeck enters News Orleans, confronts its racial conflicts, and encounters a different kind of performance altogether.

## Problems of Race

*Travels* ends with Steinbeck's journey to the South, and to New Orleans in particular. The city had been slow to implement racial desegregation of the school system following the *Brown vs. Board of Education* Supreme Court decision of 1954. It eventually moved to desegregate schools in the Lower Ninth Ward of the city, which led to a school boycott by many white parents and to large protest meetings often involving thousands of people. (Ruby Bridges, the first Black child to effectively desegregate the William Franz Elementary School, had to be escorted to-and-fro by US marshals.) Steinbeck is drawn to witness the events, even forgoing the chance to see one of his oldest and dearest friends. Following patterns already established in the book, Steinbeck views the events surrounding desegregation as primarily performative in nature. The protests are a "strange drama": "It had the same draw as a five-legged calf or a two-headed foetus at a sideshow, a distortion of normal life we have always felt so interesting that we will pay to see it, perhaps to prove to ourselves that we have the proper number of legs or heads" (189). Yet rather than moving from the unreal "show" to an engagement with the harsh reality of this political conflict, Steinbeck returns to the performative paradigm. He is sickened by the protesters' lack of principle and direction, seeing them as merely hungry for attention, for admiration: "They were crazy actors playing to a crazy audience" (195). And again: "I watched the intent faces of the listening crowd and they were the faces of an audience. When there was applause, it was for a performer" (196). And again: "The crowd, no doubt, rushed home to see themselves on television, and what they saw went out all over the world, unchallenged by the other things I know are there" (196).

We can gauge the degree to which performance predominates in the New Orleans section of *Travels* by comparing it to another nonfictional portrayal of a racial conflict published a few years later: Thomas Pynchon's 1966 "A Journey into the Mind of Watts." Pynchon describes the destructive riots in a largely Black neighborhood of LA in 1965, riots fueled by police brutality (Steinbeck would later become interested in the Watts Writers' Workshop, which developed in response to the riots). In the midst of the plastic, televised, Disneyfied production of images that Pynchon writes about in his novels, Watts represents a *real*. Even as he sees the ghetto as a social wrong, there are ways that Pynchon views it as a space to realize the nonubiquity of the postmodern illusion, an alternative of sorts. Pynchon ends his article by evoking the improvised artistic productions emerging from this neighborhood, made in some cases from the wreckage of the riots themselves, which enable members of the community to critique, resist, and ironize a mainstream society from which they are partially excluded: "In one corner was this old, busted, hollow TV set with a rabbit-ears antenna on top; inside where its picture tube should have been, gazing out with scorched wiring threaded like electronic ivy among its crevices and sockets, was a human skull. The name of the piece was 'The Late, Late, Late Show.'" What Steinbeck witnesses is also a "show" (194), a "big show" (195), a rehearsed and self-conscious performance of racist hatred from which the audience and performers "rushed home to see themselves on television" (196). We might think of Pynchon as the quintessential postmodernist writer for whom reality is always already a performative surface, yet when both writers face a racial apocalypse, it is Pynchon who finds what he describes as a spontaneous "real" amid the carnage. For Steinbeck, however, the reality of

Ruby Bridges's journey to school is overwhelmed by the "theater" of protesters, whose speeches are "not spontaneous" (196). In Pynchon's account, TV sets are repurposed as satirical protest and resistance, yet for Steinbeck the medium again dominates the message; resistance to this constructed show seems futile. It is for Steinbeck, not Pynchon, that postmodernist assumptions predominate, as the televisual fiction overtakes and dictates the vision of the real, caught in an endless feedback loop between performers and audience.

Even the African American student he encounters at the end of the episode seems trapped in the performative paradigm: "I want to *see* it," he says about social action and change (206; emphasis added). This is one of the reasons why *Travels* ends with a feeling of racial deadlock, even an apocalyptic sense that there is no easy way out. People are condemned to play roles passed down over generations, while all social actions seem to be self-reflexively about their own remediation, their own appearance on a TV screen. Ruby Bridges's skip, the curious hop that Steinbeck notices as she walks to school, is perhaps the last speck of the natural and the normal, one that is overpowered by the role she is forced to play in a tragic American drama. The New Orleans section privileges a conservative voice that urges gradual social change. Yet even this tenuous sense of hope is overwhelmed by a feeling that nothing is real. To a significant extent, Steinbeck's analysis of performativity overpowers adequate and realizable protest at social injustice.

## Conclusion

Steinbeck's travels move southwest, then further south, following a realization that a national identity, beyond sectional and racial divisions, has formed by the middle of the twentieth century (159). But following the Texas episode, he becomes less sure about what this identity is. The "American image" becomes a paradox because "certain factors are missing in the equation" (186). Something just does not add up or make sense anymore. As I hope to have demonstrated in this essay, a similar existential and metaphysical crisis is present throughout *Travels* in the "postmodern feeling" that underscores Steinbeck's responses to the culture of the Cold War, consumerist society, suburbanization and white collar labor, authorial identity, the performance of self, and the problem of race.

We can locate the center—or rather, the absent center—of these ideas around halfway through *Travels* when Steinbeck is deep in the Midwest. He turns to a topic that interests him throughout his career—loneliness—and writes three notes on the subject that he rediscovers later because they are wrapped around a bottle of ketchup and secured with a rubber band. The first note concerns the relationship between aloneness and the perception time. The third note concerns the way that loneliness tends to destroy communication and the subtleties of feeling. But the second note best encapsulates the spirit of the book as a whole: "That second note lies obscurely under a streak of ketchup, or catsup" (106). This streak captures the deconstructive spirit of the whole: the center becomes problematic, and hence meaning is rendered unstable because language is haunted by traces that make it unreadable. Like the discarded alimony note he discovers in the trash immediately following this moment (107), we are all—like Lonesome Harry—defined not by the centrality of our presence but by the signs we leave behind. The racism that Steinbeck encounters in New Orleans is another haunting trace that cannot easily be eradicated, a stain across the nation itself, obscuring its meaning and its lesson.

The brevity of the final section of the book, where Steinbeck encounters a cheerful New York City cop who gives him directions, necessarily fails to compensate for what has come before. Steinbeck may have found his home again, but the central meaning of the book remains eerily lost. Whether describing an invisible submarine, a faked shoe in a photograph, a mobile home, a dead author, a sign for Sauk Center, a plastic coating, the performance of an itinerant actor, the sentience of a dog, or simply a streak of ketchup, *Travels with Charley* turns to marginal, obscure, and decentering forces that frustrate dominant narratives and grand theories and that capture the uncertain, anxious, postmodernist mood of Cold War culture.

# 3

## "Travels with Charley:" A Mongrel Manuscript

Susan Shillinglaw

Journalist Bill Steigerwald threw down the gauntlet. In 2000 he went to the Pierpont Morgan Library, where the manuscript of *Travels with Charley in Search of America* is housed, read it, and with lip-smacking glee concluded that Steinbeck had lied in his "nonfiction" book. "Fiction all the way," he crowed in his own subsequent travelogue, *Dogging Steinbeck* (2012). "Steinbeck's a liar": gotcha. His wife Elaine rode with him in Rocinante for parts of the trip: gotcha. Steinbeck booked fancy hotels: gotcha. And the writer made stuff up, Steigerwald asserted with finality—the actor of "seedy grandeur" can't have existed, nor the hitchhikers in the South, for that matter. Lazy Steinbeck critics, he growled, hadn't held the writer's feet to the fire, hadn't even bothered to study the manuscript to see how many sections were excised before publication. Steigerwald needled Steinbeck's readers as well, those who naively trusted their beloved writer to say it like is, to remain the soothsayer of America.

Steigerwald's shake-a-fist, finger-jabbing stance got the national press attention he craved for his own project, retracing Steinbeck steps (he admits a deep yearning for trip-publicity): he spoke on NPR, snagged a *New York Times* editorial about the fictive nature of Steinbeck's book, and booked readings across the country of his own fiery text. He got "nonfiction" caught in his teeth and, like a bulldog, worried the word to a nub. But the publicity had an immediate effect: Penguin Press deleted *Charley*'s "nonfiction" categorization. And more than a decade later, embers from Steigerwald's denunciation of Steinbeck still smolder. Indeed, it may be that his attack gave rise to this collection. Certainly he challenged readers, critics, and publishers to take another look at just what Steinbeck was up to in his narrative—and in the manuscript.

I raise a glass to Bill Steigerwald, for I picked up his challenge. I'm one of those Steinbeck critics who hadn't bothered to read the *Charley* manuscript, indeed wasn't sharply aware that it was housed in the Morgan Library, whose fine collection of Steinbeck journals I had examined. Why skip *Charley*, I wondered? My COVID-19 project was to read it, consider it, and draw conclusions about what's in the manuscript and what the excised portions add to our understanding of the published text. Unlike Steigerwald's, my reading isn't constructed as a net to entrap the author; rather, it is another kind of net, perhaps a plankton net, used to filter Steinbeck's various intentions. Mimicking Steinbeck's fictional terrain (he repeatedly claimed that he wrote books in layers, intending four to five for each text), I arrange my critical discoveries in layers, suggesting five ways to consider this expansive, loose-jointed manuscript.

By way of introduction, a short digression on the physical document. Manuscript *Charley* is a mongrel. It's an assemblage of pieces seemingly composed in bits and bursts. In pen and pencil, on yellow paper and on white, with larded journals and self-referential commentary on art, politics, and family throughout, the manuscript is perhaps one of Steinbeck's most personal, revealing, and exploratory documents. He begins on a yellow legal pad (pages 1–51), writes part 2 in Barbados in a ledger book, switches to another ledger when composing the section from Chicago to the Rocky Mountains, and then abandons that ledger: "*I'm tired of the prime white ledger paper now. Yellow sheets and a pencil are best for me. Besides the lines are too close together on the ledger*" (Steinbeck 1961b, 210).[1]

And he notes that he'll follow "the page numbers of the typescript," so pagination shifts and some pages are double numbered. Subsequently, yellow manuscript pages are sometimes stapled in chunks, sometimes not, some with notes about insertion in the manuscript on the top of the stapled section. When he is writing about the actor of "seedy grandeur," the pen color changes abruptly, perhaps indicating it was written at another time or in a quick burst of inspiration.

In February 1961 John and his wife Elaine vacationed in Barbados, a three-week trip that found Steinbeck writing daily in a black journal with red spine, red corners. "*Book pages 52–102*," is written on the inside cover. "*26000*" words (he liked to count words). The journal begins, "*This will be page 52 of the report which has the working title, In Quest of America*." During that stage he composed on "*every other page for ms. and the other side for notes and day book. It's such a long time since I have used this method that it might be kind of a memory and pleasant*" (1961b, Barbados journal 4) ("a memory," most likely, of writing *East of Eden*, where he composed letters to his editor on one page, text on the opposite page.) Like the hybrid, experimental, and shape-shifting book itself, the *Charley* manuscript fluidly embraces levels of time (see ch. 7 in this book) and subject. His sharp curiosity moves from books written centuries prior to contemporary politics, to scientific experimentation, to personal anecdotes. In the Barbados journal he writes enthusiastically about his upcoming participation in Project Mohole, a complicated endeavor to drill through the earth's crust to the Mohorovicic Discontinuity and take samples of the upper mantle—thus helping to determine the earth's age and assemblage. Steinbeck saw this project as a *"whole new approach to history of the world . . . I simply wouldn't miss this no matter what"* (33). In the black Barbados journal, he is at his most personal, noting his challenging relationship with son Tom (*"Have thought so much about Tom lately"* [64]); difficulties with learning to use an aqualung; frustration with flat seas and sunburn and *"flying insects"* (44); and boredom with the *"desolate"* (74) resort beach where a privileged clientele gathers, *"clever, rich and afraid"* (90). He indulges in "a *kind of social half-life, a drugged life—too much drinking, too much sun and every waking hour full of compulsive talking"* (54) and "endless bathing" (90). Without a stint of daily writing, he admits, *"I'd go nuts."*

Unlike the manuscripts of *The Grapes of Wrath* and *East of Eden*, manuscript *Charley* meanders, shifts gears, stops, whirs along. Like the trip itself, it seems unmapped, expansive, self-revelatory.

At one point during composition of *Charley*, Steinbeck gave a portion of the text to friends for *"comment and suggestion"* and then folded their objections into the manuscript—they complained that Charley disappears from the text for a while. Steinbeck's response is *"This criticism is perhaps valid, but it is one Charley himself would never make. He has a sense of proportion"* (1961b, 2A). Fellow traveler, confidant, conversationalist, and friend, Charley is the book's ballast. He's Lennie to Steinbeck's savvy George. Indeed, a cheerful explanation of Charley's role is suggested when Steinbeck says farewell to the actor and his dog, surely an episode of writerly self-reflection: "Wait a moment. . . . What does the dog do?" Steinbeck calls out to the actor. "Oh, a couple of silly tricks," the actor responds. "He keeps the performance simple. He picks it up when it goes stale" (1997, 116). That's Steinbeck's own approach, to be sure.

In places, the manuscript itself is participatory, as if Steinbeck is writing to and with editors, readers, and agents. In manuscript, he admits that a *"small family disaster set him back ten days"* (1961, 19), although the reader of the manuscript hardly knows what happened to the family. When he switches from the white journal paper back to yellow legal pads, his typist writes him a note agreeing that yellow paper is best. On the back of the Fremont Peak section, Steinbeck scrawls a note to his agent: *"Dear Elizabeth, These pages should be added to the second section because the third changes tone and tempo. Love John*" (np). When he faces the Cheerleaders in Louisiana, he includes their actual words, knowing that "*those words will go to the publisher on the manuscript and there is not a chance in the world that my reader will see them. But the texture of the morning can not be experienced without them*" (1961b, 24). Pages are scrutinized as produced and some commentary reflects readers' response to an unfolding text—portions of the book were published in *Holiday* magazine while Steinbeck was writing other parts: "*Earlier in the record I would have hesitated to mention his* [Charley's] *difficulty* [prostatitis], *but since the first installment of these Travels with Charley was printed, I have had so many letters and cards, even telegrams sending regards to Charley from people who seem really to care about him, that I find no hesitancy in describing his difficulty to his friends*" (1961b, 212 "*following the page numbers of the typescript*"). The manuscript's intimacy is palpable.

To top off this patchwork composition, the original ending, "L'Envoi," about John and Elaine's attendance at Kennedy's inauguration, was lopped off, significantly shifting the book's tone and meaning. The actor of "seedy grandeur," again, seems an interpolated commentary on the book's intent: "His exit whetted the questions" (1997, 116). Steinbeck's dual textual exits surely raise questions. His "search for America," in fact, remained open-ended. It was for him; it is for us.

## A Haphazard Thing

This physical assemblage suggests, first, some of the fluidity and uncertainty about his project, as Steinbeck himself recognized: "There will be writing in it but I don't know what. That's one of the reasons I am so excited about it. I will not shape it. It must make its own form" (Steinbeck 1975, 672). In short, it's a narrative in search of a vessel—or even a name—to contain it. At various points Steinbeck calls it an "*undisciplined log*" (1961b, 23), a report, an account, a "*self-indulgent chronicle*" (1961b, 23) "a haphazard thing," a "wandering narrative" (1997, 88), "a barrel of worms" (1997, 159), "Operation America" (Steinbeck 1975, 668), "*In Quest of America*" (1961b, 52), and "Operation Windmills," the latter a name given to Steinbeck's journey because so many friends questioned his sanity in embarking on such a venture at age fifty-eight, shortly after recovering from a small stroke. Indeed, in the manuscript, he admits concerns about his advancing age: "*the first protests of kidneys so long kicked around like a football, the heart writing its stilted calligraphy on the cardiogram*" (1961b, 19). The book is faceted and layered and, in manuscript, expansive, exploratory, and self-revelatory. It's a recovery saga. It's a book without a map, an emergent narrative revealed through snapshots of one man's America. The trip shapes the story, and "generalities" are extended and yet tentative. The book is "warped" because it is America seen through one man's eyes—circumscribed artistic ground he also claims in *Sea of Cortez* (1951) and *A Russian Journal* (1948), his other travel narratives. It's a book in search of a genre because, he admits, "there are too many realities" (1997, 60).

Indeed, one of Steinbeck's most resonant terms is the "warp" of nonfiction. In advance of his departure, Steinbeck declares that he is "making no literary plans in advance to warp what I see. As again in the Sea of Cortez—a trip is a thing in itself and must be kept so" (Steinbeck 1975, 672). But even without a plan or a map to guide his travels, the narrative is necessarily "warped" because it gives us emphatically Steinbeck's America, the country seen through one man's eyes, and his perspective deliberately omits much of American experience: "*There are certain limitations inherent in our method, you understand that,*" he confides to Charley. "*Whole segments of American Life are cut off from us, the life of business, the life of cities, of the well to do middle class*" (1961b, 158). In *The Log from the Sea of Cortez* he writes, "We knew that what we would see and record and construct would be warped, as all knowledge patterns are warped, first, by the collective pressure and stream of our time and race, second by the thrust of our individual personalities. But knowing this, we might not fall into too many holes—we might maintain some balance between our warp and the separate thing, the external realty" (Steinbeck, 1995, 2). His approach is similar in *A Russian Journal*, where he insists that his and Robert Capa's is "A" Russian journal, not "The" definitive account of the Soviet people in 1947—his and Capa's are vignettes/photographs of ordinary Russians' lives. In asserting the artistic integrity of a circumscribed vision, his "warp," Steinbeck is on familiar ground here.

More powerfully than in the published text, this exploratory manuscript suggests Steinbeck's complex purpose: to tap into the psyche of his country as well as his own, to explore both external and internal terrain, to examine America as a text and his own artistic intentions in the text—indeed his own status as a writer who has considered the contours of fiction and nonfiction for over four decades. He writes, "*There's a wonder about traveling whether in time or space or in the mind, and if it can be both at once, why that's the best*"(1961b, 34). The manuscript expands on that notion of "the best" in travel literature—the creation of an expansive, exploratory, inclusive, emotive, incisive, descriptive document. It's a book fully embracing space (the details of his travels across America) and time (his ruminations) and his mind (what constitutes art).

In its own way, *Travels with Charley* is as much about ecological holism as *The Log from the Sea of Cortez*, where "all things are one thing and that one thing is all things—plankton, a shimmering phosphorescence on the sea and the spinning planets and an expanding universe, all bound together by the elastic string of time" (Steinbeck 1995, 178–79). In the *Log*, Steinbeck and his coauthor, marine biologist Edward F. Ricketts, insist again and again on that expansive notion of reality: "The whole is necessarily everything, the whole world of fact and fancy, body and psyche, physical fact and spiritual truth, individual and collective, life and death, macrocosm and microcosm . . . conscious and unconscious, subject and object" (Steinbeck 1995, 125). That holistic perspective also informs *Travels with Charley*, particularly in the manuscript, where human and natural landscapes are as vital to the narrative as are authorial self-reflections. In both travel narratives, Steinbeck moves restlessly from the physical to the contemplative, from fact to fancy, from truth to the nature of truth, from historical present to historical past, from real time to deep time.

Those layered intentions are immediately apparent, as Steinbeck begins his account on personal, universal, and mythic levels. On the first page, Steinbeck admits to a lifelong "disease," his own "virus of restlessness." As he packs Rocinante, a "silent, ubiquitous small boy" (Steinbeck 1997, 9) visits the truck every day, yearning to go along, he too having, in manuscript, the "*disease*" (Steinbeck 1961b, 9). This boy is indeed ubiquitous—he's like Steinbeck in his need to travel and is the first of many Americans in this text yearning to be somewhere else. Like Walt Whitman's, Steinbeck's generous embrace of America is both intimate and representative. Elsewhere in the book Steinbeck meets Mainers wishing to be in Florida (in manuscript, Steinbeck insists he must visit the state on his trip, although he doesn't make it there) and mobile home owners dismissing the idea of roots (their mode of living not unlike Steinbeck's own)—prompting Steinbeck to suggest that "we are a restless species with a very short history of roots" (1997, 81). He moves from part to whole; from self to species.

Examining Steinbeck's depiction of Cold War America, Jason Dew (2007) identifies the country's "crisis in legitimation—a crisis that can be described as America's general lack of clearly defined purpose, meaning, and identity immediately following the demise of two tangible enemies, Nazi Germany and Imperial Japan" (49). It's that American "disease" that Steinbeck sets out to chart—the country's restlessness, ennui, wastefulness, political indifference, and Cold War tremulousness. And part of that "disease" is his own—certainly the restlessness and uncertainty that propel him to take to the road. Asked by a French journalist in 1953 why American writers so persistently look to the past, Steinbeck admitted that he was startled by the question. He wrote to his agent, Elizabeth Otis, "It has occurred to me that we may be so confused about the present that we avoid it because it is not clear to us. But why should that be a deterrent? If this is a time of confusion, then that should be the subject of a good writer if he is to set down his time" (Steinbeck 1975, 485). Steinbeck took up the challenge in all of his work of the 1960s. After meeting a Vermont farmer, Steinbeck says as much in the manuscript: "*And now even our feelings were confused and the words hadn't come. What happens tomorrow is unsure. We can't even guess—and that confusion has got into every single crevice and corner of our lives. If that is so, no wonder people aren't afraid of bombs. Maybe their senses have retired from participation until the tools of thinking are provided. This Vermont farmer in the White Mountains had at least stated the problem*" (1961b, 34).

The opening pages also suggest the mythic contours of his project to plumb America's depths. He confronts a hurricane and, metaphorically, slays a dragon. As Hurricane Donna churns into Long Island Sound, the writer heroically faces the monster that would destroy his beloved cabin boat, the *Faire Elayne*. In manuscript, the approaching storm and the damage anticipated is monstrous: "*The tracking of these bumbling, evil wind screws is one of the most remarkable achievements of our time. The whorl moves slowly but within its race track winds of murderous velocity surge in a great circle. And the course may change without warning. The invader may come about and crash into the coast or it may veer off and waste its venom on the open sea*" (1961b, 12). This is an invader of mythic proportions.

Steinbeck faces down the intruder: "*The air and sky had a greenish yellow tinge, but maybe that was my eyes, blown watery by going out in it*" (1961b, 14). After, he feels the satisfaction of the conqueror, senses his warrior spirit: "*a fierce, creative gaiety, a kind of glorying in the destructive principle as though we egged Donna on and were proud of her*" (1961b, 18).

Slaying the dragon Donna, in effect, proves that Steinbeck is a worthy adventurer, a man of brawn and, as evident in the continuing quest, of brilliance. No sickly voyager he. "*I have dwelt on Donna because it too was a part of my journey to America.*" A significant part. "*Preparation and anticipation*" of a trip is, he asserts, is "*a quarter of the fun*" (1961b, 18) and a far greater percentage of the book's intent. While Donna tests the hero physically and suggests the mythic contours of Steinbeck's journey, further tests of this hero are internal, as he repeatedly confronts the doubts, the hesitations, and setbacks, as well as the insights and revelations concomitant with any journey, particularly one of this magnitude, facing down his own faltering health and that of "monster America" (20).

In manuscript, the next section, part 2, when he finally takes off on his journey, is called "*That Lonesome Road*" (1961b, 18). Loneliness is one of the mythic hero's tests, bleakness ever lurking—in his own life ("A desperate loneliness settled on me—almost a frightening loneliness" 47); in Americans' lives (Lonesome George); and in the country at large, he fears. America's future is uncertain. On his travels, he describes a plastic-wrapped nation (*"Everything for my protection and nothing for my joy"* [1961b, 50]), whose speech has flattened, whose tastes have "atrophied," whose reading is bland and undistinguished. While Steinbeck connects with many ordinary Americans, he fails to connect with others, certainly when discussing the upcoming election of November 1960.

Other tests concern creative intent, as discussed more fully later in this chapter. The writer/hero ponders the terrain of art and voices concerns about the book he's writing. Is it factual or not? Is it a blindered view of America and thus full of only partial truths? Does a love for Joseph Addison suggest anxiety of influence or a celebration of artistic forbearers, honoring a lifetime of reading and writing? All that muscular intent and wavering purpose is amply set forth in the more self-revelatory *Charley* manuscript.

## Participation

Second, while both text and manuscript are participatory, the manuscript is more insistently so—beginning on page 1. In the manuscript, following the first paragraph, Steinbeck invites his reader to join him on his "Search of America": "*In a long and wandery life, some verities have forced themselves on me. Perhaps those among my readers who have vagrant blood will find likeness of experience in a few generalities*" (1961b, 1). Throughout his career, Steinbeck insisted on an intimate, visceral, emotional connection between reader and text.

Participation was a concept that both he and his best friend and coauthor, marine biologist Edward F. Ricketts, deeply considered: to know a tide pool or a landscape or a people requires deep participation, deep engagement in what "is." One reason, I think, that Steinbeck created his exploratory genre, the play/novelette—*Of Mice and Men* (1937), *The Moon is Down* (1942), *Burning Bright* (1950)—was to bring the intimacy, immediacy, and participatory experience of the theater onto the page. Emotionally connect. Open readers up. He wished his readers to take heed so that, like migrants in *The Grapes of Wrath* who listen to stories told in roadside camps, "their participation made the stories great" (Steinbeck 2006, 325). He amplified that a few years later: "The reader if he likes a story feels largely a participation. The stories we go back to are those in which we have taken part" (DeMott 2022).

In this rambling, expansive manuscript, generalizations are a hand extended, a link between writer and audience. Generalities were his conclusions about America, a dicey proposition in 1960 since, as he knew, the subject of his book was vast and perplexing—What is America today?—and his perspective necessarily "warped" by his singular vision. While generalities are sprinkled throughout, and he alerts the reader to several as they arise, he is reluctant to make too many broad conclusions about America. He ends his introduction with this admission: "*Once I start the log of the journey I shall forgo generalities as much as possible*" (1961b, 8). And yet a few pages later he makes his first, after stocking up on liquor at a New York bottle store. The proprietor sighs, "I'd like to go anywhere" (Steinbeck 1997, 22), and in manuscript the scene continues: "*In my rear view mirror I could see him looking after me. I know the dangers in generalities but even so, after travelling all over the country I can formulate, not a theory but my first law. Nearly all Americans want to be some place else. Maybe Rocinante inflamed people and brought the longing to the surface, but I think it is there all the time in nearly all of us*" (1961b, 26).

All of us. To draw conclusions about the American people is one aim here, even if he claims to be a reluctant sage. In Maine, he posits "*one generality*" about Americans' migration from villages to smog filled cities: "*Having put my foot in the door of this generality, I must continue for what I felt here in Maine seems after my long time to be true of the whole nation and who knows the world*" (1961b, Barbados journal 37). "*There will be many more*" generalizations, he promises (37). And there are. He draws broad generalizations about Americans' custom of hunting ("Somehow the hunting process has to do with masculinity, but I don't quite know how" [1997, 45]), eating habits, reading tastes, radio reports, politics (much of the political commentary cut from the published text) and labor practices ("we Americans bring in mercenaries to do our hard and humble work" [50]).

Steinbeck's writerly terrain is filled with observations about "the people," whether in fiction or nonfiction, whether writing about "the great other side" of Russians' private lives in 1947 or drinking beer and brandy with Canadian potato harvesters in 1960s Maine, feeling "the Brotherhood of Man growing until it filled Rocinante full—and the sisterhood also" (1997, 54). And while the group of harvesters "walked" away after their brandy—past tense—Steinbeck concludes this encounter with the present tense: "But I like them" (1997, 55). Of course he does. The potato harvesters are "the people" who linger in the readers' minds in the present tense throughout Steinbeck's fiction and nonfiction. In life, in art, and on the pages of *Travels*, John Steinbeck connects with these workers and other ordinary Americans through shared food and liquor, through conversations with strangers. And he connects with readers through acute observations, his "generalities" about America and Americans. Participation is a kind of lifelong mantra for this writer. "*It didn't matter what was said,*" he muses after the potato pickers leave the pickup, "*it was the tone, the music, the lovely colored signals of communication. When such a thing is born there are no language barriers. I could have understood them if they spoke Zulu and they me if I discoursed in Pilete. I imagine such glory crowns of association, so rarely given us, are what we long for most and remember longest"* (1961b, Barbados journal 32).

We read *Travels with Charley* today, some sixty years after it was written, because this shabbily dressed, modest, restless, and curious American writer speaks to readers in personal and "lovely colored" sentences. Language connects—readers then, readers now, readers across cultures. The musical tones of speech are local and universal.

But participatory civic engagement seems blocked in America of 1960. Wary Americans didn't want to engage in "peppery arguments" (Steinbeck 1997, 26) about politics or John Kennedy's Catholicism. What generalizations could be made? Cold War Steinbeck yearns to formulate insights about his country, its politics and environmental woes: *"Nothing in nature creates the mess the human does"* (1961b, 27). But cultural indifference seems a challenge as daunting as Donna's evil force. *"I heard of a Maine lady of ninety who said something that might be the weary password of the times. She said, 'I do not care about the speculations of Sherman Adams. I do not care about the political rascality of Richard Nixon. Come to think of it I do not care about the moon.'"* And that, he concludes, *"might be an epitaph for an era"* (1961b, Barbados Journal 8).

Can he forge a participatory bond with a reluctant nation? Do generalities convince, he asks himself as he drives through Ohio and Michigan and Illinois? *"I have no more fear of generalities than I have of rattlesnakes or bubonic plague. Never in a long and wordy life have I written a general observation that has not been seized, wrestled and tromped into the ground. Even an obvious truth set down unequivocally triggers dislike, animosity and often combat"* (1961b, 90). That dark undercurrent—the shape of his own career and the health of his own nation—moves through the *Charley* manuscript.

Dis-connect is the looming national threat.

## Political Commentary

Third, much of the pointed political commentary in the manuscript is excised in the published work, nearly all of it references to Nixon and Kennedy, pre- and post-election. Steinbeck complains about voter apathy throughout the manuscript: *"Even in San Francisco only the vote getters, the professionals were vocal. The voters still were not talking"* (1961b, 262). Someone in the editorial process didn't want a sharp focus on the contemporary scene; most of Steinbeck's queries about the "Catholic issue" or Nixon or Russians were cut. When in San Francisco, Steinbeck reflects at length on American's political stance and his own, once again moving from the personal to the national and once again concluding that it's impossible to reach consensus (it's *"a mystique"*) because each person's or each institution's perceptions differ:

> *It must not be thought that my wife and I are or were non partisan observers. We were and are partisan as all get out, confirmed, blowed in the glass democrats and make no bones of it. But I must come again to a matter of sadness to me, observed all over the nation. It seems to me that for one reason or another, the greater number of people I saw, did not have political opinions, or if they did concealed them whether out of fear or expediency I do not know. It seemed further to me that the majority of people I talked to were against things but were not for anything. They had some hatreds but little love. Oh! They were four square for good government and the American Way of life. And they were against communism. I am interested in the American Way of Life and have tried to determine what it is. Is the Way described in Harpers Bazaar and Vogue? Is it the Way of Playboy or Readers Digest? Is it one thing or many? Does it mean the same thing to a West Virginia coal miner, a negro student in a Southern College, a Tammany Ward \_\_\_\_\_ and a Santa Barbara John Bircher? Do we have the American Way of Life? I asked these questions until I learned better. The truth is that the American Way of Life is a mystique. To inspect it at all is sacrilege crossed with treason. I found that those who hold the Way most dear become very uneasy when asked to explain or describe it.* (Steinbeck 1961b, 262)

He's not about to formulate answers in a country where every discussion of politics or the American way differs; the best he can do is lay out the terrain; the best he can do is express disappointment at America's hollow core; the best he can do is set out his own vivid "warp."

Much of the exchange between the young man who wants to go to New York City to be a beautician and his resistant father is omitted in the published travelogue, including this gem, the father telling Steinbeck, "*I'm a Republican. I'm going to vote for Dick Nixon. I don't like him but I'll vote for him. That's where us republicans got it over the democrats. We can vote for people we don't like. Got to because mainly we don't like anybody*" (1961b, 217).

Undaunted, Steinbeck in the manuscript takes the political temperature of the country again and again. In his three-day stop in Amarillo, Texas, he went "*questing for talk and attitudes. . . . Amarillo like the nation was split nearly even. John F. Kennedy seemed to be elected but bellicose partisanship was demanding recounts everywhere*" (1961b, np). The local men who "*hooked their boots over brass rails*" were tolerantly amused by Republican demands for recounts. It all sounds too wearily contemporary.

"*Even now,*" he writes at the top of a stapled section written after the election, "*it is difficult to remember the time of uncertainty of outcome, the recounts demanded by both sides, the charges of fraud, the screams of outraged virtue, the informed predictions on both sides that if the other won, the republic* might as well shut up show because it was finished. I've often thought that a foreigner experiencing one of our elections could report in good conscience that the United States was in a process of disintegration. Perhaps such reports did go out to Hitler and to Japan. Perhaps the same evaluations are sent to the Kremlin" (1961b, 283).

At times, John Steinbeck seems so eerily prophetic about America's political landscape that it stops you cold.

## Quirks and Diversions

Fourth, and clear from all that is cited above, the manuscript unfolds more generously, particularly in describing Steinbeck's personal quirks and diversions. Deleted passages sap some of the book's energy and joy, its political and intimate slant, as well as a good deal of Steinbeckian perspicacity. Take the initial description of Charley, for example. Immediately after Steinbeck notes that Charley can say "Ftt," the manuscript continues, "I opened the cab door and let him out, and he went about his ceremony *with the certainty of an archbishop celebrating mass*. He doesn't have to think about it to do it well. . . . *I sang the hymn I wrote to him: 'Dog of Ages, Figaree, barked a duck and peed a tree. Halleludog, Halleludog.'* He pauses to acknowledge with a small twitch of his stiff paint brush tail and then we drove on in the autumn afternoon, heading north" (1961b, 25).

Why cut that bit of flimflammery? The cuts don't destroy the passage, but they deplete it and soften the author's ebullience. Charley is an enhanced character in the manuscript, a source of humor and sorrow, a straight dog. "*Charley doesn't need words for speech. So clear was his meaning that often I find myself answering him*" (51), reads another deleted passage from the section where the two camp in Alice, North Dakota. In a book about the delicate art of communication, Charley is a patient, opinionated collaborator with his own language, "ftt." Maybe he's the ideal audience Steinbeck is searching for.

Each of Steinbeck's three travel narratives is collaborative, and Steinbeck's humor enhances his companions' quirks. In *Sea of Cortez*, each crew member as well as the balky Sea Cow outboard motor has a distinct personality, while the authors—Steinbeck, Ricketts, and in some ways Steinbeck's first wife, Carol, who went along on the 1940 voyage—are lumped into a collective and seriously inclined "we." In *A Russian Journal*, photographer Robert Capa is an outsized companion—an invented character in life and art, after all—and Steinbeck lends him a chapter in his own voice, registering the difficulties of travels with Steinbeck. Charley is similarly painted in vivid hues. While Steinbeck insisted that he didn't believe in creative collaboration, the reality is somewhat more complex. If the companion/collaborator was in a different field, such as marine biology, photography (*Bombs Away* [1942]), or film (for example, *Forgotten Village* [1941], *The Pearl* [1948], and *Viva Zapata!* [1952] are all collaborative works) then the project reflected creative fusion. Charley's field is not Steinbeck's—he's a dog, after all, as well as a foreigner with a distinctive French logic, and a gentleman at that. All this is fun but also essential to the narrative. Steinbeck needs a straight man, be it a boat's crew, a photographer, or a dog. Connecting to an audience was first embedded as connection to fellow travelers. "Me and Charley, Charley and me" go the words to the televised production from the 1960s, created by Lee Mendelson. That's the bond, as intimate as the fictional connection between George and Lennie in *Of Mice and Men*, Tom Joad and Casy in *The Grapes of Wrath*, and Lee and Sam Hamilton in *East of Eden*.

"*Only about twice on my whole trip was Charley disparaged and then it was by people no one would want to know anyway*" (1961b, Barbados Ledger 51).

When the manuscript was edited, much of the reflective, exuberant, and politically engaged Steinbeck is clipped. Less Charley. No Elaine. Indeed, the longest excised section is Elaine's delayed arrival on the West Coast, an expansive and jaunty discussion of her cancelled flights and dogged determination to join her husband, despite a rerouted plane that landed in San Francisco, not Seattle. After she finally arrives in Seattle, they spend a few days in the redwoods and then in San Francisco. It's a sprightly travel narrative: Charley isn't sufficiently impressed with redwoods; the car breaks down; a restaurant serves no cocktails, only coffee with "*steak and fried taters*"; and they have some difficulty finding a San Francisco hotel, even though Steinbeck, indulging in nostalgia about his California heritage, insists that he and his family always get a room at *their* place—"*they never forget*" that three generations of Steinbecks have stayed at "*my hotel*" (1961b, 255). Except that there are no rooms to be had: "*My little dung hill of eminence collapsed*" (1961b, 255). Steinbeck's wry comments on the vagaries of restaurant service dependably delight, as do exchanges with Charley. He imagines that when Charley returns to Sag Harbor, he'll brag to his Sag Harbor dog friends about his experience with redwood trees. And they will resist:

> "*Turn your heads fellows don't look up. Here he comes. . . . Good Old Charley Big Mouth. Just stand still, maybe he wont see us.*"
> *And I can hear the Labrador*—"*If he tells me once more about his damn redwoods, I think I shall vomit.*"
> "*Well if you ask me, I think he's off his rocker*" (1961b, 244).

Some of the froth is scooped off the manuscript.

Figure 4: Charley in Sag Harbor. Courtesy of the Martha Heasley Cox Center for Steinbeck Studies at San Jose State University.

## An Anatomy of Form

Fifth, and perhaps most significant—considering the heated discussion about whether this book is fictive or factual—Steinbeck considers his own creative terrain and, in fact, beats his critics to the punch (as he must have wryly intended). In both the book and—far more insistently—in the manuscript, *Travels with Charley* explores the terrain of art—as doggedly as he drives through American landscapes. This book might be called meta-nonfiction, an anatomy of form, a consideration of texts, authors, and genres—and the nature of truth.

The manuscript amplifies references to literary forbearers, the first being the English writer Joseph Addison, who, like Steinbeck, was an essayist, moralist, and critic, and who, like Steinbeck, addressed a broad rather than an elite audience. Steinbeck mentions Addison (in book and manuscript) in part because he aims for an Addisonian mix of history, culture, and geography in his own consideration of the American scene. When discussing the *Spectator*, Steinbeck slyly adds the date of his composition, January 29, 1961—one link between the two journals—and digresses to "comply," as did Addison, with his readers' curiosity about his physical stature.

This scene unfolds by a stream in the White Mountains. Throughout the trip, water prompts speculation. As he notes about roadside migrants in *The Grapes of Wrath*, "a certain physical pattern is needed for the building of a world—water, a riverbank, a stream, a spring, or even a faucet unguarded" (Steinbeck 2006, 195). In *Travels with Charley*, Steinbeck spins out creative worlds when he is seated in or near water; in the manuscript, reflections expand outward in ripples.

Sitting in a Chicago hotel bath, he once again invokes the *Spectator*, writing in manuscript, "*I think James Addison would approve a small analysis at this point, one arrived at in a hot tub in Lonesome George's pleasure dome.*" What follows is a long Addisonian reflection on why Steinbeck omitted his time with Elaine in Chicago from the text of *Charley*, why the "real" design of his narrative cannot contain the reality of the Chicago junket, which mars his creative pattern. At the beginning of part 3 in the text, Steinbeck writes, "Chicago broke my continuity. This is permissible in life but not in writing" (1962, 95). In the manuscript, he elaborates:

> *Point of view, tempo, timber, pitch, whatever you want to call that quality which gives a piece of writing consistency and a facsimile of life—this was temporarily distorted. I do not like Chicago for the usual reason people do not like places—because I am afraid of Chicago. I am afraid of Chicago for the equally usual reason. I do not know it.*
>
> . . .
>
> *I have never found it either necessary or desirable to set down, in addition to what was written, why it was written. But in this self-indulgent chronicle, I shall do that when I find it pleasant or desirable. If I leave Chicago out it is because it is off the line, out of drawing. In traveling it was pleasant and good—in writing it would contribute only a disunity. Readers whose lives and circumstances are chaotic, will not tolerate chaos in writing, for due to a few centuries of writing, the reality of being and reality in writing have become two separate things. Let me give an example.*
>
> *If I should set down in detail and word by word the way people talk, the result would be unintelligible to the reader. This is not speculation but exact reality. If you wish to test it do the following as I have—take a tape recorder to a restaurant, to a party to a small gathering of your friends. Record everything that is said, then from the tape write it down—every word. The result will be astonishing. The dialogue is a play you find straight from life could not be found in life. A writer must so rearrange reality so that it will seem reasonably real to the reader.*
>
> *There's a sentence for you—reasonably real to the reader. The difficulty with most stories lies in the fact that they didn't seem real to the writer. That's where it must start. A thing's happening doesn't make it seem real, sometimes quite the opposite. So many things have happened and I know they happened but they have no reality. They are less real than matters*

*imagined. But it is not the realness of reality in writing I am protesting but the circumstance that two realities do not match, having a different texture. Coexistence seems impossible. In my quixotic travels with Charley about America I paused five times, in Chicago, in Seattle, in California and twice in Texas. Then I saw and felt beloved people who knew me as I knew them. It would be quite easy to recount every moment of these stops but would be out of drawing with the rest. A book has to be one thing just as a poem does or a chair or a table. For a few days in Chicago my travels with Charley lost their identity and became something else—and no matter how delightful to me were those days, they are not at ease with the journey. In Chicago I was with the one most dear to me in the world and when that time* was over and the good byes said, I had to go through the same lost loneliness again—all over again and it was no less painful than at first. There do seem to be no cures for loneliness save only living alone. (1961b, 23/or following numbers on typescript, 145).

In this long digression, Steinbeck addresses critics, editors, readers, and himself, turning over and over and inspecting the "thing" he's creating—a thing called variously a "facsimile of life," "a book," "the journey," but not fiction or nonfiction. *Charley* is "one thing" that is shaped by the art of omission. While reality is messy, the creative act is deliberate and selective. Steinbeck here addresses his critics (as he does on other occasions) who might—and have—taken him to task for omitting parts of his trip. His is the higher authority, he insists: the work itself must seem "reasonably real" and adhere to a pattern of the artist's making. Writers of both fiction and nonfiction select details, evidence, scenes, characters. *Cannery Row*, chapter 2, discusses the same idea: "The Word is a symbol and a delight which sucks up men and scenes, trees, plants, factories and Pekinese. Then the Thing becomes the Word and back to the Thing again, but warped and woven into a fantastic pattern" (Steinbeck 1994, 17). The pattern is sometimes fictive, drawn from life, as in *Cannery Row*, and sometimes largely factual, also drawn from life, as in *Travels with Charley*. The boundaries of genre blur in Steinbeck's oeuvre.

"The design of a book is the pattern of a reality controlled and shaped by the mind of the writer," he wrote. "This is completely understood about poetry and fiction, but it is too seldom realized about books of fact" (Steinbeck 1941, 1). That's how Steinbeck opens *Sea of Cortez*, staking out his position on the territory of art. And he elaborates further on this philosophy in the *Travels* manuscript. It may well be—Steinbeck is sure of this—that we prefer the truth of artistic design, be it fiction or nonfiction, myth, romance, or journey narrative, to messy, chaotic reality. If the writer recorded things just as they occurred, Steinbeck notes, the narrative *"would roil and stir like a slow-cooking minestrone"* (1961b, 55). In short, such a book would be an indigestible stew.

From a consideration of these five aspects of the manuscript, a picture of what Steinbeck intended begins to emerge—his meta-nonfiction. After the Chicago "break in the journey," nearly halfway across the country, with a map of the United states folded in the middle where Fargo is, and halfway through his narrative, he reflects repeatedly on writing, the imagination, and the creative act. He takes stock. He considers other texts, diverse sources of inspiration: not only Joseph Addison, but also writer Bill Attwood, Herodotus, the Oracle at Delphi, the actor of "seedy grandeur," writer Sinclair Lewis, WPA guides, and, in manuscript, *The Wizard of Oz* and Mark Twain. *"Only though imitation do we develop toward originality"* (1961b, Ledger 34/156), he asserts. Self-consciously the artist, Steinbeck situates this work in a long trajectory of creativity.

While sitting by the Maple River in North Dakota, just outside Alice—population 162—Steinbeck is again drawn to watery reflection, channeling Melville as a water-gazer. He muses once again on the distinction between what our minds create and what our senses experience, the *"great duality of reality and romance."* After all, his is a Quixotic adventure, a hero's journey, as well as an actual road trip. And, as he knows, it's the narrative that will endure, just as the Wild West endures in the American imagination: *"Long after the horse has become extinct, pushed to its disappearance by the jeep, the tractor and the airplane, cowboys will still ride the ranges of the mind and their reality will increase. For it does seem that our fictions are more disciplined than the reality they are presumed to reflect"* (1961b, Ledger 29/154). Art trumps reality.

Anticipating the methods of metafiction, he creates his own version of meta-nonfiction. He considers the meaning of art, the form it should take. Texts are everywhere in this narrative. America is a text. Highway signs have "individual prose style" (1997, 62), often ungrammatical, he notes in the manuscript. Historical markers demonstrate how the nation's "myth wipes out the fact" (Steinbeck 1997, 63). By the Maple River, he takes notes on being alone (later wrapping them around a ketchup bottle—surely a sly nod to Lennie and George's riverside chat). He reads a piece of trash (a court order for alimony, "Good Lord, the trails we leave!"). All texts are intriguing to his writer, be it Lonesome Harry's detritus or a stranger's rumpled paper or Gielgud's creased letter to the actor.

He channels other writers. Pausing for some *"generality jazz"* in manuscript, he compares the America that he's exploring to the America seen by journalist Bill Attwood and his wife, who drew their careful conclusions in *Still the Most Exciting Country* (1955) after interviewing *"local officials, editors, leaders, teachers. They covered the cities as well as the country side and they came up with a wealth of information and had names, places and dates to attest it"* (1961b, Ledger 35/154). Like journalist Joseph Alsop, mentioned earlier in the text, the Attwoods interview the upper crust and *"read reports, even the fine print and figures, while I in my slipshod manner roved about with actors, gypsies, vagabonds"* (1961b, Ledger 60). Anxiety of influence is another writerly concern. *"In our contacts are we seeing anything but a fringe?"* he asks Charley. *"Fringe people, fringe associations"* (1961b, Barbados Ledger 35/157).

Surely, no reader would expect Steinbeck to interview any but the fringe. His terrain is not the Attwoods', with their broad scope and scrupulous conclusions. Their data give them no truer sense of America, if such a thing exists, than his own "warped" sensibilities. His writerly terrain is the ordinary, the commonplace, the marginalized. In *Sea of Cortez* he writes, "The rare animal may be of individual interest, but he is unlikely to be much of consequence in any ecological picture" (Steinbeck 1995, 178). True to this belief, Steinbeck avoids the "the great high-speed slashes of concrete and tar . . . called 'super highways'" (1997, 70) and seeks backroads and ordinary folk. He mostly avoids National Parks—"the unique, the spectacular, the astounding . . . we enclose and celebrate the freaks of our nation and of our civilization" (Steinbeck 1997, 123). Most conversations are with workers, focused on the present, but punctuated by youth who push to the future: the young man on the ferry who talks about nuclear warfare; the son yearning to go to New York; the hitchhiker eager to see racial change "soon." These young voices of the future shape the arc of Steinbeck's trip around America, internal and external. Perhaps the incidents didn't occur as they did, when they did, if they did. But Steinbeck's truth, articulated so fulsomely midway through his journey, is loyalty is to the work of his mind, to the pattern of this narrative, to the scope of this work, which encompasses the past, the present, and the future we are all approaching.

As Cecilia Donohue has noted (2017), Steinbeck's methodology is hardly representative in this book: "His avoidance of personal snapshots of U.S. urban life constitutes an evasion of a major American issue—everyday urban living" (70). But he admits as much in the manuscript, assumes the role of critic, and scrutinizes his own investigatory chops, his journalistic methodology. Charley, he sighs, *"I find myself doubting the validity of my method. In the first place I can't prove anything I say I have seen because the only record I am leaving is a New York license and an illegible signature in an occasional camp ground or motel. How can I be sure that what I see is really there or that I am not totally missing something that is"* (1961b, Ledger 36/158). Again and again he circles back to the creative endeavor itself, part of his own, personal Search for

America—who is looking, what is he seeing, is it accurate? The manuscript, in particular, is as much about Steinbeck's perplexities about genre and method as about the actualities of a road trip. "*In other words, Charley,*" (his interlocutor), "*my questions have foaled not answers but more questions. But maybe that's what an answer is—a question with a downward inflection*" (Ledger 41/161).

In this midtext reflection, the actor of "seedy grandeur" offers another aesthetic consideration. He's a shadow Steinbeck. Like Steinbeck, he's respectful of his lowly audience, a borrower of words, a lover of dogs, and a restless artist whose "exit whetted the questions" (Steinbeck 1997, 116). This episode might as well be the book in miniature. The actor articulates what Steinbeck has long translated into art: the dramatic power of words spoken to an audience, moving through time and space (Shakespeare's words through Gielgud through the actor to Steinbeck). The performative act is discussed, performed, memorized, replicated—a hall of mirrors and soundscapes and texts. In the manuscript, after parting company with the actor, Steinbeck recalls *Huckleberry Finn* and the King and the Duke's version of Hamlet's soliloquy: "*I memorized it once,*" he admits, and "*the flow of sound and rhythm*" remains (1961b, Ledger 49). As he recites his lines, Charley is his audience, "*watch[ing] me cautiously until I had finished reciting*" (51).

Writing to an audience he had cultivated for three decades, Steinbeck hoped they would, like Charley, approach his exploratory journey/journal with participatory curiosity and abiding patience. Steinbeck's journey is as much about America's shifting identity as it about his own existence as an American: a writer, social commentator, weaver of stories; a playwright and journalist and diarist; a collaborator. *Travels with Charley* is a meditation on art, politics, history, culture, race, America. "ALL," as *Sea of Cortez* suggests. "*Maybe I'm too old, and surely I'm too ignorant,*" he muses as he looks forward to the Mohole project when writing *Charley* in Barbados, "*but I'm the best they've got because my mind can look ahead. I can foresee what is ahead*" (1961b, Barbados journal 90).

*Travels with Charley*, the text and the far more expansive manuscript, is an emergent narrative, a story of physical stamina, artistic resolve, and America's health and well-being, in 1960 and in the future. Resolutions are withheld (Jones 2021; Shillinglaw 2013). The conclusion is as murky as the Joads's future, with the migrant family huddling in a California barn, starving, pelted with rain. That image has been replicated across the decades. So has the image of the snarling Cheerleaders in New Orleans, the most disturbing and powerful episode in the book and far more so in the manuscript. Steinbeck simply didn't know how that raw story ended—the country's political, social, and racial future. In his refusal to draw conclusions about America's racial scourge, it may be that Steinbeck is more prescient here than at any other moment in this narrative: "the more I inspected this American image, the less sure I became of what it was" (Steinbeck 1997, 186).

The trip collapses in Louisiana. If this is a hero's journey, the hero is deflated—not defeated, as some suggest, when he faces an "evil wind screw" that is far more insidious than Donna's destructive force: the country's racial legacy. As at the beginning of *Charley*, Steinbeck first connects on a personal level, recalling conversations with southern friends and his childhood acquaintance with the Black Cooper family, each sibling respectable and successful. But as he knows, "*a noninvolved person, no matter how sensitive or oozing with empathy finds himself stopped as by the invisible walls of the fairy castles so prevalent in medieval stories, a wall whose invisibility in no way weakens its strength*" (Steinbeck 1961b, 23). While he admits that, as a nonsoutherner, he is "basically unfitted to take sides in the racial conflict" (Steinbeck 1997, 188), he does, as he must, when he faces his final challenge in a search for America.

With their howls of protest, the Cheerleaders are a societal storm, and Steinbeck can arm himself only with words, not a physical plunge into the Long Island Sound. In the manuscript, he includes a passage he knows that his publishers—and readers and his country—cannot confront. As a witness, he records the dark drama that plays out in the heart of America. Today we have phone videos; back then, we had Steinbeck's unflinching words: "*I don't know how the sick sadness of the morning can be felt without those words. I am going to write down the exact expressions screamed in a banshee voice, a voice in which hysteria was very near the surface. Those words will go to the publisher on the manuscript and there is not a chance in the world that my reader will see them. But the texture of the morning can not be experienced without them*" (Steinbeck 1961b, 24).

What may not be as clear in the published text as in the manuscript is that the most insidious venom of these Cheerleader women is directed at the white man and his little girl, at those who dare to cross the color line:

> "*You mother fucking, nigger sucking, prick licking piece of shit. Why you'd lick a dog's ass if he'd let you. Look at the bastard drag his dirty stinking ass along. You think that's his kid. That's a piece of shit. That's shit leading shit. Know what we ought to do. Strip down them fancy pants and cut off his balls and feed them to the pigs—that's if he's got any balls. How about it friends?" The cheer lady raised her red and gleaming face and the crowd behind the barrier roared and cheered and pounded each other with joy. The nervous strolling police watched for any break over the barrier. Their lips were tight but a few of them smiled and quickly unsmiled. Across the*

> *street the U.S. Marshalls stood unmoving. The grey man's legs had speeded for a second but he reined them down with his will and walked up the school pavement.*
>
> *The crowd quieted and the next cheer lady had her turn. Her voice was the bellow of a bull, a deep and powerful shout with flat edges like a circus barker's voice. No need to set down her words, the pattern was the same, only the rhythm and tonal quality was different. And any one who has been near the theatre would know that these speeches were not spontaneous. They were tried and memorized and carefully rehearsed. And it was theatre. I watched the intent faces of the listening crowd and they were the faces of an audience and when they applauded, it was for a performer.* (24)

This tragic chorus inverts the comedic actor's soliloquy. This performance is an American tragedy. The Cheerleaders, he concludes, leave "*New Orleans misrepresented to the world . . . unchallenged by other things I know are there*" (1961b, 25). He knows that humans are also good. He knows, as he conveys in the novel he has just concluded, *The Winter of Our Discontent* (1961), that the light never quite goes out, even when it seems that it might.

The subsequent conversations with the "enlightened Southerner," the "old Negro" who he offers a ride, the lank-haired racist, and the "young Negro student" round out Steinbeck's pattern in the South—four representative voices that bracket the madness. Perhaps those conversations didn't occur in the order presented, and perhaps he made up some. But a higher truth—artistic, emotional, personal, and national—is contained in a narrative pattern that defies categories. Steinbeck ends his book with a patchwork of opinions, true. But that narrative pattern replicates the physical form of the manuscript, the artistic pattern of the book, the internal landscape of the writer and the choral voices heard throughout the narrative. Steinbeck faces turmoil, listens, sees, and records—and admits that the outcome is emerging. If we insist on categories for this exploratory text, we miss the internal patterns. Often creative expression seeps out of categories, and insisting on categories may, in the end, leave us blinded.

When I was director of the National Steinbeck Center in Salinas, we were awarded a 2016 NEA Big Read grant to organize a community consideration of Claudia Rankine's *Citizen*, a meditation on race in America—through essays, poetry, photographs, posters, and websites. On the back cover, the book is catalogued as "Poetry." It's more than that, far, far more. Those texts that we can't confine or label are the ones that may well shake us to the core. *Travels with Charley*, whatever its category, should do just that, and the manuscript, in particular, illuminates some uncomfortably dark corners.

## Note

1. Throughout this essay, all manuscript quotations are in added italics. The manuscript is housed at the Pierpont Morgan Library in New York City, MA 2199. My gracious thanks to Philip Palmer, Robert H. Taylor Curator and Department Head of manuscripts at the Morgan Library for providing me links to the manuscript throughout the period of COVID seclusion. His generosity knew no bounds.

# 4

## Myth and Observation
### The Dual Axes of *Travels with Charley*

CHARLES ETHERIDGE

Throughout his career, Steinbeck was always Steinbeck. Although the subjects of his work varied, both his fiction and nonfiction are remarkably consistent in method. Steinbeck's writing always exists at the intersection of myth and close observation. Everyday life and objects are imbued with mythic significance, and, at the same time, Steinbeck presents as full, nuanced, and clear a picture as possible. This pattern occurs throughout his major work, with *Travels with Charley* admirably representing a culmination of Steinbeck's fruitful grounding of his work at the place where myth and observation meet. Steinbeck was never content, however, to use the same method over and over, choosing rather to refine his narrative modus operandi in each new work. In *Travels*, Steinbeck develops this intersection by building on two works of classic literature: Miguel de Cervantes's *Don Quixote*, which serves as the basis for the mythic axis, and Joseph Addison's the *Spectator*, which provides the basis for the observational axis.

### THE MYTHIC AXIS

Before discussing Steinbeck's well-documented use of myth, it might be helpful to define what is meant by the term "myth" in this context. During the period Steinbeck was active, the study of myth was largely the purview of disciplines such as psychology and anthropology. Psychologist Carl Jung originally introduced the term "archetype" in 1919, defining it as "the primordial image" or "a factor determining the uniformity and regularity of our apprehension." He later refined his definition to "a pervasive idea, image, or symbol that forms part of the collective unconscious" (qtd in Button 2019,

27). Cultural anthropologists embrace a definition of myth that "embraces any backdrop of shared conceptions that are imposed on the understanding of everyday reality—starting with religion, but also including everything from folklore to science" (O'Neill 2018). Structuralist anthropologist Claude Lévi-Strauss (1963) wrote that "myth is language, functioning on an especially high level where meaning succeeds practically at 'taking off' from the linguistic ground on which it keeps rolling" (210). Although psychological and anthropological approaches to myth were eventually applied to literary studies, these definitions were concerned with understanding human psychology and human systems. As will be discussed more fully later, however, part of Steinbeck's genius was to anticipate the way advances in social science could create new methods for storytelling. Thus, for the purposes of this study, it is important to define myth from what Peter N. Dunn (1972) called "its literary side," which he defines as "an established pattern of significant narrative, which forms either the whole work or an important part of it" (2).

The importance of myth to Steinbeck's work has been well documented—from the 1970s onward, this topic has been explored as a staple of his writings. Jackson J. Benson's 1977 study "John Steinbeck: Novelist As Scientist" provides a thorough analysis of the way the author used his fiction to create a number of ways to explore reality; one in particular was myth, which Benson conflates with "religion," which he believes "advocates the importance of man within a context which is religious in tone, material, and general attitude" (250). In other words, myth is based on belief. Similarly, writing about humankind's "mythopoeic heritage," Todd M. Lieber (1972) concludes that Steinbeck's best work "is that which can penetrate to the sources of human thought and behavior and present in the form of some objective correlative the archetypal and mythopoeic knowledge that lies deep in the mystery of human experience" (275). Peter Lisca's landmark 1978 study *John Steinbeck: Nature and Myth* explores the topic thoroughly. Numerous studies deal specifically and explicitly with Steinbeck's fascination with myth, including the 1933 *To a God Unknown*—a richly mythic book with a character named Rama after one of the avatars of the Hindu god Vishnu (LeMaster 1971, 8–11). *Tortilla Flat* deliberately translates Arthurian myth to Steinbeck's California (Levant 1974, 53). Further, scholars have identified numerous mythic sources for *The Pearl*—ranging from Christian myth to Hindu *sruti*—and, of course, others point to Steinbeck's incomplete attempts to render a contemporary language to retell Thomas Malory's *Le Morte d'Arthur*, published posthumously as *The Acts of King Arthur and His Noble Knights* (1976). Steinbeck's nonfiction contains mythic elements as well; in *The Log from the Sea of Cortez*, Steinbeck writes of the myth of the pearl, which later becomes the basis for *The Pearl*. *A Russian Journal* compares Georgia (the republic of the Soviet Union) to Eden, and in that same work Steinbeck notes that Stalin has achieved mythic status, like that of Augustus Caesar (1948, 164).

Any student of Steinbeck knows that this partial list barely scratches the surface of his fascination with myth. Not incidentally, during his early career in 1932, he was briefly acquainted with Joseph Campbell, perhaps America's best-known scholar of myth and author of *The Hero with a Thousand Faces*, which lays out the theory of the archetypal or "composite hero" who is shared by many world cultures, which Campbell called the "monomyth" (1968, 37). Steinbeck read passages from *To a God Unknown* to Campbell, who offered suggestions, and the two found a great deal in common with one another (Benson 1984, 223–24; Souder 2020, 121–23). Campbell felt that he "may have learned more from Steinbeck about the relevance of myth than vice versa" (Benson 1984, 223); Steinbeck also demonstrated to Campbell that "as far as the fiction writer was concerned, nature power was the generator of myth" (Benson 1984, 223). Clearly, myth is one of the major forces driving Steinbeck's work.

Steinbeck scholars have long identified the Bible, particularly the Old Testament, and Malory's *Le Morte d'Arthur* as the two most important sources for his use of myth; and more recently they have noted the influence of Hinduism and Taoism on his work. Another equally powerful source of myth for Steinbeck is *Don Quixote*—a picaresque novel that is itself a myth with its insane but Christlike figure roaming the earth endeavoring to right wrong and celebrate good. Steinbeck reread this book often, particularly when he was writing *Viva Zapata*, *The Wayward Bus* (which he called the Mexican *Don Quixote*), and *East of Eden* (Benson 1984 571–72, 637, 650–51). He read Cervantes both in English translations and in Spanish (Benson 1984, 571, 880).

The parallels between *Don Quixote* and *Travels with Charley* are explicit. Steinbeck dubbed the anticipated journey "Operation Windmills," a clear reference to Don Quixote's habit of tilting at windmills—a phrase that has come to mean the willingness to take on causes that cannot be won but that are worth fighting for anyway. Steinbeck further frames the "adventure" of his tour of America in mythic terms by naming his camper "Rocinante," and, in case the reader is unfamiliar with the reference, he ensures that the allusion is not missed, adding, "which you will remember is the name of Don Quixote's horse" (1962, 7). Written by Miguel de Cervantes Saavedra and published in two parts (1605 and 1615), *Don Quixote* is, among other things, the tale of an old man who decides to become a *caballero andante* or knight-errant—a rambling knight with no clear destination who goes off on a quest to revive chivalry by rescuing damsels in distress and righting wrongs. In the process, he often ignores the reality in front of him and imbues the mundane with heroic significance.

Setting the narrative of *Travels with Charley* within the framework of *Don Quixote* is instructive. The comic, mock-heroic manner in which the narrator frames the protagonist is reminiscent of the manner in which Steinbeck frames himself. Cervantes describes the old man, Quixada, as having given "himself up to reading books of chivalry with such ardour and avidity that he almost entirely neglected the pursuit of his field-sports, and even the management of his property" (1887, 2). Having lost his wits due to an excess of reading, Don Quixote "hit upon the strangest notion that ever madman in this world hit upon, and that was that he fancied it was right and requisite, as well for the support of his own honour as for the service of his country, that he should make a knight-errant of himself, roaming the world over in full armour and on horseback in quest of adventures, and putting in practice himself all that he had read of as being the usual practices of knights-errant; righting every kind of wrong, and exposing himself to peril and danger from which, in the issue, he was to reap eternal renown and fame" (1887, 145–46).

When Quixada takes on the identity of a knight errant, he renames himself Don Quixote.

Steinbeck often viewed himself ironically and spoke of himself in self-deprecating terms, in much the same way that the narrator of *Don Quixote* refers to the old man. Steinbeck often used Pigasus, the winged pig, as a symbol for himself, and, after signing books, would often draw a small pig with wings. His wife Elaine said that, according to Steinbeck, "the little pig said that man must try to attain the heavens even though his equipment be meager. Man must aspire though he be earth-bound." It is not a stretch to imagine Steinbeck identifying with Cervantes's old man, who had too much time on his hands and a head too full of books. Early in *Travels with Charley*, Steinbeck describes himself as "a wayward man" and, when discussing travel within the context of his own age, he writes, "Once a bum, always a bum" (1997, 3). Later, Steinbeck will describe his journey in terms of the Spanish participle *vaicilando*, which he defines as someone's "going somewhere but" not caring "whether or not he gets there" (50). Thus, the task he sets for himself, "to try to rediscover this monster land" (5), may be described as "quixotic," or impractical, or unrealistic. As if to amplify his own connection to Don Quixote, Steinbeck had "the name 'Rocinante' painted on the side of [his] truck in sixteenth-century Spanish script" (6). Cervantes describes the old man's horse as a "hack" or ordinary horse that shows "more quartos than a real" (meaning its hoof has more than eight cracks, since a quarto is one-eighth of a real) and more "blemishes than the steed of Gonela"—a well-known sixteenth-century jester (1887, 147). The narrator describes the horse as "tantum pellis et ossa fuit," or "only skin and bones." This deprecating Latin description calls to mind Steinbeck's own Latin motto: "Ad astra per alia porci," or "To the stars on the wings of a pig." Furthermore, "rocin" actually means "work horse" or "draft horse"(Cervantes 1887, 147n). Just as a workhorse presents an ironic contrast for a man who styles himself a *caballero andante* (literally, a "wandering horseman"), a camper mounted on the back of a pickup truck seems an ironic steed for a wealthy, famous writer who claims he is taking the trip because "I did not know my own country" (1997, 5).

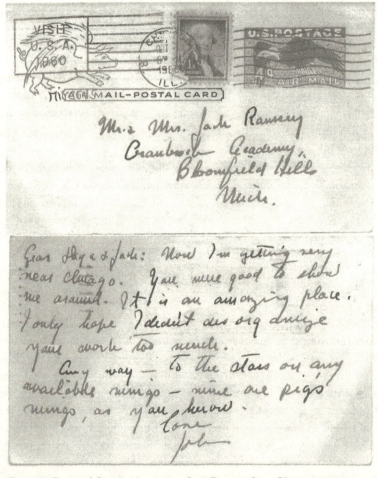

Figure 5: Postcard Steinbeck wrote to Jack Ramsey from Chicago, postmarked October 6, 1960. Brad Bennett collection. Courtesy of the Martha Heasley Cox Center for Steinbeck Studies at San Jose State University.

Steinbeck's use of the name "Rocinante" and the invocation of *Don Quixote* have further implications. According to Cervantes scholar Ricardo Marín Ruiz (2015), the author "pursued a more serious and transcendental aim than parodying medieval romances." Rather, Ruiz believes, Cervantes wanted "to unveil the archaic and deceitful nature of chivalry books" (439, 440). According to Ruiz, Cervantes adopted characters from these books "to strip them of their extraordinary condition and relocate them in realistic situations" (440). Whereas chivalric romances included impossibly idealized horses, Rocinante "is the only non-human creature in the novel that is subjected to the above-mentioned degrading transformation. Thus, the singularity of this horse does not lie in his strength, bravery or powerful and fast galloping, but in his being deprived of these qualities, just as it happens to human characters" (440). Put more simply, by the ironic reversal of the idealized, noble steed with the portrayal of the *caballero andante*'s steed as a real, flawed work horse, Rocinante comes to symbolize the values of "generosity, and loyalty" (441). It could also be applied to Steinbeck as well. Ruiz's analysis closely parallels Steinbeck's understanding of the book: as he wrote to his friend and editor Pascal Covici, "It turns out that the book is not an attack on knight errantry but a celebration of the human spirit" (qtd. in Benson 1984, 650). According to Stephen George, "ultimately, the appeal of Cervantes and the knights' code of chivalry was personal. John Steinbeck saw Don Quixote as a symbol of himself" (2006, 55).

After Steinbeck establishes the mythological context of *Charley*, he continues with the language of myth. When recounting the events surrounding Hurricane Donna, which required him to prepare his Sag Harbor home for the storm, he pays special attention both to Rocinante and to his boat, *Fayre Elayne*, which he mentions seven times in rapid succession (11–13). As mentioned earlier, his third wife was named Elaine and he followed the tradition of many pleasure craft owners the world over by naming his boat after his spouse. The spelling, however, is significant, for the feminized craft is a "fair maid," consistent with chivalric stories, such as *Don Quixote* and *Le Morte d'Arthur*. In addition, using the archaic spelling of the word "Fayre" and of his spouse's name "Elayne" explicitly invokes the language of Malory's *Le Morte d'Arthur*, one of Steinbeck's favorite books since childhood. Furthermore, there are five women named Elayne in *Le Morte d'Arthur*. One explicitly called "fayre maid" is Elyane of Astolat (or Ascolat), who is enamored of Lancelot. Another Elayne is Galahad's mother, the daughter of King Pellas. The use of Arthurian myth continues as Steinbeck arrives in Deer Isle, Maine, which he says is "like Avalon" (42). Avalon is the mythic island where Excalibur was forged and where Arthur was taken after he was gravely wounded. Steinbeck further notes that the inhabitants of Deer Isle pronounce "double vowels . . . as they are in Anglo Saxon" (41), linking the place to the language of Arthurian myth and adding to the sense of mythical place he creates as he continues on his journey.

Steinbeck explicitly links the American consciousness with myth, observing that "there are customs, attitudes, myths and directions and changes that seem to be part of the structure of America" (44). Many of these have to do with the pioneering spirit of which he often wrote (such as in "Leader of the People"). He notes that these ancestors "wrestled this continent as Jacob wrestled the angel," adding a biblical element to the American myth he is defining. But, as is typical in *Travels with Charley*, comic inversion quickly comes into play, as it does in much of his work. He discusses the everyday in terms of great seriousness, imbuing the mundane with significance. There are a number of reasons for this. Steinbeck was consistently self-deprecating in his humor and in the way he talked about himself. Since he appears as a major character in his own book, it's not surprising that he took the opportunity to view himself ironically. But this use of ironic inversion is also completely fitting within the mythic context established in *Don Quixote*, as Ruiz noted, by stripping chivalric characters "of their extraordinary condition" and relocating them, "in realistic situations" (440).

These mythic references echo throughout the narrative. When dealing with the myth of the American outdoorsman, for example, Steinbeck notes dryly that "every American is a natural-born hunter." He then dryly describes hunters "without talent, training, or practice" who try to show their prowess with firearms. He speculates, "Somehow the hunting process has to do with masculinity, but I don't know quite how" (44–45). This section concludes with a story of a rural New Yorker who painted both sides of animal with "the word cow" and a Wisconsin hunter who "shot his own guide," thinking he was a deer (45). Throughout the *Travels* narrative, Steinbeck collects myths, "stories told and retold," such as tales of lost treasure in the desert (163). Or he continues to speak of the everyday in mythic terms, such as when he likens a family's Thanksgiving get together in Texas to a feast attended by Petronius, a Roman official known for a profligate lifestyle.

The mythological references, especially those to mythic quests, run throughout the book. The "birthplace of Elvis Presley" is equated with the "birthplace of Homer," imbuing a contemporary pop star with the aura of an ancient Greek author of mythological stature. Charley finds a "particular literature" on bushes and tree trunks, which, Steinbeck muses, might be "as important in endless time as these pen scratches I put down on perishable paper," making his dog's ablutions coequal and, perhaps, more important, than the literary work he is writing (108). Steinbeck finds that, in his own mental geography, Fargo, North Dakota, is one of the "fabulous places of the earth, kin to those magically remote spots mentioned by Herodotus and Marco Polo and Mandelville" (104). At one point, Steinbeck bumps into an itinerate actor, who had a "seedy grandeur" that would have been appropriate in "the time of chivalric myth" (112).

Not surprisingly, these mythic references reach a crescendo when the author returns to his native California among the redwood trees. As Cervantes does with Rocinante in *Don Quixote*, Steinbeck mythologizes his animal companion, Charley, who, upon discovering *Sequoia gigantica* is likened to "Galahad who saw the Grail" (143). Steinbeck speculates that, like Galahad, Charley "might be translated mystically to another place of existence, to another dimension, just as the redwoods seem to be out of time and out of ordinary thinking." The motif or ironic inversion continues, for whereas Galahad could heal the sick and received a mystical visit from Joseph of Arimathea, Steinbeck wants his dog to urinate on a redwood tree. When Steinbeck says, "Look, Charley. It's the tree of all trees. It's the end of the Quest," Charley sneezes, wanders around, and eventually does his business on a hazelnut bush (144). The ironic inversion is again reversed when Steinbeck goes to great lengths to ensure that Charley does his business on "the serene grandfather of Titans," ultimately succeeding.

At the end of *Don Quixote*, the old man returns to the village of La Mancha and dies, having renounced chivalry. At the end of *Travels with Charley*, the aging author gets lost trying to find his way home, wailing to a policeman, "I want to get home" (209). When the policeman guides the author through traffic and shows him the way home, Steinbeck's journey comes to a far less bleak end than does Don Quixote's, but both are ignoble ends for a knight errant. Mythically, the narrative framework of *Travels with Charley* is informed by Cervantes's work as Steinbeck imbues the mundane with mythic significance to comic effect, then inverts the comic elements by suffusing them with dignity. As he says, "I am happy to report that in the war between reality and romance, reality is not the stronger" (105).

## Observation

If the mythic view—imbuing the mundane with significance by acknowledging echoes with larger human stories—is one axis that governs much of Steinbeck's work, the other axis is close observation. Just as Steinbeck introduces the mythic axis by framing his book in terms of Cervantes's *Don Quixote* by naming his vehicle "Rocinante," so he introduces the "observational" axis by invoking Richard Addison and his *Spectator*, published as a collection of essays in 1711.

After writing of a childhood "love for Joseph Addison which I have never lost," he describes being in "the White Mountains in 1960, sitting in the sun" and opening "the well-remembered' first volume (30). Steinbeck cites the Latin quote Addison used: "Non fumum ex fulgore, sed ex fumo dare lucem Cogitt, et speciosa dehinc miracula promat" (31), taken from Horace, but never translates it. The quote, which Addison provides a translation of, is relevant not only to Addison but to Steinbeck's journey and to his narrative method:

> One with a flash begins, and ends in smoke;
> The other out of smoke brings glorious light,
> And (without raising expectations high)
> Surprises us with dazzling miracles. (Addison 1858, 1)

*Travels with Charley* is, arguably, a "dazzling miracle" that surprises "without raising expectations." Steinbeck quotes the entire first paragraph of Addison's essay, noting that "a Reader seldom peruses a Book with Pleasure 'till he knows whether the Writer of it be a black or a fair Man, of a mild or cholerick Disposition, Married or a Batchelor." In order to "gratify this Curiosity" Addison concedes that "I must do myself the Justice to open the Work with my own History" (qtd in Steinbeck 1997, 31–32).

Steinbeck says he must "obey" Addison "within reason" because a "Suggestion from the Master is a Command not unlike Holy Writ," and he says he will "comply" (31). He gives the date he writes as January 29, 1961, then gives a full description of himself: "tall—six feet even" even though he acknowledges that he is a "dwarf" next to the other men in his family. Furthermore, he is "wide of shoulder" and "narrow of hip," his hair is "a grizzled gray," his "eyes blue," his "cheeks ruddy," and he wears "a beard and moustache" and his beard has a "dark skunk stripe up the middle" with "white edges," which "commemorates certain relatives." Furthermore, he admits, his beard is "pure unblushing decoration," and he likens his pride in his beard to "a peacock [who] finds pleasure in his tail" (32).

Although Steinbeck acknowledges the influence of Addison, his observational style is both dissimilar and similar to the eighteenth-century master's approach. Addison gives a personal history, noting that he was "born to a small hereditary estate" (2), that he had the "reputation of a very sullen youth" (3), and that now, as an adult, his "face is well known at the Grecian" (6). In contrast, Steinbeck mostly concentrates on his own physical description, focusing on his face, his beard, and his height. Whereas Addison describes himself in society, Steinbeck describes himself as a physical or biological specimen, as one might expect from the author of *Sea of Cortez*, a writer whose techniques depended partially upon biological observation. However, there is a deeper similarity in terms of observational style between

Addison and Steinbeck. Addison goes on to note, "I live in the world as a Spectator of mankind, than as one of the species; by which means I have made myself speculative statesman, soldier, merchant, and artizan" (1858, 7). Addison, then, viewed himself as part of a larger system, choosing to separate himself from it so he could comment on it. In this way, Addison's view is similar to Steinbeck's "detached" perspective that is characteristic of his 1930s works. In "Novelist As Scientist," Jackson Benson notes that Steinbeck's use of science "put him in a position of isolation," similar to the way Addison describes himself (1977, 248).

Steinbeck also viewed himself as part of a system, but his technique was biological or scientific, with his perspective informed by what biologists call "system theory." It is important to understand that, unlike nearly every other American author, Steinbeck had some scientific training, having taken a summer session marine biology course at the Hopkins Marine Station in Pacific Grove, California. Stanford University's Hopkins Marine Station, founded in 1892, is the oldest marine laboratory on the West Coast of the United States, and it has been an influential center for thought in the environmental sciences since the late nineteenth century. While studying at Hopkins, Steinbeck was exposed to the work of William Emerson Ritter, who coined the term "organicism," which is the belief that "a proper understanding of living organisms, broadly construed, differs fundamentally from the understanding of non-living things. Organicists typically oppose mechanistic or reductionist views of living things" (McDonough 2016). Put more simply, organicism is the theory that patterns and principles can be applied to all systems in life. Modern environmental scientists adopted Ritter's views and now use the term "systems theory" to describe the idea of viewing individual organisms as part of a larger whole.

Ritter's influence can be seen in much of Steinbeck's mature work. For he wrote his fiction "ecologically," reflecting the work of one of the first biologists to apply system theory—the idea that patterns and principles can be applied to all systems in life. As Ritter used the term, "the comprehensive study of nature when man is fully included in nature must be pursued with a mental technique adequate to conceive individual objects (of which the conceiving human being itself is one) and all objects to be so related to one another as to constitute the general order of nature, the universe" (qtd in Benson 1984, 243). Simply put, Steinbeck humans are part of larger biological system.

When he was in his twenties, Steinbeck worked at a fish hatchery in Tahoe, and later, when he moved to the Monterey area, he became close friends with Edward F. Ricketts, a noted marine biologist and owner of Pacific Biological Laboratory. Ricketts would "collect, prepare, and ship animals to schools to be used for exhibition, experiment, and dissection in high school and college biology and zoology classes" (Benson 1984, 194). While he lived near Cannery Row, Steinbeck would spend many afternoons at the lab, and Steinbeck's first wife, Carol, worked for Ricketts part time for a few months. The friendship between Ricketts and Steinbeck has been well chronicled in Richard Astro's 1973 *John Steinbeck and Edward F. Ricketts: The Shaping of a Novelist*, which details the influence Ricketts had on the author's work, and also in Jackson J. Benson's definitive 1984 *The True Adventures of John Steinbeck, Writer*, which provides a great deal of biographical information. More recent scholars such as Katharine Rodger (2004), Eric Tamm (2005), and Donald Kohrs and Richard Astro (2021) have authored detailed studies of how the collaboration process between Steinbeck and Ricketts worked. Ricketts himself was the model for a number of Steinbeck's characters, including Doc in *Cannery Row* and *Sweet Thursday*, as well as "young Dr. Phillips" in his short story "The Snake," which was apparently inspired by an actual event that happened to Ricketts at Pacific Biological Laboratories.

Ricketts was Steinbeck's friend and collaborator; the two are coauthors of *Sea of Cortez*, an account of a specimen collecting trip the two took to the Gulf of California in 1940. In this book, Steinbeck and Ricketts maintain that "it is advisable to look from the tide pool to the stars and then back to the tide pool again" (1941, 217). By looking at the tide pool, one can look to the stars to gain larger truths and then look back to the tide pool and understand them more fully.

Steinbeck's evocation of Addison, while at the same time viewing himself as a biological specimen that is part of a system, forms the other main line of inquiry in *Travels with Charley*. His expressed intention "to look again, to try to rediscover this monster land" (5) begins by evoking system ecology: "Two or more people disturb the ecologic complex of an area. I had to go alone and I had to be self-contained, a kind of casual turtle carrying his house on his back." Thus, he adopts Addison's method of acknowledging his place as part of a larger system while at the same time expressing an intention of standing apart, of being an observer.

Steinbeck specifically equates this biologically systemic "double vision"—a back and forth between an awareness of the whole system and its individual parts—with the process of writing. On the first day of his journey, he consults a map: "And suddenly the United States became huge beyond belief and impossible even to cross. . . . It was like starting to write a novel" (20). As a writer, Steinbeck realizes he must "write one page and then another" or "I know I can never do it." By thinking about the journey one day at a time, he realizes this approach is the only way he can face "the bright-colored projection of monster America" (20). Just as one can move from "the tide pool to the stars," as he states in *The Log from the Sea of Cortez* (1951, 217), one can begin to comprehend the whole of the country only by closely examining the individual parts as they are encountered.

His fascination with systems remains consistent early in his journey, as he muses about the "hundreds of towns and cities" in "every climate and against every kind of scenery," noting that they are "all alike" because "American cities are like badger holes, ringed with trash" (22). As he most often does in his work, Steinbeck provides a catalog—in the literary sense of the term, a poetic listing, à la Walt Whitman or in the more literal sense, the catalogs of species provided in *Sea of Cortez*—of what he observes, including "boxes, cartons, bins, the so-called packaging" that create mountains. Then, as he does in his other work, he speculates about what these individual things measure—in this case, they are evidence of "our wild and reckless exuberance of our production" (22).

In the America Steinbeck sought to discover, he found that "the best of learning" was to be found "on the morning radio, which [he] learned to love" (28). The radio, he writes, "takes the place of the local newspaper." Steinbeck is struck by the broad representation the radio brings: "Every town of a few thousand people has its station," and these morning radio shows have taken "the place of the old local newspaper." By listening to the radio, the author is able to gain a glance into the tidepool, the individual systems that exist around each new area he visits. He learns what is unique, such as "social doings, prices of commodities, messages," as well as what is the same, or what each system has in common (29). Because he is Steinbeck, the observations are sometimes humorous: the hit song "Teen-Age Angel" seems to be played in nearly every place he visits; another common denominator is "ads for Florida real estate," some of which "went out on a limb and promised that it was above sea level" (29).

Recognition that nonprint media are in the process of changing the way observation and reportage are transmitted and recorded is an underappreciated aspect of *Travels with Charley*. If the book is something of a summation of Steinbeck's career, his attempt to get to know his country once again and record it, Steinbeck's observations remain sharp and prescient. Just as *The Grapes of Wrath* anticipated systemic social science methods developed by Gilbert Ryle and Clifford Geertz decades later (Etheridge 2009, 673), *Travels with Charley* hints at the discussions of electronic media that will transform society in works such as Marshall McLuhan's *Understanding Media: The Extensions of Man* (1964). Not only does Steinbeck have his pulse on the way society is changing, but his methods anticipate new ways of talking about how that society will change in the future.

A useful example of this observation comes from his concern that these new forms of media are the reason that "regional speech is in the process of disappearing, not gone but going" (82). When Steinbeck was younger, he observed, "I could almost pinpoint a man's place of origin by his speech." However, "forty years of radio and television must have this impact. Communications must destroy localness, by a slow, inevitable process" (82). In other words, the mass media are imposing a uniformity on language, which will, eventually, impose more uniformity in other areas. Steinbeck's observations about language sound a great deal like McLuhan's statements that the creation of print culture, which he calls "the typographic principles of uniformity, continuity, and linearity," had resulted in "homogenization" (1964, 6). McLuhan further states that these technologies demand "that we behave in uniform and continuous patterns" (7), which create a "typographic cultural bias" (8), causing us to "assume that uniform and continuous habits are a sign of intelligence." Uniformity becomes a cultural good, and it devalues other ontologies, other ways of being in the world.

Steinbeck is "saddened" by the "inevitability" that "radio and television speech" will become "standardized." Like McLuhan—whose book appeared a few years after *Charley* was published—he links the standardization of language with the standardization of thought, noting that "the idioms, the figures of speech that make language rich and full of the poetry of time and place must go" (106–7). At the same time, Steinbeck admits that some of his regret for the loss of local languages is nostalgia because "it is the nature of a man as he grows older . . . to protest about change," but the "lines of change are down." Those who try to hold change back are "the sad ones who waste their energy" by resisting the inevitable, with the inevitable results of "bitterness in loss and no joy in gain" (83).

Often, Steinbeck is puzzled by the changes he finds, unable to figure out how they fit into a larger system. In such cases, he relies on what he and Ricketts called nonteleological or "is" thinking, simply recording the observations he has made and then admitting he doesn't understand. Such is the case in his observations about mass production, a theme to which he returns throughout the book. For he simultaneously expresses admiration for the American energy and efficiency that mass production illustrates while also lamenting the negative effects of that production, such as the endless waste produced or the loss of regional cultures and the homogenization of thought created by mass media. "Maybe," Steinbeck states, "understanding is only possible after" (84). Steinbeck seems be saying that there is no way to understand American's wastefulness. As part of his detached perspective, he simply describes what he encounters and lets the reader draw the obvious conclusions—here, about waste, and later, about race.

This inability to comprehend the changes, the inability to ascertain how the individual elements fit into a system, is most evident in the closing chapters, when Steinbeck goes to New Orleans while the city is attempting to integrate its schools. A group of white women, dubbed the Cheerleaders, regularly stationed themselves at the police barricades set up near a school entrance and shouted racial epithets at a small African American girl as she was escorted to school by US marshals. Steinbeck expresses despair at what he sees: "In a long and unprotected life I have seen and heard the vomitings of demoniac humans before" but these women's screams fill him with "a shocked and sickened sorrow" (195). Even more shocking to him was the total absence of "the ones whose arms would ache to gather up the small, scared black mite" (196). Steinbeck compares the scene to the "demented cruelty of egocentric children" (195)—which characterizes the Cheerleader—with the many good and kind people he knows in the city. Steinbeck, the great observer, felt "something was wrong and distorted and out of drawing" (196). He does not editorialize further, but, as an observer, he shows the Cheerleaders' cruelty, allowing readers to draw their own conclusions.

As he leaves New Orleans, he feels sickened by what he saw and, later, when he writes about the event, he notes, "Even setting this down on paper has raised the weary, hopeless nausea in me again. It was not written to amuse" (260). Steinbeck, as usual, looks at individual cases to try to make sense of the larger system. He tries to engage people, both Black and white, with little success. He offers a ride to an elderly African American man who is reluctant to get into his truck and who, while polite, resists Steinbeck's attempts to engage him in conversation. In further encounters, a young white man hurls epithets at Steinbeck when he expresses his disapproval of the Cheerleaders. And a young African American student Steinbeck encounters admires Martin Luther King Jr. but laments that his methods will "take too long" (206).

Steinbeck tries to understand the larger whole based on its individual parts—he tries to move from the tide pool to the stars—but he cannot look up and find the metaphorical stars, the light, in the darkness of segregation-era Louisiana. He asks, "What was I learning?" He speaks of the weight of "savage fear" that permeates the American South, noting that this fear is part of the system: "Everyone, white and black, lived in it and breathed it—all ages, all traces, all classes. To them, it was a fact of existence" (203). But he is also quick to note his own failure, lamenting, "I want to be very clear about one thing. I have not intended to present, nor do I think I have presented, any kind of cross-section" that might be construed as "'a true picture of the South" (206–7). The most he can say for certain is that "it is a troubled place and a people caught in a jam." The systemic problems—racial prejudice, poverty, and legally codified oppression—that have created conditions in the South that have started to boil over resist Steinbeck's desire to systematize and understand. When systems break down, however, he falls back on non-teleological thinking. Like the volumes of trash created by American cities and the homogenization imposed by mass media, the horror of racism that controls the South simply "is," and, for him, understanding is not yet possible. As an out-of-control forest fire may engulf a region, so the South finds itself smothering in its own anger and what Steinbeck later calls in *America and Americans* a malaise of stifling "withdrawn separateness" (1966, 59).

As already noted, the sense of being lost is the way in which Steinbeck resolves the mythological axis of *Travels with Charley*—the knight errant must return home with the help of a policeman. The same sense of being lost, of not knowing, brings the observational axis of the book back to its origin. Steinbeck returns home having seen a great deal but, like Don Quixote, having not fully understood what he has seen. I'm not sure he doesn't understand; perhaps he refuses to draw conclusions? Although at one level, this ending might be perceived as unsatisfactory, it is nonetheless an ending that is consistent with the methods he has used throughout his major works. By his use of myth, Steinbeck has imbued his journey across the American landscape with deeper meaning—by creating echoes of other powerful stories by invoking *Don Quixote*, the Bible, and *Le Morte d'Arthur*. At the same time, he has closely observed people and their impact on the nation's landscape—both as individuals and as members of groups. Hence, he has painted a thumbnail portrait of the America he has found—a microcosm, or miniature, of the larger whole. Ultimately, although Steinbeck tries to balance the two axes of myth and observation, he tilts in favor of the mythic. Like Rocinante, he is real and flawed. Like the knight errant Don Quixote, he is occasionally foolish and lost, but always cherishing the values of loyalty, chivalry, and kindness. Although he is occasionally bitter about what he has found, he expresses a profound love for his country, both in his observations of what it is and his mythic vision of what he hopes it could be.

# 5

## Steinbeck Laughing

*Travels with Charley* as American Picaresque

CARTER DAVIS JOHNSON

*Travels with Charley* presents a somewhat puzzling question of genre. On the one hand, Bill Steigerwald (2012) has emphatically lamented Steinbeck's fictional embellishments, dismissing the book's initial label of nonfiction as a fraud. On the other hand, the book's clear relationship to Steinbeck's transcontinental trip disqualifies it as fiction in the usual sense. Trying to navigate between these poles, William Groneman (2012) suggests that we might categorize *Travels* as popular history or as a nonfiction novel. He ultimately presents the label of "Classics" as a consolation (82). Instead of relegating *Travels* to an amorphous, unrecognized genre, however, perhaps we can best understand the text as a picaresque novel.

The picaresque tradition centers on a wandering hero whose misadventures provide occasions for social critique. Wandering the country in his modern truck, dubbed Rocinante, Steinbeck, in the manner of Don Quixote, becomes a picaro himself. Embracing the picaresque elision of fact and fiction, Steinbeck (2012) creates an avenue of discovery for "the small diagnostic truths which are the foundations of the larger truth" concerning America in the days of the Cold War (6). To establish the text within this tradition, in this essay I emphasize several similarities between *Travels* and Royall Tyler's *The Algerine Captive*, perhaps the first American picaresque novel. While both works align with the foundational elements of the genre, they maintain a distinctively American element: an optimistic call for national unity built on a shared conception of an American identity. By understanding *Travels* within the American picaresque tradition, scholars can circumvent the largely inconsequential arguments about degrees of facticity, allowing the rich cultural commentary to occupy the forefront of interpretation.

Figure 6: John Steinbeck laughing, 1957. AP photo. Courtesy of the National Steinbeck Center, Salinas, CA.

Perhaps the most fundamental attribute of the picaresque novel is the elision of fact and fiction. In his study of the genre, Luigi Gussago (2016) remarks that picaresque novels often take the form of "mock autobiographies in which the narrator has no claim to reliability or coherence" (3). Such is clearly the case in Tyler's *The Algerine Captive*. Despite the narrator's self-identification as a "biographer of private life," his name (Updike Underhill) invites the reader's skepticism (Tyler 1816, iv). As the novel moves from initial genealogy to comedic wandering, the narrator's reliability as true biographer unravels. The reader recognizes the fictional elements of the text through repeated caricatures, sardonic tones, and situations that are too narratively convenient. In order for these fictional elements to be effective within the genre, readers must believe that the fiction is indicative of actual experience. Tyler crafted the novel's text as a relief in the broader background of fact. In other words, the fictional world of Updike Underhill is situated within the factual world of the late eighteenth century. Cathy Davidson (2004), in her book *Revolution and the Word: The Rise of the Novel in America*, comments on this picaresque elision: "Tyler confuses the issues further by claiming his fiction is factual and by pretending that he writes, valiantly, against the mass popularity of fiction. Fiction masquerading as fact and railing against fiction" (292). This complicated relationship is foundational to the picaresque genre. Gussago describes it as the combination of "vision and brutal reality," approaches to life that "converge and at times mesh into a continuum" (2016, 1). Within the picaresque novel, the tension between artistic liberty and facticity is continually negotiated.

In *Travels*, Steinbeck embraces a similar narrative strategy. Despite the fact that Viking originally pitched the book as nonfiction, Steinbeck explicitly alerts the reader to the nature of his account: "And in this report I do not fool myself into thinking I am dealing with constants. . . . For this reason I cannot commend this account as an America that you will find" (77). Steinbeck never claimed to write a quantitative account of the United States. He was not so naive as to think that individual perceptions are wholly objective and exhaustive. Steigerwald (2012) emphasizes that Steinbeck wrote the book "virtually without notes and nine months after his trip ended" (242). This argument suggests that exact notes and precise details would have provided greater accuracy. Steinbeck (2012), however, was not concerned with taking notes: "I knew very well that I rarely make notes, and if I do I either lose them or can't read them. I also knew from thirty years of my profession that I cannot write hot on an event. It has to ferment" (11). Steinbeck did not regurgitate facts; rather he let the content of his trip ferment, transforming his observations into broader depictions of culture. Furthermore, he was skeptical of the journalistic purity to which Steigerwald tries to hold him accountable. Steinbeck writes, "I've always admired those reporters who can descend on an area, talk to key people, ask key questions, take samplings of opinions, and then set down an orderly report very like a road map. I envy this technique and at the same time do not trust it as a mirror of reality" (2012, 76). Steinbeck recognized the dangers of false constants. He distrusted clean-cut answers that claimed to have a definite and complete understanding of the "facts." Instead, he pursued a broader and more multifaceted understanding of life, a philosophical pursuit outlined in *Sea of Cortez*. In the introduction to the log, he presents a type of cognitive dualism: one might describe a fish by its scientific classification, or one might convey the subjective experience of encountering it. He seeks to synthesize the factual and the phenomenological: "Spine-count description need not suffer because another approach is also used. Perhaps out of the two approaches, we thought, there might emerge a picture more complete and even more accurate than either alone could produce" (Steinbeck and Ricketts 2009, 4). For Steinbeck, the world was composed not only of factual truths but also of experiential ones. This type of dualism denies a metalanguage that displaces the subject outside of the world he criticizes. Steinbeck was skeptical of the "myth of permanent objective reality," writing, "If it exists at all, it is only available in pickled tatters or in distorted flashes" (2009, 3). To present the world as a mere summation of facts would be a reductive depiction.

Consistent with his concerns in the *Sea of Cortez*, Steinbeck's ambition in *Travels* moved beyond the realm of facts and orderly reports. His trip was not an expedition for quantifiable data. Rather, he was interested in qualitative and intangible attributes. We observe this distinction in his opening words: "I had not heard the speech of America, smelled the grass and trees and sewage, seen its hills and water, its color and quality of light. I knew the changes only from books and newspapers. But more than this, I had not felt the country for twenty-five years" (2012, 5). Steinbeck sought a truth that surpassed "books and newspapers"; he searched for the je ne sais quoi that resists determinacy but manifests itself as a visceral and palpable expression of culture. Steinbeck was interested in the American zeitgeist of the middle century, a concern he further explored in *America and Americans*, published four years later. In *Travels*, the aging writer seeks to discover the metaphysical health of a nation. Rather than turning to the Bureau of Labor Statistics, he looks to interpersonal conversation and observation, the old habits of a novelist.

The picaresque genre is an apt match for Steinbeck's expressed ambitions, as it offers an avenue by which to pursue the qualitative truths that may be disclosed by culture. The genre allows for generalizations and essences. It is muddy and contradictory. It melds fact and fiction. The picaresque maintains the flexibility to describe a situation precisely without depicting anything undoubtedly verifiable. The narrator's claims are not accountable to the vindication of surveys and statistics. Through this flexibility, the author presents intangible truths composed of a conglomeration of opinions and experiences. Additionally, the ability to hold multiple and even contradictory perspectives allows the narrator to careen "wildly between extremes, exploring the inherent danger of one polarity only to be propelled into the pitfalls of the other" (Davidson 2004, 249). In an essay exploring the relationship of *Travels* to another American picaresque novel, *Huckleberry Finn*, Christian Knoeller (2005) states that "Steinbeck writes with reference to a tradition where almost anything goes, seemingly as wide-eyed—if not so naive—as Twain's narrator" (27). Knoeller is correct concerning the relationship with *Huckleberry Finn* and the wide latitude of the picaresque genre. Steinbeck, however, is writing not merely in "reference to a tradition" but *in* the tradition itself.

While the convergence of fact and fiction is a fundamental attribute of the picaresque, social commentary is its fundamental purpose. Although there is controversy concerning the etymology of the genre's title, "the words *pícaro/picaño* presumably derive from the Spanish verb *picar*—to prod with a *pica*, a large spear" (Gussago 2016, 4). This traditional explanation is an appropriate metonym for the pointed cultural critique that defines a picaresque novel. One of the sharpest commentaries in *The Algerine Captive* is Updike's description of southern religious practice. Updike describes a parson who publicly beats a slave on the way to church, "accompanying every stroke, with suitable language." He then preaches "an animated discourse . . . upon the practical duties of religion." The service concludes with a blessing before the "parson and people hastened to the horse race" (Tyler 1816, 81). Tyler explicitly ridicules the ugly hypocrisy of the parson and congregation, sarcastically remarking that Updike carried "a certain staple of New England . . . called conscience" (82). Not only does Tyler attack hypocrisy, a long-standing critique of organized religion, he also condemns racial cruelty. This scene is particularly attuned to the differences between northern and southern religious practice. Although Updike is presented as more sympathetic than these southern "Christians," he later displays a similar superficiality. When he encounters an Islamic scholar in Algiers, Updike is invited to enumerate and defend his theology. But his apologetics are shallow and rely mostly on cultural inheritance, ultimately reflecting the hypocrisy that he condemns. Did Tyler attend the service he described? Perhaps. Nonetheless, to question the historicity of the sermon or the exact transcript would distract from the chapter's social commentary.

Like *The Algerine Captive*, *Travels* centers on social critique, pointedly culminating in a searing attack on racial cruelty. Although the text functions as a travelogue, the trip itself inhabits a periphery role. The logistical details, as Steigerwald criticizes, are secondary or even missing in Steinbeck's account. But these logistics become an issue only if they are mistakenly viewed as the text's primary concern. In *Travels*, the physical movements fundamentally serve as prompts for Steinbeck's sustained social commentary. This commentary, the true source of the book's delight, inspects the nation through a series of relaxed musings. The aged writer, unworried by chronology or facticity, pursues whichever digressions appear most fecund or noteworthy. Embracing the picaro's physical and metaphorical wandering, Steinbeck makes logistics subservient to both narrative and critique.

Over the course of his journey, Steinbeck aims his *pica* at many targets, one of which is religion. Describing a church service he supposedly attended, Steinbeck mirrors Tyler by attacking hypocrisy as well as emphasizing regional difference. In a rural Vermont sanctuary, Steinbeck listens to a sermon on the reality of hell and the need for some "basic reorganizations." He describes the minster as "a man of iron with tool-steel eyes and a delivery like a pneumatic drill." Similar to Tyler, Steinbeck focuses on the individual preacher, using his personality as a synecdoche for the congregation. However, he does not criticize the same type of hypocrisy. Instead of depicting a hypocritical parson, he presents the Vermont church as a representative of authenticity, contrasted with a culture of hypocrisy. The church becomes a bastion that opposes corruption, not a manifestation of the problem: "The service did my heart and I hope my soul some good. It had been long since I had heard such an approach. It is our practice now, at least in the large cities, to find from our psychiatric priesthood that our sins aren't really sins at all but accidents that are set in motion by forces beyond our control. There was no such nonsense in this church" (78). While Steinbeck's tone verges on the ironic, his primary criticism targets this "psychiatric priesthood," not the church. He expresses frustration with a glorified humanism that reduces evil to the accidental. In contrast to this abdication of responsibility, Steinbeck presents a preacher who "spoke of hell as an expert, not the mush-mush hell of these soft days, but a well-stoked, white-hot hell served by technicians of the first order" (78). Latent in this description is a doctrine of sin that presupposes the individual's moral culpability: one does not arrive in hell by "accident." While indulging stereotypes of zealous rural preaching, Steinbeck thwarts expectations by praising the hardness of the sermon and lamenting the softness of the "psychiatric priesthood"—presumably meaning a priesthood that soft-pedals the foibles and sins of the times.

He further complicates the perspective by undermining his praise with caricatures of fire-and-brimstone preaching. As the reader is pulled into the familiar caricature, however, Steinbeck oscillates back toward underhanded praise: "But this Vermont God cared enough about me to go to a lot of trouble kicking the hell out of me. He put my sins in a new perspective. Whereas they had been small and mean and nasty and best forgotten, this minister gave them some size and bloom and dignity. . . . If my sins had this dimension there was some pride left. I wasn't a naughty child but a first rate sinner, and I was going to catch it" (78–79). It would be impossible to define Steinbeck's perspective on Christianity by reading this passage. Moreover, it would be foolish to try. He berates the "large city" trend of self-apologizing determinism and applauds the sincerity of the rural congregation. Yet his praise fluctuates between sincere appreciation and back-handed compliments. Steinbeck's elusive perspective is not due to a lack of perception. His social commentary is cheeky and ironic, getting at the reality that exists beyond a single service in Vermont. He participates in a picaresque tradition that criticizes from beyond accusations of seriousness.

The move beyond serious, factual reporting brings us to another hallmark of the picaresque: satire. Closely tied to the genre's broader purpose of social commentary, irony and satire are primary characteristics of the picaresque. Furthermore, like all good satire, there are elements of truth within the seemingly unbelievable depictions. Returning to the elision of fact and fiction, the emphasis falls on the joke's punchline, not on the factual gaps. There are numerous instances of satire throughout *The Algerine Captive*, with one notable example occurring in chapter 12. Attempting to display his classical education in a southern town, Updike writes an ode to a young lady. But in the process of conveying these "high sounding epithets of the immortal Grecian bard," Updike offends the lady's suitor (Tyler 1816, 49). After accidently accepting a challenge to a duel, Updike immediately regrets his decision. His friend, however, reassures him, "You consider this little affair too seriously. . . . There is no more danger in these town duels than in pounding our great mortar. Why, I fought three duels myself in Carolina before I was seventeen" (52–53). The Carolinian outlines the proceedings, assuring the frightened Updike that the match will only involve a few intentional misses. Yet before the duel even occurs, the town intervenes, making them "drop an affair which we had neither of us any heart to pursue." The whole ordeal gives Updike a reputation as a "*man of honour*" (55).

Tyler accomplishes several things within this short chapter. Primarily, he parodies the practice of dueling, his satire undercutting its association with a badge of honor. He emphasizes the gilded nature of Updike's dispute and the social capital involved. Although *The Algerine Captive* was published in 1797, Tyler's criticism of honor is particularly un-Romantic. He communicates a somewhat cynical, albeit playful, perspective on heroism and honor in Southern society. Thus, he makes his satire feel more akin to a modernist text than an early American one. Secondly, Tyler uses satire to contrast regional differences within the United States. He creates caricatures that represent and help define their environments. Not only is Updike's friend an entertaining personality, but he also functions as a representative of the South. Tyler's characters are closely connected to the attitudes of their environments.

We observe a similar use of satire in *Travels*. Commenting on the relationship between Americans and hunting, Steinbeck notes that "there are any number of good and efficient hunters who know what they are doing; but many more are overweight gentlemen, primed with whisky and armed with high-powered rifles" (57). This description of American hunters may be understood as a humorous yet accurate generality; in so, it would be a falsifiable claim. Consistent with the picaresque tradition, however, Steinbeck presses beyond falsifiability into the overtly satirical:

> In Wisconsin, as I was driving through, a hunter shot his own guide between the shoulder blades. The coroner questioning this nimrod asked, "Did you think he was a deer?"
> "Yes, Sir, I did."
> "But you weren't sure he was a deer?"
> "Well, no sir. I guess not." (Steinbeck 2012, 57)

Following his somewhat serious exposition on the masculine instinct to hunt, Steinbeck seamlessly transitions into this fictional account. Surely this hunting incident, if it occurred at all, did not occur as he was "driving through," and he certainly did not access the dialogue from a court report. Nonetheless, following the broader picaresque tradition, he relates his exaggerated and comedic anecdote with the mock authority of an eye witness. Steinbeck indulges his propensity for satire by creating the ballad of a trigger-happy midwesterner. Similar to Tyler's duel episode, Steinbeck integrates geographic region into his satire. Attuned to the fictional quality of the story, we are not prompted to ask, "Which part of Wisconsin?" Rather, we understand that Wisconsin serves as a synecdoche for the rural Midwest. This regional perspective is further implied by Steinbeck's placing the story between separate anecdotes about New York State and Maine. Furthermore, when speaking of something as culturally diverse and ambiguously demarcated as an American region, Steinbeck does not give a consensus but a characterization.

Continuing his satire of the American hunting ethos, Steinbeck announces his concern about Charley's safety. He supposedly springs into action: "I wrapped Charley's tail in red Kleenex and fastened it with rubber bands. Every morning I renewed his flag, and he wore it all the way west while bullets whined and whistled around us." Although a gratifying spectacle for the imagination, this image of Rocinante driving through a barrage of gunfire is obviously fictional. If held to standards of factual accuracy, this scene misses the mark. Nevertheless, the fictional nature of the scene is not indicative of insincerity or manipulation. The story of Charley as a brave flagbearer, draped in its ironic Romanticism, is a moment of humorous social commentary. As if we missed the joke, Steinbeck writes, "This is not intended to be funny" (58). Like Tyler, Steinbeck seamlessly moves between sincerity and sarcasm. His blend of satirical fiction and travel narrative helps give the text its unique and charismatic quality. The reader is constantly slipping between the details of the trip, the speculations of an aging writer, and the wry satire of American life.

Thus far, the comparison between *Travels* and *The Algerine Captive* has emphasized a shared alignment with the picaresque tradition. This argument for the genre of *Travels* could have been accomplished, however, using other picaresque texts such as *Don Quixote*, *Don Juan*, or *Moll Flanders*. Why compare *Travels* and *The Algerine Captive*? The purpose of this comparison is to emphasize their shared American departure from the European tradition. This departure is most explicitly expressed in the writers' assertion of an identifiable and real American identity, a stabilizing force within the otherwise disorientating picaresque narrative.

Commenting on the typical conclusion of picaresque novels, Davidson (2004) writes that "the picaro's ritual homecoming, like Odysseus's, is not necessarily final, as if the hero's wanderlust has only temporarily abated" (250). On a surface level, both novels comply with this genre convention. Updike returns from Algiers with the intention to "unite myself to some amiable woman" and "pursue my practice, as a physician" (Tyler 1816, 240). Despite his intentions, the ending is left essentially unresolved. Updike has a plan, but as previously observed, his plans usually amount to very little. In a similar manner, Steinbeck (2012) concludes *Travels* while lost in New York: "And now I'm back in my own town, where I live—and I'm lost" (277). As Davidson describes the scene, the wandering is unresolved. In like manner, the final scenes of a European picaresque novel are typically accompanied by allegorical indeterminacy. The hero's inability to settle reflects the inability of the narrative to decide on a distinct perspective. The picaresque novel cannot establish a single paradigm or moral framework; the reader is lost alongside the picaro, forever condemned to wander in uncertainty.

While Tyler and Steinbeck both nod to the genre's typical conclusion, they ultimately defy it by providing a telos for their picaro's wandering. After presenting a myriad of indefinite commentaries, both writers provide a resolute and definitive perspective. They exhort a national unity that is constituted and sustained by a unique American identity. By presenting national unity as a meaningful social goal, both texts become didactic in a manner that is foreign to the picaresque. Because of the multiplicity of indeterminate perspectives in the European tradition, the idea of social progress is an oxymoron. Tyler and Steinbeck, however, suspend their use of irony to vindicate the American identity. By offering a clear instance of resolution, both Tyler and Steinbeck diverge from the "goalessness" of the European tradition.

In *The Algerine Captive*, we notice the cogency of Tyler's overarching American exhortation through the reconciliation of the book's two portions. Although Updike's captivity can seem disconnected from the preceding commentary on domestic life, it is actually crucial for understanding the text as a whole. The first half of the book displays the shortcomings of American society, emphasizing the disconnect between American ideals and their manifestation. While Tyler identifies a sundry of problems characteristic of the United States, he uses the second half of the book to contrast American principles with foreign authoritarianism. Through Updike's captivity, Tyler presents American ideals as fundamentally admirable, even if their manifestation is riddled with hypocrisy, inconsistency, and exclusion. These ideals, while not immune to failed implementation, form the basis for national unity.

In order for American ideals to unify, however, they must be manifested by Americans. Tyler's hope for unity is contingent on the individual. At the end of the book, Updike announces his desire to achieve the "enviable character of an [*sic*] useful physician, a good father, and worthy FEDERAL citizen" (Tyler 1816, 240). In Updike's declaration, Tyler situates the responsibility of national unity at the individual level. When individuals manifest American ideals, the American identity transcends political, social, and regional divisions. For Tyler, the hope of national unity was contingent on the individual's fulfilling the American identity.

In his work of the 1960s, Steinbeck likewise argued for the existence of a distinct American identity. He was particularly attuned to its separateness from European heritage. In his final publication, *America and Americans*, he discusses this identity in regard to the formation of American literature. Steinbeck (2002) writes that the source of American writers "was identical; they learned from our people and wrote like themselves, and they created a new thing and a grand thing in the world—an American literature about Americans" (388). Steinbeck recognized a vein of writing that contained a distinct identity. The writers were not European expatriates but co-participants in a new, shared experience. In *Travels*, we observe a parallel description of the American identity: "For all of our enormous geographic range, for all of our sectionalism, for all of our interwoven breeds drawn from every part of the ethnic world, we are a nation, a new breed. Americans are much more American than they are Northerners, Southerners, Westerners, or Easterners. . . . This is not patriotic whoop-de-do; it is carefully observed fact. California Chinese, Boston Irish, Wisconsin German, yes, and Alabama Negroes, have more in common than they have apart. . . . The American identity is an exact and provable thing" (210). Steinbeck's conception of national unity was not defined by historical or genealogical identity. His brief list of Americans is ethnically, culturally, and regionally diverse. For Steinbeck, the American identity represented a "new breed," unified around a shared collection of ideals. Furthermore, his hope for unity, like Tyler's, was tethered to the individual American's cherishing and holding onto these ideals.

We can observe this connection between unity and extension in Steinbeck's condemnation of the "Cheerleaders" in Louisiana. Reflecting on their racial harassment, he describes an abdication of identity: "These were not mothers, not even women. They were crazy actors playing to a crazy audience" (258). The Cheerleaders not only forfeit their identities as mothers and women, they also forfeit their identities as Americans. They eschew the values of equality for all that undergirds American ideals. Although Steinbeck resists offering a solution for that "troubled place" called the American South, his reluctance primarily concerns the "dreadful uncertainty of the means" (273). He believes that the end, however, is something more definite, citing the dialectical "something new" of Monsieur Ci Gît (264). Though not fully elaborated upon, this "something new" denotes a multiracial citizenry that is capable of moving beyond harmful racial binaries. In this new condition of American society, ideals of human dignity eclipse the barriers of race. Both Tyler and Steinbeck were resolutely optimistic about the possibility of national unity, a possibility dependent on the individual.

The picaresque offers the opportunity to ridicule, criticize, lament, and laugh at the absurdity of life. While both *Travels with Charley* and *The Algerine Captive* exhibit these essential characteristics, Steinbeck's and Tyler's vision of national unity defies the fractured reality of the European picaresque. In both works, we encounter a picaresque tradition that is uniquely American. Rather than a failed attempt at nonfiction, *Travels with Charley* is a continuation of the American picaresque tradition. Becoming a wandering picaro himself, Steinbeck embodied the hope and danger of the open road, a symbol that invokes the freedom and possibility of the American ideal. Blending the lines between essence and actuality, he joins Tyler in providing a glimpse into the country's soul—that certain entity which inhabits the immaterial junction of the individual, the region, and the nation.

# 6

## Operation Windmills

*Travels with Charley* and *Don Quixote*

WILLIAM P. CHILDERS

Although there is no clear evidence that Steinbeck had read *Don Quixote* prior to the 1940s, after World War II he returned frequently to a book that had become one of his favorites, as he indicated to Elizabeth Otis in a letter dated March 23, 1954: "Rereading *Don Quixote* again. That good, good book. It takes on new shapes every time I re-read it" (DeMott 1984, 25). In finding his footing during the early years of the Cold War, Steinbeck underwent an individualist turn, to which his growing interest in *Don Quixote* was undoubtedly linked. He appropriated Cervantes in various writing projects, some of which would remain unfinished. Far from representing an unambiguous embracing of chivalric values as a solution to the dilemmas of the present, however, this reception was multifaceted, encompassing issues of narrative technique, European cultural tradition, emerging media, and dominant "myths" of the national psyche, such as the Western genre and the romantic idealization of the antebellum South. In particular, Steinbeck views *Don Quixote* as both literary parody and social satire, an interpretation that bears its ultimate fruit in *Travels with Charley in Search of America*, whose intertextuality with Cervantes he acknowledged to Pascal Covici on June 20, 1960, three months before setting out on his journey: "I know you approve of the trip and know how necessary it is to me but there are others who find it so Quixotic that I am calling it Operation Windmills and have named my truck Rocinante" (Steinbeck 1975, 671).[1]

The first published work for which Steinbeck explicitly states his intention of adapting or imitating Cervantes is *The Wayward Bus* (1947). He wrote to Pat Covici on July 12, 1945, that it would be "something like the Don Quixote of Mexico" (Steinbeck 1975, 283). Here the shared element is the use of a frame-tale to hold together multiple narrative strands, as in the long middle section of part 1 of *Don Quixote* (Cervantes 1949, chs. 23–46). From the beginning, then, *Don Quixote* provides Steinbeck not only an ironic version of the chivalric myth but also a toolkit of techniques for structuring the interaction among author, book, characters, and reader. In the same year, 1947—the four-hundredth anniversary of Cervantes's birth—Steinbeck and photographer Robert Capa traveled to the Soviet Union, resulting in the publication, in early 1948, of *A Russian Journal*. According to Capa (1947), "We decided to make an old-fashioned Don Quixote and Sancho Panza quest—to ride behind the iron curtain and pit our pens, lances and lenses against the windmills of today" (195). As the author-narrator, Steinbeck is the Quixote figure, and the image-man, Capa, is his Sancho sidekick. *A Russian Journal* constitutes an antecedent to *Travels with Charley* insofar as Steinbeck is already using the mad knight's adventures as a template for his own travels.

The following year, 1949, Steinbeck wrote Elaine Scott of his impressions as he read the final chapters of part 2 of *Don Quixote*, apparently for the first time: "And suddenly it turns out that the book is not an attack on knight errantry but a celebration of the human spirit" (Steinbeck 1975, 382). This comment reveals his growing awareness of the complexity of Cervantes's strategy vis-à-vis the reader, for whom the pretense of the book's being an "attack on knight errantry" constitutes authorial misdirection. This understanding of the vicissitudes of a long novel's requiring active reading undergirds Steinbeck's most ambitious mature work, *East of Eden* (1952), begun shortly after he finished reading *Don Quixote* in its entirety. As originally written, the entire textual web of *East of Eden*—including the author's direct addresses to his own sons, Thom and John, and the self-reflexive journal in the form of letters to his editor, Pascal Covici—constitutes his rejection of the Cold War modernist consensus against excessive authorial intrusion into fiction, epitomized, for example, in the enshrining of both Henry James and Ernest Hemingway for their impersonal, disciplined technique (Bennett 2015, 142–74). *East of Eden* is an unabashed reconstruction of the writer as moralist, in a time when such a public role had been declared passé. In this reconstruction, the "mark high and bright" set by Cervantes proves decisive. What holds the multigenerational saga and the layers of authorial and narrative commentary together, in the end, is the authorial will. Steinbeck recognized Cervantes as his predecessor in this regard and understood the "Prologue" to part 1 of *Don Quixote* as a manifesto of sorts, declaring the interdependent autonomy of author and reader. Thus, the first draft of the dedication to Pascal Covici (later replaced by a shorter text) was a pastiche of Cervantes's 1605 "Prologue," paying homage simultaneously to the great Spanish novelist and to his longtime friend and editor, who less than two years earlier had sent him the new Viking edition of *Don Quixote* (Steinbeck 1969, 179–82).

Throughout the 1950s, Steinbeck worried both publicly and privately over what he perceived as a crisis in American society. McCarthyism, consumerism, the looming threat of nuclear war, and a general sense of complacency resulting, paradoxically, from postwar prosperity, all combined to persuade him that the nation had become shallow and hypocritical, morally sick.[2] He fretted about his own status, how critics, editors, and the public only seemed to want him to write another *Tortilla Flat* or *The Grapes of Wrath*, but he also worried that he might be "finished" as a writer. Ultimately, this concern was less an expression of personal ego than a desire to write something relevant in response to the current crisis, as he had done during the Great Depression. He recognized that the problems of conformity and hypocrisy could not be dealt with by protest fiction in the same way *The Grapes of Wrath* had addressed the wealth gap caused by unbridled capitalism. The underlying cause of this post–World War II crisis was moral decay resulting from too much, not too little, and this could only be addressed, finally, through satire. The problem nagged him throughout the decade and into the next, giving rise to a curious back-and-forth between past and present, Europe and the United States, romance and satire. The culmination of this dialectic would be his last two major books: the bleak satirical novel, *The Winter of Our Discontent*, and *Travels with Charley in Search of America* (1962). In the run-up to these achievements, *Don Quixote* sometimes appears on one side of the equation, sometimes on the other; in the end, its inherent ambiguity allows it to function as a kind of bridge between the two sides, facilitating their resolution.

The stages of this development can be reconstructed, though they were not publicly known at the time. In 1954 Steinbeck planned a book project following the route of Don Quixote through La Mancha and other parts of Spain, described in a letter to Elizabeth Otis dated February 24, 1954: "Remember the book I told you I want to write next year . . . Footsteps of Don Quixote—with pictures? *The country has not changed much.* The windmills are still there and the castles" (Quoted in Benson 1984, 745–46; emphasis added). This explicitly European approach to Cervantes is rooted nostalgically in Spain's past. On June 17, however, he wrote from Paris indicating a change in direction: "Most writers in America, and I myself among them, have gone almost entirely in the direction of the past. . . . With something of a shock I realize that I have written about nothing current for a very long time" (1975, 485). The outcome of this reflection is *The Short Reign of Pippin IV* (1957), a political satire, unusual for Steinbeck. In *Pippin*, the notorious political instability of the French Fourth Republic leads to a restoration of the monarchy, creating hilariously anachronistic juxtapositions of medieval pomp and modern-day Paris. The resulting farce recalls Don Quixote's revival of chivalry, though the unwilling Pippin IV is also in a bit like Sancho Panza when he becomes governor: a private citizen thrust suddenly into power, veering between wanting to do what is best for his subjects and feeling vexed by the trappings of office.

Shortly after *Pippin*, Steinbeck threw himself into an ambitious project of adapting Sir Thomas Malory's *Le Morte d'Arthur* into modern prose, which would occupy him for most of three years (1957–59). Like the abandoned "Footsteps of Don Quixote," this undertaking entailed once again immersing himself in the European past. It also concerned chivalric romance, the genre that Don Quixote reads obsessively until it drives him mad, making him believe he can become a knight errant. After working exclusively on *Le Morte d'Arthur* for months, Steinbeck suddenly decided he needed to distance himself from it and began yet another Quixote-related project in September 1958, "Don Keehan, the Marshall of Manchón." The textual parallels with the opening chapter of *Don Quixote* are unmistakable:

> This gentleman of ours was close on to fifty, of a robust constitution but with little flesh on his bones and a face that was lean and gaunt. [ . . . ] They will try to tell you that his surname was Quijada or Quesada—there is some difference of opinion among those who have written on the subject—but according to the most likely conjectures we are to understand that it was really Quejana. (Cervantes 1949, I.1, 25–26) Don Keehan was going on fifty. He never got married. [ . . . ] He was always skinny but as he got older he dried up and seemed to get longer and thinner like a rattle snake in a cold winter. [ . . . ] The Keehans changed their name back in gold rush times. They had a hundred leagues of land granted by the Spanish Crown and their name was Quejana. (*Don Keehan*, quoted in Williams 2015, 124–26)

This was to be a satirical novel, set in the West, about a modern-day Quixote who goes crazy, not from reading chivalric romance but from reading Westerns and watching them on television. Moreover, in October 1958 Steinbeck was already trying to interest Elia Kazan and Henry Fonda in a movie project based on this novel, making it a complex feedback loop across genres (parody Western) and media (from television to literature to film). One of the main ideas distracting Steinbeck from Malory and leading him to take up "Don Keehan" was the similarity between the age-old chivalric romance and the contemporary Western, whose presence on television in the '50s and into the '60s fascinated and irritated him. Ultimately, "Don Keehan" is part of a vast critical reflection on the persistence of past forms in present-day fiction, and, correspondingly, literary tradition versus mass media, in which Steinbeck's own imagination and his relations with his readership are engaged. As we will see further below, in the manuscript of *Travels with Charley* the "adult Western" remains a concern, alongside another extension of chivalric romance, the antebellum South. For the last two months of 1958, Steinbeck worked intensively on "Don Keehan," then abruptly abandoned it.

With hindsight, all these abandoned projects, "Don Keehan," "Footsteps of Don Quixote," and the Malory translation-adaptation, despite Steinbeck's enthusiasm for them, were less ends in themselves than pieces of a larger work-in-progress, exploring language, literary technique, and the tension between identification with and demolition of the hero through parody and self-reflexive critique of the mythic underpinnings of fictional narratives. All of this led, in the end, not to a modern adaptation of *Don Quixote* or the *Mort d'Arthur* but to a new, slyly satirical way of writing by means of which to address issues of the present day.

Since the mid-1940s, then, *Don Quixote* had been a constant presence in Steinbeck's reading and writing life, influencing works with no overt connection to it, such as *The Wayward Bus*, *A Russian Journal*, and *East of Eden*, as well as forming the explicit basis for several unfinished projects, including "The Wizard of Maine," "Footsteps of Don Quixote," and "Don Keehan, Marshall of Manchón." The few critics who have addressed the matter mainly view his interest in Cervantes as reinforcing his lifelong passion for Malory and chivalry (George 2006, 54; Schultz and Li 2005, 271). Yet Steinbeck's reception of *Don Quixote* actually focuses at least as much on its comedy, ambivalence, and complex interaction with the reader. In "Culling All Books," Robert DeMott suggests that Cervantes stood for artistic freedom and that *Don Quixote*, alongside *Tristram Shandy* and *Moby-Dick*, achieved a "formless form" by means of an intrusive narrator (1981, 47). DeMott's entry on Cervantes in *Steinbeck's Reading* is also a useful starting point (1984, 25–26). As the unused dedication to *East of Eden* amply demonstrates, Cervantes's use of authorial irony to situate himself, as a free creator, above the fray, beyond the reach of the conventional rules and expectations of his day aided Steinbeck in similarly situating himself strategically vis-à-vis the media landscape of the early Cold War. Insofar as he was interested in Cervantes's treatment of chivalry, this was inseparable for him from the element of parody and satire; that is, Steinbeck turned to Cervantes precisely when he turned *away* from Malory, in order to bring the chivalric into contact with debased late twentieth-century life (in *Pippin*, in "Don Keehan," and in *The Winter of Our Discontent*). The reconstruction of this complex reception of Cervantes, unknown to the reading public at the time, prepares us to see the name Rocinante in *Travels with Charley* as the jumping-off point for recovering a self-consciously literary and satirical reading of the travelogue, especially the manuscript version, leading us beyond the homespun Americana of the Woody Guthriesque narrator in the published version.[3]

As readers of *Travels with Charley* know, John Steinbeck crossed the United States in 1960 in a camper he nicknamed "Rocinante" after Don Quixote's horse. At first glance this is merely a joke regarding what others considered the impracticality of the trip. Some may recognize a deeper affinity between Cervantes's hero and Steinbeck's rugged individualism, or between the episodic, seemingly aimless wandering of the mad knight across La Mancha and Steinbeck's equally meandering path from Maine to California and back to New York. This essay goes further, demonstrating the pervasive role of *Don Quixote* in the original manuscript of *Travels with Charley*. Cervantes's novel self-consciously brings together multiple genres by means of pastiche and parody, juxtaposing the elevated genres of romance with the low-comic picaresque in a mutual critique with satiric overtones concerning seventeenth-century Spanish politics and society. Steinbeck was well aware of the complexity and self-conscious literariness of Cervantes's masterpiece, as is amply attested by his decades-long engagement with *Don Quixote*. To fully appreciate its function as a model for Steinbeck's travelogue, however, it is necessary to read the manuscript of *Travels with Charley* held at the Morgan Library (Steinbeck 1961a), as numerous passages not included in the published version contribute to the richness of this intertextuality. I will therefore have frequent recourse to the manuscript in these pages.

The starting point for this discussion is necessarily the name "Rocinante," the only direct textual link retained in the published book (though the manuscript includes others). This name is insistently repeated, a total of seventy-five times; the sheer frequency of repetition elevates the importance of this "baptism." Moreover, the naming of the camper takes place as part of a sequence of preparations paralleling those of Don Quixote before his first sally, when he scours and repairs his armor, invents names for his horse and himself, and ponders his choice of a lady (Cervantes 1949, I. 1, 29).[4] Thus, after explaining how he ordered and readied his armor-like "turtle shell," the author-narrator of *Travels with Charley* baptizes the vehicle Rocinante and then, like Cervantes's protagonist, frets about his own name—for he has been warned that, "since my photograph was as widely distributed as my publisher could make it, I would find it impossible to move about without being recognized" (1962, 7). From the start, the author's declared intention is to travel incognito, leaving his previously established identity behind, as Alonso Quijano does when he becomes Don Quixote de la Mancha. Yet he writes the name of Don Quixote's horse across the back of his camper, symbolically putting on display the very thing he wants to hide—the "quixotic" nature of his quest and literary vocation: "I was advised that the name Rocinante painted on the side of my truck in sixteenth-century Spanish script would cause curiosity and inquiry in some places. I do not know how many people recognized the name, but surely no one ever asked about it" (7).

Thus "Rocinante" constitutes, from the first, an inside joke, a secret sign establishing complicity between the author-narrator and the reader, a joke in which the characters met by the narrator on his journey do not share. This difference between the reader's point of view and that of the characters is also a fundamental structural element of *Don Quixote* right from the first chapters. A further layer of irony is introduced, though, when Steinbeck disguises himself as an outdoorsman: "I racked a shotgun, two rifles, and a couple of fishing rods in my truck, for it is my experience that if a man is going hunting or fishing his purpose is understood and even applauded" (7). The hunting and fishing gear matches his persona to the camper as surely as Don Quixote's suit of armor to his steed, though it helps him to blend in, rather than making him stand out. In both cases, what is ultimately disguised are the author's own intentions. Knight errantry was no more Cervantes's purpose in writing than hunting and fishing are Steinbeck's. In this sense he is aligned less with the protagonist of *Don Quixote* than with its author, who uses his character's chivalric pose for his own satirical aims.

The ironic linking of the camper to a pseudo-chivalric "quest" is heightened by attributing equine traits and responses to it. Most of the time, certainly, "Rocinante" is simply used to refer to the camper-truck as an object that is driven, parked, and maintained. A first step toward the conversion of this inanimate object into a character is the use of feminine pronouns, *she/her*: "if [Hurricane] Donna struck. . . . there was one added worry—Rocinante, sitting among the trees. In a waking nightmare I saw a tree crash down on the truck and crush her like a bug. I placed her away from a possible direct fall, but that didn't mean that the whole top of a tree might not fly fifty feet through the air and smash her" (12). This alone would not suffice to constitute Rocinante as a full-fledged character, since it is a common usage with ships and sometimes other vehicles and does not, by itself, imply personification. In a number of passages in both the manuscript and the published book, however, emotions and other sentient traits are attributed to the camper, primarily in relation to movement. The three principal examples in the published book are evenly spaced near the beginning, middle, and end: "Even Rocinante, dirty and pine-needle-covered as she was, seemed to leap over the road with joy" (57); "The road surface tore viciously at my tires and made Rocinante's overloaded springs cry with anguish" (139); and during the return journey, "Rocinante could be fleet, but I had not driven her fast. Now she leaped under my heavy relentless foot" (244). This last occasion appears to be a deliberate echo of the *original* Rocinante's response when he realized he was returning home from the inn where Don Quixote had been farcically dubbed a knight during his first sally: "He guided Rocinante toward the village once more, and that animal, realizing that he was homeward bound, began stepping out at so lively a gait that it seemed as if his feet barely touched the ground" (Cervantes, 1949, I.4, 41).[5] Another passage along the same lines was deleted from the manuscript; just after the truck is repaired in Oregon, "*Rocinante rode higher now, and she seemed to bound along on confident tip toes*" (1961a, 248; 1962, 168). In a more subtle instance removed earlier, Steinbeck playfully pretends that the camper sulks when he comes back from calling his wife on a pay phone, reestablishing his former identity, name, and responsibilities and thereby betraying the fantasy world of the quest: "Afterward Rocinante was doubly silent and Charley sensing a change would smell me over suspiciously. I must have carried an odor of names and events" (1961a, 95; 1962, 103). Rocinante is "doubly silent" because her silence as an inanimate object that has no voice is compounded (in the author's imagination) by her obstinate *refusal* to speak (even if she could).

Thus Rocinante is associated with escape from the mundane sphere of names and events into a realm of fantasy and adventure. From the start, however, the camper is also constituted as a space for building community, echoing the function of the titular vehicle in *The Wayward Bus* (1947), Sweetheart, which is similarly feminized and given a temporal-spatial function and a thematic role, as the literal "vehicle" for the creation of a band of pilgrims on life's allegorical journey. In Maine, the author-narrator regales a group of French-Canadian migrant workers with authentic French cognac:

> The cognac was very, very good, and from the first muttered "Santé" and the first clicking sip you could feel the Brotherhood of Man growing until it filled Rocinante full—and the sisterhood also.
>
> They refused seconds and I insisted. And the division of thirds was put on the basis that there wasn't enough to save. And with the few divided drops of that third there came into Rocinante a triumphant human magic that can bless a house, or a truck for that matter—nine

people gathered in complete silence and the nine parts making a whole as surely as my arms and legs are part of me, separate and inseparable. Rocinante took on a glow it never quite lost. (1962, 63)

Rocinante's function here is akin to that of the inn in chapters 32–46 of the 1605 *Don Quixote*, where a handful of characters in conflict are gathered under the aegis of Don Quixote's parodic knighthood and formed into a harmonious group. This sheltering structure figuratively stands for the literary realm itself, understood as a portable space where liminal *communitas* can be staged.[6] The notion that the "glow" Rocinante here acquired was never quite lost authorizes us to read this layer of meaning into the entirety of *Travels with Charley*, indeed, to infer that the book, as a project, aspires to offer such a space for rebuilding community to its American readership in the second decade of the Cold War.

Most importantly, the camper Rocinante is associated with the freedom of the road. Even if the transcendent idealism of the Quest is ironically undercut, the picaresque feeling of open-endedness is maintained, just as it is in *Don Quixote*. Metonymically, Rocinante symbolizes the longing for adventure rooted in dissatisfaction with one's present existence. Insofar as the author-narrator is on any sort of mission, it is in opposition to the complacency Steinbeck felt was corrupting US society from within. Rocinante helps bring to the surface the latent discontent of those he meets. The most direct statement of this was unfortunately deleted from the manuscript; it follows the encounter with the store owner at the start of the journey, when the author-narrator orders liquor to share with those he meets on the trip. The shopkeeper looks longingly at Rocinante and wishes out loud that he could go along:

> "You don't even know where I'm going."
> "I don't care. I'd like to go anywhere."
> *In my rear view mirror I could see him looking after me. I know the dangers in generalities but even so, after travelling all over the country I can formulate, not a theory, but my first law. Nearly all Americans want to be someplace else. Maybe Rocinante inflamed people and brought the longing to the surface, but I think it is there all the time in nearly all of us.* (1961a, ms 26, ts 29; 1962, 24; italics here, and throughout this chapter, indicate manuscript passages omitted from the published book.)

The fact that "Rocinante inflamed people and brought the longing to the surface" explains the lingering gazes of a number of those met on the journey—beginning with the author's son's schoolmates—although the meaning of these looks is only implicit without the deleted passage:

> It can be imagined what effect Rocinante had on two hundred teenage prisoners of education just settling down to serve their winter sentence. (1962, 26)
> I pulled up to speak to him, saw his eyes wash over Rocinante, sweep up the details, and then retire into their sockets. (1962, 139)
> The door was open, and I saw his eyes go over Rocinante and linger on the license plate.
> "You really from New York?"
> "Yep."
> "I want to go there sometime." (1962, 153)

In this last instance, the young hairdresser from Idaho (to whom I return below), the desire for escape has a specific goal, New York City, a beacon of culture and tolerance in the gay youth's eyes. In the other cases, though, "Rocinante" names a vaguer longing, a general feeling of dissatisfaction, produced by the juxtaposition of reality and imagination in a framework that is intrinsically literary, insofar as it depends on verbal articulation to give it concrete form. They stare at the camper, and presumably read the name written across its back, but fail to recognize in "Rocinante" the rootedness of their desire in a novelistic representation that splits their subjectivity between their present existence and the lives they imagine for themselves.

"Rocinante" is just the tip of an iceberg. The relationship between Steinbeck's travelogue and Cervantes's novel runs deep, but much of that context was eliminated or severely curtailed when the manuscript was edited for publication. This is especially true for the central Cervantine trope of bringing together the elevated world of the romance genres (chivalric, pastoral) and the comically debased everyday world of early modern Spain, as represented in the picaresque novel. A similar mixing of genres to produce a double-edged satire that slyly turns the idealized past against a comically debased present is visible in the manuscript of *Travels with Charley*, though it is largely obscured in the published book, in favor of a more escapist nostalgia. In the original version Steinbeck uses ironic metaliterary commentary to highlight his awareness of genre and his relationship to the reader; and he incorporates critical reflection on the appeal of romance genres alongside satirical comments on technological progress, consumerism, and the weakening of democratic institutions by mass media. All of this was cut from the manuscript or greatly toned down, resulting in a more marketable narrative, but one in which the satire is muted, and the overall effect is less overtly Cervantine.

Writing *Travels with Charley* in the first person, Steinbeck incorporated asides of the sort he sometimes jotted down, during previous writing projects, in journals or letters to his editor or agent: supplementary texts on the writing process, which make fascinating reading alongside, for example, *The Grapes of Wrath*, *East of Eden*, or *The Acts of King Arthur*. In accordance with editorial practice of the time, these passages, in which he negotiated his reader's expectations and situated his text in relation to others' writings, were mostly omitted; yet precisely this kind of paratextual and metaliterary positioning is one of the things Steinbeck explored in his prolonged interaction with Cervantes. As discussed earlier, the unused dedication-prologue to *East of Eden*, deliberately modeled on the prologue to part 1 of *Don Quixote*, is a fundamental locus for this connection.

Steinbeck's first-person text is closer to what is nowadays called autofiction than to a purely factual account. He is aware of this and deliberately problematizes the truth status of his narrative, confronting directly the tension between anecdote and generality. Not long after leaving Chicago, he wonders aloud to Charley, "I came out on this trip to try to learn something of America. Am I learning anything? If I am, I don't know what it is. So far can I go back with a bag full of conclusions, a cluster of answers to riddles?" (1962, 125). This passage invites comparison with the moment when Don Quixote, in his third sally, meets up with a carrier transporting images of saints and, contrasting his own failures with their achievements, admits that "up to now, I do not know what I have won with all the hardships I have endured" (1949, II.58, 886). An omitted passage at this point in the manuscript shows Steinbeck deliberately rejecting a naively factual approach:

> I was talking aloud to Charley. He likes the idea but the practice makes him sleepy.
>
> *There are certain limitations inherent in our method, you understand that. Whole segments of American Life are cut off from us. . . . In our contacts are we seeing anything but a fringe? Fringe people, fringe associations. I do wonder if it is not true that we have overlimited ourselves. Several years ago, Bill Attwood and his wife, after years in Europe, toured America and wrote a book on their findings. But they went in their own persons, interviewed local officials, editors, leaders, teachers. They covered the cities as well as the countryside and they came up with a wealth of information and had names, places, and dates to attest it. On this occasion, Charley, as on several others, I found myself doubting the validity of my method. In the first place I can't prove anything I say I have seen because the only record I am leaving is a New York license and an illegible signature in the books of an occasional campground or motel. How can I be sure that what I see*

*is really there or that I am not totally missing something that is?* Just for ducks, let's try a little of what my boys would call this generality jazz. (1961a, ms 157–58, ts 175–76; 1962, 126)

A key phrase here is "a wealth of information," the implicit flip side of which is a poverty of ideas. The book referred to is William Attwood's *Still the Most Exciting Country* (1955), a report whose modest length belies an impressive number of interviewees. Ultimately, Attwood presses a barrage of information into the service of Cold War boosterism, affirming, for instance, that racism is on the wane in the United States, that juvenile delinquency is confined to major cities, and that the nuclear physicists at Los Alamos are working to make war obsolete once and for all. Among the Pollyannaish claims in Attwood's book, one that must have rankled Steinbeck is that television, according to librarians across the country, was not causing people to read less, only to read less *fiction*:

> What has TV done to America?
> It has altered reading habits. All the librarians we talked to were agreed that just as many, if not more, books were being circulated, but that fiction is far less popular. Novels used to account for about sixty per cent of withdrawals; now the figure is closer to thirty. People are getting the make-believe stuff on their screens and are reading books for information. . . . The best-sellers are now biographies and inspirational guides on how to be happy and how to be a better salesman. (Attwood 1955, 32–33)

*Still the Most Exciting Country* belongs to the same genre as John Gunther's compendious *Inside U.S.A.* (1947), whose authoritative voice Steinbeck subtly mocked at the beginning of *A Russian Journal*: "In late March, I, *and the pronoun is used by special arrangement with John Gunther*, was sitting in the bar of the Bedford Hotel on East Fortieth Street" (1948, 3, emphasis added). To speak with any credibility about the postwar United States, one almost had to ask Gunther's permission. His monumental, 979-page book is a more ambitious undertaking than Attwood's; but however sophisticated its social, political, and cultural analysis, it ends up homogenizing everything into the seamless monolith of its author's thoroughly researched viewpoint. Opposing such patriotism backed by a marshalling of "facts," Steinbeck knows, risks confinement to "the fringes"—merely anecdotal knowledge from which it is impossible to generalize. And in the HUAC era, if the anecdotes serve to question the status quo, one risks having one's views dismissed entirely.

By 1960, however, a countergenre had emerged to the ostensibly factual, complacently patriotic journalism of Gunther and Attwood. Steinbeck had a copy in his personal library of Henry Miller's *The Air-Conditioned Nightmare* (1945), a demolition of mainstream American society anticipating Kerouac's *On the Road* (1957), which Steinbeck is known to have read as well (DeMott 1984, 80, 157). These books belong to a new kind of countercultural travelogue, the nihilistic inversion of "See America First" reportage, which in the years following *Travels with Charley* would come into its own as the "New Journalism." This genre produced such classic antiheroic narratives as Norman Mailer's *The Armies of the Night* (1968), Tom Wolfe's *The Electric Kool-Aid Acid Test* (1968), and Hunter S. Thompson's *Fear and Loathing in Las Vegas* (1971). These two genres are mirror images of one another; or, perhaps more accurately, one aspires to be a "straight" mirror to society, and the other sets itself up as an aggressively distorting, funhouse mirror. According to the one, while the United States may have its problems, they are all on their way to being solved, and it is "still the most exciting country"; the other rejects the dominant values of Anglo American society and finds redemption only in the underground: avant-garde artists and writers, bebop, or, in *On the Road*'s final gesture of refusal, Mexico.

Steinbeck responds to this opposition of extremes through a self-reflexive, ironic narration, explicitly associated with *Don Quixote* in a key passage near the middle, where he reflects on the shaping of his journey by the choices he makes about what to put in and what to leave out. In its published form it opens part 3, and reads simply, "Chicago was a break in my journey, a resumption of my name, identity, and happy marital status. My wife flew in from the East for her brief visit. I was delighted at the change, back to my known and trusted life—but here I run into a literary difficulty. Chicago broke my continuity. This is permissible in life but not in writing. So I leave Chicago out, because it is off the line, out of drawing. In my travels, it was pleasant and good; in writing, it would contribute only a disunity" (1962, 111).

Some eight hundred words are cut from the manuscript at this point, a fascinating digression concerning, precisely, the unity and form of the account of "*my quixotic travels with Charley about America*" (1961a, ms 150). The adjective "quixotic" here indicates a reaffirmation at this crucial point of the association between this book and Cervantes's novel. In the reflections excerpted here, Steinbeck makes it clear that he is concerned less with what he saw and heard than with how to construct a representation that will not be merely factual but poetically true, discursively unified:

> Chicago broke my continuity. This is permissible in life but not in writing. *Point of view, tempo, timbre, pitch, whatever you want to call that quality which gives a piece of writing consistency and a facsimile of*

> life—this was temporarily distorted. . . . *In my usual writing, everything is tested, approved or rejected, every sentence, every word, every intention, every rhythm, is planned, tried as surely as though I used test tubes and controls instead of paper and pen.* . . . *If I could cut one single word and still achieve my purpose, that word would be cut.* But another man can come along, not knowing the intent of my purpose and digest out great portions perhaps knowing he removes whole layers of my intent but finding them not so necessary as I have found them. [ . . . ] *If I leave Chicago out, it is because it is off the line, out of drawing. In traveling it was pleasant and good— in writing it would contribute only a disunity.* Readers whose lives and circumstances are chaotic, will not tolerate chaos in writing [ . . . ]. *A writer must rearrange reality so that it will seem reasonably real to the reader.*
> 
> There's a sentence for you—reasonably real to the reader. The difficulty with most stories lies in the fact that they didn't seem real to the reader. [ . . . ] But it is not the realness of reality in writing I am protesting but the circumstance that two realities do not match, having a different texture. Coexistence seems impossible. In my quixotic travels with Charley about America I paused five times, in Chicago, in Seattle, in California and twice in Texas. Then I saw and felt beloved people who knew me as I knew them. It would be quite easy to recount every moment of these stops but it would be out of drawing with the rest. A book has to be one thing just as a poem does or a chair or a table. *For a few days in Chicago my travels with Charley lost their identity and became something else—and no matter how delightful to me were those days, they are not at one with the journey.* (1961a, ms 147–50, boldface added; 1962, 111)

The difference in "texture" corresponds to the difference between, on the one hand, an ordinary trip taken in company with others, compromising between their perceptions and expectations and one's own, and, on the other, the quixotic journey taken alone in Rocinante, with the freedom to set aside preestablished identity and live for a time half-immersed in imagination, moving in a liminal space ("the fringes") associated, however ironically, with the chivalric quest.

At the end of this latter journey the author-narrator, reflecting on its overall shape and, again, on the uniqueness of each traveler's experience, refers to the whole as "project windmills," alluding, of course, to the episode in which Don Quixote attacks them. That sentence was stricken from the text, probably because it presupposed an earlier reference to this "code name," which had not in fact appeared previously, though Steinbeck referred to his trip privately as "Operation Windmills," for example in a letter to Covici dated June 20, 1960 (1975, 671). But removing the phrase erased the thread connecting *Don*

*Quixote* to the question of how to carve a quasi–chivalric quest narrative from the background of a nonfictional account of an ordinary trip:

> In the beginning of this record *of my travels with Charley* I tried to explore the nature of journeys, how they are things in themselves, each one an individual and no two alike. I speculated with a kind of wonder on the strength of the individuality of journeys and stopped on the postulate that people don't take trips—trips take people. That discussion, however, did not go into the lifespan of journeys. This seems to be variable and unpredictable. Who has not known a journey to be over and dead before the traveler returns? . . .
>
> *Project Windmills bears out my premise. It* [My own journey] started long before I left, and was over before I returned. I know exactly where and when it was over. Near Abingdon, in the dog-leg of Virginia, at four o'clock of a windy afternoon, without warning or good-bye or kiss my foot, my journey went away and left me stranded far from home. (1961a, ms *39, ts 360; 1962, 243. Note: the ms pagination starts over with p. *1 during the Texas episode.)

"Quixotism" and "tilting at windmills" are thus associated with the vain attempt at forging a single whole, a "quest," out of the disparate experiences the author-narrator has on "the fringes." Moreover, he abandons these "fringes," these solitary wanderings, several times along the way to travel in more comfortable style, accompanied by his wife, Elaine. Here it is helpful to recall Cervantes's struggle with the coherence of his vast novel and his reflection on the problem of the unity of part 1 at the beginning of part 2, when he has Don Quixote and Sancho Panza debate the matter with Sansón Carrasco, who has brought them news of a book based on their previous exploits. Objections from readers to digressions and lacunae are fielded by the characters themselves in a tour de force that has appealed especially to postmodernists (1949, II.2–4, 525–35).[7] Steinbeck's metaliterary reflections on "the journey" and its meanings are similarly concentrated in a pause around the middle of the account (Chicago-North Dakota), when the author-narrator looks back on the path he has followed, and ahead to what remains, mimicking Cervantes's technique.

Another example, later on, is an unpublished digression of over four hundred words explaining Charley's absence from certain episodes on the West Coast when Steinbeck was traveling with Elaine. As those scenes were either cut altogether or she was airbrushed out (literally by changing "we" to "I" and omitting specific sentences describing her words and actions), this passage no longer made sense and therefore also had to be eliminated. The digression is recognizably similar in tone to the "explanation" Cervantes has Sancho Panza give at the beginning of part 2 for why his donkey disappeared and then reappeared in part 1 (1949, II.3–4, 532–34). Sansón Carrasco speaks up for certain readers who had objected, like the ones who ostensibly complain here about Charley's being left out of certain episodes:

> *Having come so far in my narrative, I offered the text to one or two whose judgement I trust for comment and suggestion. For a writer with a forest of material to sort out may well get lost in the trees. Not comment, but complaint was soon forthcoming as follows.*
>
> *"While you pleasured yourself with high living with memories and prophecies, with politics and self-indulgence, what of Charley? He has not been mentioned. You can't retire him at will."*
>
> *This criticism is perhaps valid, but it is one Charley himself would never make. He has a sense of proportion. When Charley and I traveled alone together, the dog was indeed man's best friend. But Charley knows better than any one that when the wife is present, he is man's second best friend, and he finds this a normal relationship and perhaps a better one.* (1961a, ms 282A; 1962, 182)

This passage continues with a discussion of Charley's point of view on human affairs, strongly reminiscent of Berganza's perspective in Cervantes's *Colloquy of the Dogs*: "*He has always been a tolerant observer of the follies and inconsistencies of the higher species.* [ . . . ] *In my more human and frail moments, I have thought I saw Charley's quick smile of amusement. But he accepts our species for what it is. And if some well-intentioned but misguided bumblehead of a fairy godmother should offer to change Charley into a human, I think he would laugh himself sick.* [ . . . ] *And I hope that will answer the criticism that Charley has been ignored*" (1961a, ms 282A–282B; 1962, 182). The reference to the "fairy godmother" who offers "to change Charley into a human" recalls the witch Cañizares in *The Colloquy of the Dogs*, who tells the Berganza he is really a human being under a spell that has made him take a dog's form. This is one of several places where *Travels with Charley* echoes *The Colloquy of the Dogs*, a text Steinbeck clearly knew, as he wrote Elizabeth Otis on June 25, 1962, that he was thinking about writing a play to be titled "A Colloquy of Bugs," based on the theory that if a nuclear holocaust destroyed humanity, the cockroaches would survive. It was to be "somewhat in imitation of *A Colloquy of Dogs* by Cervantes" (Steinbeck 1978, 105).

There is, then, a split inscribed in the manuscript between the two sides of the author-narrator—on the one hand he is the "quixotic" traveler on a "quest" for America in Rocinante, and on the other, the writer grappling with the problem of giving those experiences a coherent shape and meaning, self-consciously confronting the implications of the movement in and out of the romantic imagination, and inviting the reader to follow the permutations of his meditations on form, genre, representation, media, and myth. It is no oversimplification to say that the former involves identification with Don Quixote and the latter with Cervantes. Most importantly, the identification with Don Quixote is not only ironized, it is incorporated into an envelope of metaliterary reflection derived at least in part from Steinbeck's prolonged exposure to Cervantes's consummate literary artistry, which had taken him far beyond an interest in the antihero alone. The problem is that only tatters of this envelope survived the editing process, and all connections between it and *Don Quixote* were erased.

The first version of *Travels with Charley* is thus a more ambitious work—in both literary and social terms—than the book that appeared in 1962. For that very reason, it threatens to unravel, and surely what the editors at both *Holiday* and Viking trimmed away seemed to them not to fit the central theme. This trimming distorted the true nature of this book, more a critical meditation on the *image* of the United States and how it is constructed than a nonfiction account of an actual trip. The trip is a necessary pretext. The reader of the published book might well feel betrayed to learn now, decades on, that there are significant differences between the narrative and the actual journey, which was edited to appear a seamless, authentic account. But the attentive reader of the manuscript will not be in the least surprised, given the hints dropped along the way alerting us to the fact that *any* coherent narrative is the product of artifice.

One of the themes that gives unity to this meditation in its original form is the way certain romantic myths of American life, such as the frontier West or the antebellum South, are related to the reality of the country. The analogous relationship in early modern Spain is that of chivalric and other romance genres to everyday life, which is the central theme in *Don Quixote*. Steinbeck had recently been grappling with yet another version of the same tension in his work on the fifteenth-century adapter of Arthurian romance, Sir Thomas Malory, discussed earlier. A key reflection on these themes originally followed the comment that "Fargo," even after Steinbeck visited the town and saw how little the reality conformed to the image in his mind, still retained the set of associations it had for him before he saw it:

> And I found with joy that the fact of Fargo had in no way disturbed my mind's picture of it. I could still think of Fargo as I always had—blizzard-riven, heat-blasted, dust-raddled. I am happy to report that

in the war between reality and romance, reality is not the stronger. [ . . . ] *I was delighted with my discovery about Fargo, for it confirms and strengthens the great duality of reality and romance. And it explains many things also—how the south can be what it is and at the same time a magnolia scented dream. And it reassures us that long after the horse has become extinct, pushed to its disappearance by the jeep, the tractor and the airplane, cowboys will still ride the ranges of the mind and their reality will increase. For it does seem that our fictions are more disciplined than the reality they are presumed to reflect. It has been my experience and probably that of most writers, that having written a story a friend or a critic on reading it, cried out—"This is not true to life. This character would not have done thus and so." Let then the writer protest—"But that's not made up. I got that incident, that man, out of the morning paper."*

*This changes nothing. "It's not true to life for a book," the critic says. And there you have our lonely duality. The external real can do anything and does, but our romances are governed by permanent and unchanging laws. And in accepting both, we need have no sense of a split world at all, else there would be no moss draped magnolia south, no adult westerns.* (1961a, ms 155, ts 169–70; 1962, 122)

Rather than a "split world" of fantasy and reality, Steinbeck's focus is the role of imagination *in* the social and cultural "real world." In contrast to the purportedly "factual" accounts of Attwood or Gunther, but without falling into the nihilism of, say *The Air-Conditioned Nightmare*, he follows Cervantes's example and situates his narration between these two extremes, at the intersection of reality and romance. The overlaying of romance onto reality is indicated in the text through the ironic use of chivalric epithets such as "the Lily Maid" and "my lady wife" to refer to Elaine Steinbeck, or "the gallant Rocinante" to refer to his camper. Regrettably, the former were *all* removed in the editing process, sometimes because Elaine Steinbeck's very presence was deleted (in the West Coast episodes) and at others because the chevaleresque tone was jettisoned (in the Texas section).[8] "Gallant" and "gallantry" are also used several times in relation to Charley, most notably in the brief episode of the "rather stout and bedizened Pomeranian of the female persuasion" toward whom "his French blood flared up, and he proceeded to gallantries" and, eventually, "toward romance," provoking a violent reaction on the part of the smaller dog's owner (1962, 38–39). This scene is unmistakably patterned on a similar moment in *Don Quixote* when Rocinante, catching the scent of some mares grazing nearby, "suddenly felt the desire to have a little sport with the ladies" and "trotted briskly over to them to acquaint them with his needs" (1949, I.15, 108). In both texts, sexual response in animals is described using elevated language normally reserved for romantic love, thereby debunking the pretense that humans' sublimation of desire is anything more than a disguise for naked libido. Again, romance motifs are inserted into the real world, producing a comic-parodic effect that undermines our pretentious vanity.

At times Steinbeck reflects on his practice as a writer in relation to conventional genres and emerging media, emphasizing that he is not simply trying to write a "true account" of a trip across the country but to use the travelogue as an opportunity to diagnose the malaise afflicting the United States and intervene to address it. These overlapping themes are introduced in an intriguing deleted passage that comes relatively early:

> Then I had a waiter in and bespoke soup and a steak and a pound of raw hamburger for Charley, and I overtipped mercilessly. *With my coffee I turned on the large television set, and watched girls wash their hair, and saw an adult Western and I saw the debate between Richard Nixon and John F. Kennedy. Being a democrat, I wanted Kennedy to win but in a sense I mourned the passing of a simpler time. Many years ago when Hoover was president it was generally known that he read detective stories. I was very poor and needy then and I wrote a detective novel and just before the pay off I inserted a chapter addressed to President Hoover asking for a post office. For one reason or another that book didn't get printed but in effect it amounted to the right of petition. For eight years now I have known that if I had wanted to make contact with the President* [i.e., Eisenhower] *I had only to write a Western and incorporate my message just after the chase and just before the pay off. If Kennedy should be elected, it would not be so simple. It's said that he reads widely in many fields and it would be difficult to be sure you were getting to him. Maybe a book aimed at his daughter to be called A Child's Garden of Politics.* (1961a, ms 78, ts 109–10; 1962, 80)

Around 1930, as a matter of fact, Steinbeck did write an unpublished detective novel, "Murder at Full Moon," actually a horror-crime hybrid involving werewolves, which Gavin Jones has assured me does have a chapter addressed to Hoover. Moreover, during the Eisenhower years he began but did not finish a Western parody-satire, "Don Keehan, the Marshall of Manchón," discussed earlier, which is patterned directly on *Don Quixote* and concerns a middle-aged man who has seen too many Westerns on television (Williams 2105). However tongue-in-cheek, then, Steinbeck engaged in a writing practice that deliberately exploited readers' addiction to specific forms of genre fiction to surreptitiously insert a political "message." And he associated that addiction with Alonso Quijano's love for chivalric romance, which led to his transformation into Don Quixote. As a writer Steinbeck intentionally intervened in public life, and the choice of this or that conventional communicative mode could be a mask for another strategic purpose, meant to be transformational for the reader. This is true of *Travels with Charley* itself, which uses the outward form of a travelogue to intervene in the public life of the nation.

The casual reader of *Travels with Charley* can be forgiven for failing to appreciate the irony with which the Woody Guthriesque nostalgia for the Dust Bowl values of his *Grapes of Wrath* days is evoked, in order to gain a critical leverage against the present—in exactly the same way as nostalgia for chivalry functions in *Don Quixote*. As we have just seen, the theoretical musings that undergird this juxtaposition of romance and reality were mostly omitted, leaving behind only occasional stumps of the amputated passages. So too were some of the sharpest satirical barbs from the homespun Will Rogers voice of the author-narrator: attacking consumerism; questioning militarism (the Bomb); and pointing out the dependence of political power on the power of media, with the disheartened citizenry's correspondent loss of faith in supposedly democratic institutions. Let us examine a few of these.

First, the manuscript of *Travels with Charley* shuttles between mocking rejection of ultramodern consumerism and retreat into the "great outdoors." Vestiges of this remain in the published book, for example in the discussion of mobile homes, which Steinbeck represents as a paradoxical attempt at packaging the wilds. But even these vestiges have been toned down, as this example shows, concerning the vending machines at rest stops:

> It is life at a peak of some kind of civilization. The restaurant accommodations, great scallops of counters with simulated leather stools, are as spotless as and not unlike the lavatories. Everything that can be captured and held down is sealed in clear plastic. The food is oven-fresh, spotless and tasteless; untouched by human hands. I remembered with an ache certain dishes in France and Italy touched by innumerable human hands.
>
> *Back to the vending machines, they have a much fancier name than that but I have forgotten it. Only one product was missing, but before I can get this printed, it will be there—a coin machine with an oxygen mask where for a price one could breathe ten or twenty times—a boon for heart attacks and hangovers—with a disposable mask, of course.* (1961a, ms 80, ts 113; 1962, 82–83)

Selling oxygen in a vending machine with a disposable mask would be the ultimate conversion of raw nature into a hygienic consumer product. Its absurdity struck someone, apparently, as excessive, and it was axed. Similarly, the critique of consumerism in relation to travel—"one goes, not so much to see but to tell afterward"—was driven home by an anecdote that must have seemed too pointed, too much in line with the stereotype of the "crass American" the State Department was struggling to eradicate around the world: "I don't know what made me turn sharply south and cross a state line to take a look at Yellowstone. Perhaps it was a fear of my neighbors. I could hear them say, 'You mean you were that near to Yellowstone and didn't go? You must be crazy.' Again it might have been the American tendency in travel. One goes, not so much to see but to tell afterward. *My wife once saw two women rushing into the Uffizi in Florence. One said, 'We have twenty minutes,' and the other panted, 'All right. You look and I'll check.' The purpose was obvious. In the future, if asked if they had seen such and such they could consult the catalogue and find out*" (1961a, ms 169, ts 204; 1962, 145). Thus the satire is frequently toned down, and the overall effect is less a critique of consumerism than the endearing cantankerousness of a middle-aged man resistant to change.

Much of the back-and-forth between modern civilization and rustic camping out was sacrificed when scenes involving Elaine Steinbeck were cut. This made the narrative more homogeneous and emphasized more the "authentic" image of a man traveling alone with his dog, but it also flattened its meaning. The most important example occurs when the author-narrator books a room at the Seattle airport to await his wife's arrival from New York:

> I wonder why progress looks so much like destruction.
> *I had some difficulty finding the airport since it serves both Seattle and Tacoma and is called logically enough SeaTac. It is so far from the city that it has become a city in itself. The enormous runways designed for jet traffic surrounded by motels of airport architecture, glass and plastic and stainless steel. In one of these, I registered to await my wife. It was a triumph of the modern. In my room, one whole side of which was glass, everything was built in. My big bed withdrew into a wall in the daytime as a snail slides into its shell. The bedside cabinet was a mass of buttons and little lights controlling radio, television, telephones and a great many other conveniences I never penetrated. [ . . . ] I could be in my bed and by pushing buttons draw in the beauty and culture of our time. Gun Smoke. Have Gun Will Travel. I Love Lucy. I love Dinah Shore, I love Barbara Stanwick. The greatest engineering minds in the history of the world had made these marvels available to me. Just looking at all those buttons brought home to me what a primitive life I had been leading.* (1961a, ms 228, ts 233; 1962, 162)

The most palpable sarcasm is reserved for mass media entertainments made possible by ultramodern technology, precisely the "make-believe stuff" for which Attwood reported people were turning to screens, "the beauty and culture of our time," which it took "the greatest engineering minds in the history of the world" to bring to his hotel room: *Gunsmoke*. The following pages describe Elaine Steinbeck's difficulties in getting to Seattle, despite the fact that it was initially supposed to be an easy trip, corresponding to the advertising copy she had read, which promised she would be *"treated like . . . royalty . . . her every wish anticipated by beautiful stewardesses and gallant stewards"* (1961a, ms 229, ts 234; 1962, 162). She ends up being rerouted to San Francisco, where her luggage is lost and she has to get on another flight. When she finally arrives she is tired and upset. The whole incident is turned into one more example of the incongruity between reality and the romantic ideas that float in our heads and are used to manipulate us, to sell us things, commodify our time, our attention, our lives.

Similarly, Cervantes uses Don Quixote as well as a slew of secondary characters, including but not limited to Sancho Panza, to show how people are led astray by idealized notions of heroism, military glory, social status, wealth, and romantic love, as well as by fears, especially fear of the racial other (Childers 2010). In *Travels with Charley*, the primary fear that is used to manipulate the public is nuclear war, which means both the Bomb and "the Russians." In a passage that made it past the editors' scrutiny, Steinbeck depicts himself insinuating to a Minnesota storekeeper that "the Russians" are just serving the function of giving people something to fear:

> "You think then we might be using the Russians as an outlet for something else, for other things."
> "I didn't think that at all, sir, but I bet I'm going to. [ . . . ] You've given me something to think about in a sneaking kind of way." (1962, 129)

This "sneaking kind of way" of providing "something to think about" indicates the author-narrator's method, not just with other characters, but with his readers as well. One such "something to think about" that was sneaked into the manuscript with a certain frequency, but curtailed in the book, was the Arms Race itself. "The Bomb" is mentioned explicitly just twice in the published version: during the visit to Deer Isle, Maine, when Miss Brace's cat George is said to feel such intense hatred of everyone else that he would be happy "if the bomb should fall and wipe out every living thing" except his owner (1962, 47); and when the author-narrator sees the evacuation route signs along the highway in Minnesota, "the planned escape route from the bomb that hasn't been dropped . . . a road designed by fear" (1962, 117).

The nuclear deterrent Attwood thought would end all war is referred to more obliquely as well in the encounter with the submarine crewmember ("And now submarines are armed with mass murder, our silly, only way of deterring mass murder" 1962, 21), and in a passage on the overwhelming pace of technological change ("now a force was in hand how much more strong, and we hadn't had time to develop the means to think, for man has to have feelings and then words before he can come close to thought and, in the past at least, that has taken a long time" 1962, 31). This last example, however, shows how the theme was developed further in the original text, for the manuscript continues: "*And now even our feelings were confused and the words hadn't come. What happens tomorrow is unsure. We can't even guess—and that confusion has got into every single crevice and corner of our lives. If that is so, no wonder people aren't afraid of bombs. Maybe their minds have retired from participation until the tools of thinking are provided*" (1961a, ms 33, ts 38; 1962, 31). It is actually the *lack* of fear of a nuclear holocaust that worries him. People have grown too accustomed to the idea to really feel afraid. Thus, while visualizing the "well-stoked, white-hot hell" of the Vermont preacher's sermon, Steinbeck ponders this numbness: "*Maybe we've seen too many blast furnaces, watched motion picture mushroom clouds rising from atomic explosions of the unthinkable and therefore unbelievable heat of the sun*" (1961a, ms 72, ts 96; 1962, 71). Endless mass media repetitions of the apocalypse have normalized what initially seemed unspeakably terrifying. Kubrick's *Dr. Strangelove* (1964) is still two years away, but Americans have already learned to "stop worrying and love the bomb." Elsewhere the author-narrator imagines the ancient Greeks, doom having been prophesied at Delphi, "*and when that happened, why it was time to dig a bomb shelter*" (1961a, ms 160, ts 182; 1962, 130). Finally, he tells the young gay man and his father, in Idaho, emphasizing the importance of hairdressers, "*If a hydrogen bomb were going to be dropped on Tuesday at two o'clock in the afternoon and if it were completely announced and certain, and if fifty thousand women had hair appointments on Tuesday at two o'clock—fifty thousand women would be killed under driers*" (1961a, ms 221, ts 224; 1962, 157). This hyperbole was presumably deemed too irreverent (and perhaps sexist as well), but it reinforces the notion, hinted at repeatedly, that the danger of nuclear annihilation, perhaps precisely because it was numbingly present at all times to the collective imagination, was not taken seriously. Part of the way Steinbeck tried to counter that complacency was by slipping in repeated reminders, much as Cervantes did with the wanton, wasteful violence of war, which he nonetheless never openly denounced, even though he repeatedly undermined it with ironic evocations of vainglory and futile heroism.

A significant aspect of Steinbeck's satire in *Travels with Charley* are numerous references to the presidential campaign and election of 1960 between Richard M. Nixon and John F. Kennedy, nearly all of which were removed before publication, as they made the book too topical and too partisan (Steigerwald 2013, ch. 2). Steinbeck's main interest in the election, though, is what he perceives to be the prevailing mood among voters: a mixture of cynicism, distrust, and passive resistance. The impact of mass media—radio broadcast speeches, televised debates, and telephone pollsters—was corrosive, and Steinbeck shows a sophisticated awareness of the tropes and techniques of representation used to manipulate public opinion:

> *Every election brings forth phrases like incantations. The most used one of the 1960 election was to me irritating and even insulting. I don't know who used it first but I heard it first in a Nixon speech. The phrase is "spell it out." "I'm going to spell it out." "He spelled it out." I think it intends to mean I'm going to speak simply and directly, but actually we spell out messages to keep secrets from children. The c-a-n-d-y is in the t-o-p d-r-a-w-e-r. To me it means that the speaker holds my intelligence in contempt so that he must reduce his message to baby talk. The phrase has for me an overtone of dishonesty.*[9]
>
> *On the television screen the faces of the contestants grew daily more gaunt and haunted with pure poisonous fatigue. I don't know whether the public demands it, but certainly the candidates believe that agony and sacrifice is demanded of them. There was one other innovation. The facial make-up for television cameras became more important than the message. There are people who still believe that if Nixon had had another make-up man he might have won. And maybe they are right.* (1961a, ms 263–64, ts 272–74; 1962, 176)

In writing *Travels with Charley* Steinbeck strove to counterbalance this influence of mass media by means of a self-reflexive, critical narrative subsuming the political discourse of radio and television within a broader framework—rhetorically pitting authentic orality against broadcast media.

The last major topic of the book, opposition to desegregation in New Orleans, even if not directly related to the election, is also a political issue, and one that Steinbeck frames as a question of media representation: the nauseating television, newspaper, and magazine coverage commanded by the sensationalizing, obscene "Cheerleaders." The media transform such local stories into mirrors for national identity: "And *not only is* the South a limb of the nation, *but* its pain spreads out to all America. *To avoid the south would be to ignore one of the most if not the most important single factor that moulds the American image*" (1961a, ms *12, ts 326; 1962, 216). To critique of the role of new media in forging a national image or identity and intervene deliberately to revise that image moves a writer far beyond the entertainment industry or the modernist literary establishment. Unmolding this "American image," penetrating into its mystique, discovering the shared roots in romantic myth of the "wild West" and the "magnolia-draped South," was a project not for a fact-based journalist but for a novelist steeped in fantasy and fiction. In *Travels with Charley* the tangible physical journey per se had more to do with the rhetorical legitimation an eye-witness account provides than with anything Steinbeck would actually see and hear. The real substance of the narrative is a critique of the impact of representations masquerading as facts—though it appeared two years before McLuhan's *Understanding Media* popularized the new slogan "the medium is the message" (1964, 7).

The use of the contrast between "romance" and "reality" to establish a satirical critique of American life that neither nostalgically upholds the past nor unreasonably condemns the present is the foundational layer of Steinbeck's Cervantism in *Travels with Charley*. Upon this foundation he constructs a socially conscious but tolerant and flexible persona who can see both sides of an issue and, rather than taking a stand of his own, can put it before the reader as an open question. This is a contemporary version of Cervantes's famous "perspectivism," a hallmark of his style for which Steinbeck had shown an appreciation as early as *A Russian Journal* and *East of Eden*. And finally, having constituted the author-narrator as such a socially engaged but ideologically neutral observer of American life, he further deploys this Cervantine structure to situate himself as a writer vis-à-vis important literary trends of the moment, such as the emerging Beat movement (as represented by Kerouac) and still-dominant Modernism (Faulkner); and beyond even the status of "literature" as such, the underlying, "timeless" encounter of the lone performer with the audience in the context of the new media of the time, through the character of the itinerant Shakespearean actor (1962, 130–36).

The character Steinbeck establishes for himself in *Travels with Charley* is closer in role and outlook to the author of *Don Quixote* than to its protagonist, especially as presented in part 1, where the would-be knight is primarily represented as a bellicose lunatic. The author-narrator here is not really "fighting windmills"; in fact, his attitude in interacting with other characters is far from the belligerent, confrontational stance of the mad knight who insists on imposing his chivalric vision on everyone he meets. The ironic invocation of "Rocinante" as an inside joke between author and reader aligns him more with Cervantes, whose ability to sympathize with and humanize all parties across religious, class, and gender divides has led to endless debate about his own ambiguous views. One particularly apt example of this perspectivism in *Travels with Charley* is the episode of Robbie, the young man who lives with his father, at whose motel complex the narrator stays in Idaho. As the manuscript clarifies, Robbie's mother abandoned the family, evidently a number of years ago. Robbie has studied to become a ladies' hairdresser; he dreams of visiting New York City for the cultural scene. The implication is clearly that he is homosexual. The father gruffly demands the author-narrator's opinion of his son's chosen profession, and by way of answer the narrator builds up the influential role of the hairdresser in any community, where women confide in him and take his views seriously. What is most interesting about the scene is how studiously the author-narrator avoids confrontation with the father, an avowed Republican and somewhat of a misogynist, at least to judge by his comments about Robbie's mother. The defense of hairdressing as a respectable vocation is couched in terms the father can accept. The author-narrator strategically de-escalates the tension within the family, "sneakily" giving the father "something to think about." He depicts himself as a secret ally of the gay youth but not as an open combatant against his father. The author-narrator's behavior here is close to Don Quixote's in part 2, for example in the meeting with the gentleman in the green-colored greatcoat (*caballero del verde gabán*), whose son wants to be a poet (1949, II.16, 608–10). Don Quixote gives a long, prudent speech about child-rearing, parental guidance, and the dignity and worth of poetry, which culminates, "In conclusion, then, my dear sir, my advice to you would be to let your son go where his star beckons him" (610). In fact, that episode could easily have been a conscious or unconscious model for this scene in *Travels with Charley*.

The other interesting thing about this scene is that it was edited down from about fifteen hundred words to roughly half that. Most of what was removed concerns electoral politics or the Bomb (some of which is quoted earlier) or is related to Robbie's mother, mention of whom was entirely removed. Without the shadow-presence of the absent wife and mother, some subtlety in the interaction among the three men is lost and the characters, especially the father, are flattened as a result. The cuts diminish this scene, both in terms of its length and its artistry. In the original it stands out as a deliberately paradigmatic instance of the author-narrator's approach to the issues faced by those he meets on the road, and thereby, metonymically, by US society in general. He intervenes productively, introducing his tolerant, liberal-minded views in a nonthreatening manner that can worm its way into a person's viewpoint. The goal of this strategic intervention is to strengthen what Arthur M. Schlesinger (1949) called "the vital center" of Cold War cultural politics, the precise opposite of the polarization that, by 1960, had begun to take hold (and has only grown worse since). This centrist literary strategy, I would argue, is the basis of Steinbeck's successful self-reconstruction as a writer and public figure at the end of his life; the sophistication with which he deployed it has been underestimated by excessively doctrinaire critics.[10]

Read in its manuscript form and in the light of its appropriation of *Don Quixote*, *Travels with Charley in Search of America* emerges as an experimental hybrid between narrative and essay. Though it incorporates rhetorical gestures derived from the genre of the journalistic travelogue as a report on contemporary America, such as Attwood's *Still the Greatest Country*, it does so in a manner that marks its distance from that approach just as decisively as Cervantes marked his from the chivalric romance. What Steinbeck explores in its pages, really, is the deeper, more troubling question, What is it still possible to do with a book? Given the nature of the malaise facing the country—conformity, complacency, a mass-media image of national homogeneity that does not conform to reality but passes itself off as reality—what impact can a writer have? Lurking behind the entire project is the recognition that the problems of the Cold War era do not lend themselves to muckraking journalism or proletarian protest fiction. Though nothing definitive emerges from this exploration, Steinbeck suggests a continuing role for the novelist as a self-conscious critic of the ways deep-rooted myths—like those of the Old West or the Old South—continue to impinge on our desires and perceptions, leaving us susceptible to mass media manipulation. Implied as well, therefore, is a role for the reader in cultivating that awareness and joining with the writer in a necessary though perhaps futile effort at resisting through critical reflection. As we have seen, the author-narrator provides numerous examples in which he interacts with men whose views are more conservative than his own and subtly engages in a deliberate practice of slyly opening their minds.

I have tried to show that in significant ways *Don Quixote* provides a blueprint for this practice, and that this function is by no means limited to the so-called myth of the quixotic hero. On the contrary, in my reading, Steinbeck's *Travels* emerge as more Cervantine than quixotic, that is, more ironic in their evocation of the chivalric "quest," which serves a satirical purpose of establishing for the author-narrator an oblique point of view, from "the fringes." The leverage against the status quo this provides is hedged around in the manuscript by what I have called a metaliterary "envelope," of reflection on the nature of coherent literary representation, its ties to romance models, and its inherent artificiality. The reader familiar only with the offhand remark at the beginning of *Travels with Charley* to the effect that Rocinante is the name of Don Quixote's horse may well be surprised by such grandiose claims. But, as outlined in this essay, Steinbeck had a much longer and more complicated history with *Don Quixote* than is generally known, going back to the mid-1940s. As this essay shows, one of the reasons it is little known is that the evidence for it is almost entirely found in posthumous or still unpublished writings.

The preceding exploration contributes to the ongoing process of, in Gavin Jones's formulation, reclaiming John Steinbeck, in this case as a more self-conscious artist than his detractors would have us believe. His critique of Cold War modernism in some ways anticipates postmodernism but is probably better understood as a sui generis attempt at maintaining an aspect of the writing of the '20s and '30s that had largely been eclipsed behind the postwar emphasis on form: its serious engagement with social and political issues beyond the text, despite a playful exterior, and despite insistence on the autonomy of art. If the younger Steinbeck was indeed writing "for the future of humanity" as Jones puts it, in *Travels with Charley*, *The Winter of Our Discontent*, and even the underrated *America and Americans*, we find him writing for the future of the United States. Is it too late for us to take heed?

## Notes

1. I wish to publicly thank María Molestina, the head of reader services at the Morgan Library, for her generous assistance in the research for this essay.

2. These concerns appear in several pieces from the '50s and '60s collected in *America and Americans and Selected Nonfiction* (Steinbeck 2004), including the title essay (317–404), "The Trial of Arthur Miller" (101–4), and "Dear Adlai" (108–9), and in letters from the same period (Steinbeck 1975, 527–703).

3. I discuss Steinbeck's decades-long engagement with Cervantes in greater detail in "A Mark High and Bright" (Childers 2023).

4. Quotes from *Don Quixote* are taken from Samuel Putnam's translation (Cervantes 1949), as that is the edition Steinbeck is known to have read after Pascal Covici sent him a copy. Citation is given by part (I or II), chapter, and page.

5. In the only previous study of the intertextuality of *Don Quixote* and *Travels with Charley*, Marín Ruiz (2015) compares this aspect of the representation of Rocinante with appropriations of Rocinante by John Dos Passos and Graham Greene.

6. British anthropologist Victor Turner developed the concept of *communitas* to refer to social bonding outside of established structures, which he associated with the "liminal" experiences of rites of passage (1977). I previously employed the book on pilgrimage he cowrote with his wife, Edith Turner (1978), to account for the role of liminal *communitas* in Cervantes's *Persiles y Sigismunda* (Childers 2006, 84–124).

7. The antimodernist strain in Steinbeck leads to this convergence with postmodern metafiction, though it is an overstatement to call him a postmodernist avant la lettre. On Steinbeck's "weak modernism," see Jones (2021, 108–28).

8. "My lady wife" does occur once in the 2012 edition of *Travels with Charley* (203), in "L'Envoi," which retains this stylistic tic precisely because it was *not* submitted to the same editing process in 1962 as the rest of the manuscript; it was discarded early on and is not even included in the *typescript* at the Morgan Library. This shows how arbitrary it was to include "L'Envoi" at the end of *Travels with Charley* in the latest Penguin edition, without incorporating any more of the deleted material. What is needed is a critical edition of the manuscript and typescript, to finally give a full picture of the book Steinbeck originally wrote.

9. Nixon did indeed use this phrase in speeches in the autumn 1960 campaign, for example in Plainfield, New Jersey, on October 4 (1960a) and in New York City on October 5 (1960b).

10. Most notoriously and cruelly, in 1962, the announcement of John Steinbeck's Nobel Prize gave Arthur Mizener an occasion to dismiss Steinbeck's "moral vision of the thirties" (Mizener 1962, 4) and "tenth-rate philosophizing" (44). More recently, Philip Lopate, reviewing Souder's biography, superciliously opined that "Steinbeck's reputation seems stuck a few notches below greatness" (2021). See Jones's introduction, "Loving and Hating Steinbeck," for a cogent reflection on the "reasons for the critical disdain toward Steinbeck" (2021, 2), which has its basis in the formalist biases of high modernism.

Part II

# TRAVELS AS JEREMIAD

1960s America and Today

# 7

## Steinbeck and the "Longue Durée" of Deep Time in *Travels with Charley*

BARBARA A. HEAVILIN

In *Travels with Charley in Search of America*, as Steinbeck and the French poodle Charley near the end of their quest in search of America, the author thinks ahead longingly to the coming of Christmas and returning home. This journey, he writes, had begun long before he left home and ended before he returns: "I know exactly where and when it was and when it was over. Near Abingdon, in the dogleg of Virginia, at four o'clock of a windy afternoon, without warning or good-by or kiss my foot, my journey went away and left me stranded far from home" (Steinbeck 1997, 208). He does not feel the deep cold of approaching winter or see the beautiful countryside as he blindly bulldozes across West Virginia and plunges onto Pennsylvania's "great wide turnpike": "There was no night, no day, no distance. . . . After Abington—nothing. The way was a gray, timeless, eventless tunnel. . . . New Jersey was another turnpike. My body was in a nerveless, tireless vacuum" (209). As he goes on his way, he reflects that "at the end of it was the one shining reality—my own wife, my own house in my own street, my own bed" (209). Here Steinbeck has entered a nontime, a nonspace, emptiness where time seems to stop: "My body was in a nerveless, tireless vacuum." He is in a liminal space between his trip that has just passed and his homecoming in the near future. The present does not register, as his way has become "a gray, timeless, eventless tunnel."

Throughout *Travels*, Steinbeck has similarly explored time and space and the lens they provide for observing the world and human beings. Just as he reflects on that inward, nontime, liminal, in-between space that human beings all encounter on occasion, so he looks outward as well. And his gaze into the "longue durée," or long view, extends far across continents and into spaces of deep time. These reflections on time past, time future, and the present moment create a layered perspective that helps readers consider not only Steinbeck's era but our own. This deep-time slant achieves that mystical vision of wholeness he set forth in *Sea of Cortez* (1941), first published some nineteen years before *Travels* was published in 1962: "All things are one thing and that one thing is all things—plankton, a shimmering phosphorescence on the sea and the spinning planets and an expanding universe, all bound together by the elastic string of time. It is advisable to look from the tide pool to the stars and then back to the tide pool again" (178–79). Here the long view to the stars and the immediate vista of the tide pool become one, joined "by the elastic string of time."

Wai Chee Dimock's 2006 *Through Other Continents: American Literature across Time* defines "deep time" in relationship to American literature, often viewing this body of work as a kind of "shorthand, a simplified name for a much more complex tangle of relations, . . . better seen as a crisscrossing set of pathways, open-ended and ever multiplying, weaving in and out of other geographies, other languages and cultures. These are input channels, kinship networks, routes of transit, and forms of attachment—connective tissues binding America to the rest of the world" (3). American literature thus threads through "the long durations of those cultures into the short chronology of the United States" (3). The effect is to thicken and lengthen time, even revealing "abiding traces of the planet's multitudinous life" (3). On a continuum that runs through all races, nations, and species, Dimock believes, these phenomena create one world, to which all peoples in all times belong (195). In the case of Steinbeck, his present time, while grounded in the tide pool—or in a close survey of America in 1960, the time of his journey—is also connected to the universe, the stars above—or even to his thoughts and feelings expressed throughout his trip across America. To obtain a true, clear picture across time and space, Steinbeck suggests, requires a contemplation of a continuum between the two, and both in relationship to the whole.

Exploring the effect on time of such a continuum in the *longue durée* (long view), Fernand Braudel's 1980 "History and the Social Sciences: The Longue Durée" states that time seems to slow, to border on the "motionless," even a "semistillness" (33). In this long view, by means of semantics, words, and meanings, in *Travels* space and time continue ad infinitum, creating what Robert Pogue Harrison's 2003 "The Origin of Our Basic Words" calls a "literary culture" that binds people together and creates a "civil society" existing across time—one that includes those now living, those who have died and gone before, and those who are not yet born. The limits set by human finitude are thus transformed "into a field of historical relations," establishing a civil society woven of words (85). In *Travels*, Steinbeck builds such a society, such a field of relations. With his country's well-being at the forefront of his mind and deep in his heart, in this book Steinbeck embraces deep past, past, present, future—creating a "'lexical' civil society" made of words, meanings, deep time, wide spaces, such as that Harrison envisions.

Holding deep time and the longue durée as a mirror in which Americans may see themselves more clearly and address serious issues more assiduously, Steinbeck muses on the inexorable passing of time and inevitable future consequences when humanity reaches a point of no return: "I do wonder whether there will come a time when we can no longer afford our wastefulness" (22). And as the nation faces such monumental problems as the threat of nuclear warfare during the Cold War of the 1960s, he worries, too, because "we haven't had time to develop the means to think" (27). How do we learn how to think about these things? It takes time, and the question still looms in our own day as the United States and NATO face off with Russia over the war in Ukraine and live under the threat of World War III. Throughout *Travels*, Steinbeck is acutely conscious of time—geological time, a lifetime, present time environmental abuse encroaching on the future, and, most direly, time to develop "the means to think" (Steinbeck 1997, 27) about the looming global threat of nuclear war. Always, this concern gives the reader perspectives by which to compare ideas across continents and frames of eras of time, sometimes going back eons into deep time. Throughout his journey with Charley, Steinbeck is deeply concerned with four categories associated with time: (1) the prehistorical and historical, (2) the human experiences of beauty and death, (3) the development of a civil society, and (4) an inward move to transcendence over time and place.

## Prehistory and History

First, like Dimock and Braudel, Steinbeck looks back into prehistory and history—with his somber tone especially echoing that of Jewish history during the time of the prophet Isaiah—and he finds a sense of wholeness, of kinship with people and times long ago. In what Braudel has dubbed the motionlessness and semi-stillness "of the long, even of the very long time span, of the longue durée" (Braudel 1980, 27), Steinbeck peers into deep time and historical time, a view resulting in things connecting so that ties to other times may be observed. This temporal and spatial perspective provides a different way of seeing ourselves in the light of other ages, other countries, other backgrounds, and, as a result, seeing ourselves united with the ages—"a global civil society" (Dimock 2006, 5). "It is the slow tempo of time," Braudel believes, "that gives a true sense of history: a structure of everyday ties" (qtd. in Dimock 2006, 5). Dimock similarly envisions the wholeness of "a global civil society" and an earth that must be mapped across time and space—an inclusiveness that embraces both contemporaries and those from other times, other places.

In a July 1961 letter to his editor, Pascal Covici, Steinbeck voices concerns that echo Dimock's and Braudel's comments about the longue durée. That letter serves as an important prefatory introduction to *Travels* and reflects the writer's mood and carries over into the somber tone of the book. Steinbeck looks across human history and supplies a temporal and spatial map, most pointedly in his reflections on the biblical prophet Isaiah, with grave implications for our own day and times.

After he returned home from his trek across America, Steinbeck confides in Covici about his deep concern with writing the *Travels* book. Dispirited, he confides that other than its "geographical design and its unity of time," its focus seems "haphazard": "The little book of ambulatory memoirs staggers along, takes a spurt and lags. It's a formless, shapeless, aimless thing and it is even pointless. For this reason it may be the sharpest realism because what I see around me is aimless and pointless—ant-hill activity. Somewhere there must be design if only I can find it. I'm speaking of this completed journey now. And outside of its geographical design and its unity of time, it's such a haphazard thing" (Steinbeck 1989, 702). The letter shows his concern for focus on "unity of time"—a concern that will go deeper than just a chronological account of time on a trip with a dog across America. For time itself becomes a focus as Steinbeck gazes beyond the present day and back into deep time, peering on occasion into the future. Thereby, he brings new insight and meaning into our current condition, "holding the mirror," as Enlightenment writers in the eighteenth century would have it, providing a perspective by which we may observe ourselves in relationship to other societies in other times, other places.

Steinbeck is perturbed by threats America faces from without and within—a Cold War standoff between the United States and Russia, a malaise of moral inertia across the nation. Further, he is much concerned with the passing of time—both his own aging and the threat of decay overshadowing his country and encroaching on its people. As the letter to Covici continues, verbs and participial verbals create an unending continuum in time that begins in the past, continues to the present, and gazes steadily forward into the future. His concern with time here is palpable: "Thinking and thinking for a word to describe decay. . . . Through time the nation has become a discontented land. I've sought for an out on this—saying it is my aging eyes seeing it, my waning energy feeling it, my warped vision that is distorting it, but it is only partly true. The thing I have described is really there. I did not create it. . . . The haunting decay is there underneath it" (Steinbeck 1989, 702–3).

With "aging eyes," "waning energy," the distortion of "warped vision," and dread of "haunting decay," Steinbeck fears that time has taken its toll on him and could be partly to blame for his perception of the nation's discontent and the erosion of ethical mores eating away at its very fiber. Then he looks into deep time, far into the past of human history, to biblical days and ancient Jewish history for a comparison to what he is witnessing—for a perspective that will give us a way of seeing ourselves in our own day: "Well, there was once a man named Isaiah—and what he saw in his time is not unlike what I have seen, but he was shored up by a hard and durable prophecy that nothing could disturb. We have no prophecy now, nor any prophets" (Steinbeck 1989, 703).

As though talking to himself, he begins with "Well" as a precursor to his thoughts, pausing to weigh his own words. Drawing on his Episcopalian background and upbringing, Steinbeck goes back to deep time, some seven hundred years before the birth of Christ, to biblical times, the country of Israel, and Isaiah, one of the most revered of the Old Testament figures to this day. With that one recognizable name, Isaiah, he creates a time machine of sorts, a means of connecting, comparing nations across time. At the time, Israel was in great fear of an encroaching invasion by the Assyrian Empire, and Isaiah brought light into the darkness, bringing hope by pointing toward the coming of a Messiah who would preserve peace and bring prosperity. Memorialized by Handel's *Messiah*, the message is still treasured today by classical musicians as well as by Jews and Christians—and in general by lovers of music the world over. Steinbeck's readers would recognize the reference to a future time of endless peace: "The people that walked in darkness have seen a great light: they that dwell in the land of the shadow of death, upon them hath the light shined. . . . For unto us a child is born, unto us a son is given. And the government shall be upon his shoulder, and his name shall be called Wonderful, Counselor, the mighty God, the everlasting Father, the Prince of Peace. Of the increase of his government and peace there shall be no end" (Isa 2: 6–7 [King James Bible]). Here Steinbeck provides a spatial and temporal perspective across continents and deep time. The magnitude of Isaiah's prophecy gives great gravitas to Steinbeck's sad comment on our own times based on his observations during his travels with poodle Charley: "We have no prophecy now, nor any prophets."

In light of the Isaiah reference in this letter to Covici, then, we can perceive our own day and times with greater clarity. At the time, the Cold War with Russia threatened America from without, while the country was also threatened from within by a weakening moral fiber brought on by overindulgence and environmental abuse. Now there is no Isaiah to prophesy a coming Messiah bringing peace and light. And we are "the people that walk in darkness," with no prophecy of light to come. This venture into deep time that tells of Isaiah's prophecy of hope for the Israelites as they face dire times lends contrast to Steinbeck and Charley's travels in search of America. Early on, then, even before publication of *Travels*, Steinbeck was musing on deep time, his somber mood and tone carrying over into his book.

Steinbeck's diagnosis of the "haunting decay" of his beloved country and the postmodern loss of prophets, however, does not tell the entire story of *Travels*. Nor does it foretell what will be a joyous homecoming and a sense of hope for renewal at the story's end when he returns home to Sag Harbor, just as Christmas is coming. For Steinbeck himself is a prophet of sorts—a bard who diagnoses "the haunting decay" at heart of the nation's malaise and seeks a panacea, pointing toward some hope, if small. Kathleen Hicks's chapter in this volume proclaims, "Even if it is nigh impossible to believe Americans, much less the world, can come together to confront the challenges of our times successfully, at least there is comfort in knowing it is possible for humans still to find hope after the storm" (chapter 8). Steinbeck's studies in deep time, across the longue durée, show grounds for such hopefulness.

Steinbeck's prehistorical and historical perspective enables Americans to establish a sense of connection to other times and a means of measuring their own. Some of Steinbeck's observations in *Travels with Charley* are in the form of meditative pensées, in which he briefly reflects on a topic, in one case in particular musing on the final outcome of the human condition following a nuclear holocaust. And he chooses theater, a lifelong interest, as a focal point. A probably imagined encounter with an itinerant Shakespearean actor provides opportunity for reflection on the long history of theater, leading to his hopeful prediction that acting will survive even in the event of a nuclear holocaust and the death of the written word. In this excursive pensée into deep time and into a future he foresees, he covers millennia. After a brief discussion on Shakespeare and acting, the actor continues on his way home, and Steinbeck muses on the probability of the survival of acting after a holocaust. His opening sentence modifier is followed by a dash ("So it went on—") and sets up a time sequence, a continuum. He ponders the longevity of the acting profession, the history of writing, and fear of a bleak future when the written word is no more: "So it went on—a profession older than writing and one that will probably survive when the written word has disappeared. And all the sterile wonders of movies and television and radio will fail to wipe it out—a living man in communication with a living audience" (Steinbeck 2007, 116). And here we may consider the bastions of writing in a civilized and peaceable world—libraries, schools, universities, the corner newsstand, the backs of cornflake boxes, Sunday funnies, and on—accompanied by a fearful, cold dread of the nuclear annihilation of the written word. And against the backdrop of this bleak vista, Steinbeck looks to a future time after holocaust, and he prophesies the survival of theater, and with it, of human beings and the human spirit—"a living man," "a living audience." It is a prophecy that the light of hope will survive, coming out of the darkness, triumphing over the seeming doom.

There are four movements in time here. First, his take on "a profession older than writing" harks back to medieval times, the fall of Rome, the onset of the Renaissance—some thousand years of theater—and images of mystery and morality plays performed in churchyards. Second, he moves to present time with all its "sterile wonders of movies and television and radio." (Clearly, he is a lover of theater and live performance.) Third, there is a frightful prophecy of future time if nations do not settle differences peaceably. He writes, "A profession older than writing . . . will probably survive when the written word has disappeared." Then the images freeze as, after the excursion across continents into deep time and back into present time, we see the writer Steinbeck as he sits, writing, and invites the reader to contemplate the end of writing, and, with it, the demise of all the concomitant institutions dependent on the written word—from libraries and universities to newsstands. Fourth, there is a further shift in time beyond the death of writing and civilization as we know it. For theater and acting, "a profession older than writing," Steinbeck believes (or has to believe, if he is to cling to hope in the survival of humanity), "will probably survive when the written word has disappeared": a living man will act before "a living audience." Applause. Typically, Steinbeck leaves us with some hope, however thin—note the word "probably" in this prophecy.

## Beyond History and Time: Beauty and Death

In addition to historical time, Dimock writes of time in relationship to human experiences, such as beauty or death, that may not be based solely along boundaries of time and space. For in some experiences in the presence of deep beauty or the overwhelming sadness of death, time seems to cease. In *Travels* Steinbeck poignantly depicts experiences that go beyond history and time. In Wisconsin he encounters awe and glorious beauty similar to that of Romantic poet Wordsworth's depiction of an experience with the sublime in "Lines Composed a Few Miles above Tintern Abbey" (1798). Wordsworth writes of seeing "into the life of things" and feeling "a presence" that dwells in "setting sun," "round ocean," "living air" (lines 8–50; 92–95). Note the quality of time here as it reaches a stasis in which time itself has no meaning—only a dwelling presence as the poet sees into "the life of things" as time slows, halts. Such is Steinbeck's experience with the beauty of Wisconsin.

As Wordsworth sees "into the life of things" in "Tintern Abbey," going beyond admiration of the place's beauty to sublime awe in face of something much greater than the human, so Steinbeck describes a time in Wisconsin when he sees "into things, deep in," rising above the mundane. Bordering on the transcendental, Steinbeck's experience with the glory of Wisconsin's great beauty begins with reminiscences of what he had heard about in the past: delicious cheeses, pictures he does not exactly recall, but which he "must have seen." The state's terrain changes rapidly in a "variety of Field and hill, forest, lake." He thinks across seasonal time in this place, surmising that summers here may "reek and rock with heat, the winters may groan with dismal cold." And he focuses on one early October day when every tree, every hill is set off, separately, to glow in "butter-colored sunlight" (97–98)—a vista of earth and sun similar to Steinbeck's inclusive vision in *Sea of Cortez*, as he gazes from the tide pool to the stars and back again.

Then a sharp shift from present time to deep time occurs in a key sentence: "There was a penetration of the light into solid substance so that I seemed to see into things, deep in, and I've seen that light elsewhere only in Greece" (97). Like Wordsworth, Steinbeck seems to see into "the life of things." He transcends time and space, seeing deep, past eons, into origins of hills, lakes, forests, and across continents to another place, Greece—birthplace of Homer, *The Iliad*, and *The Odyssey*—where light penetrates solid substance. Next, he abruptly returns to the present rural scene of farm animals, corn, and pumpkins on this magical day.

As he continues his travels, he mulls again over deep time as he discovers alongside the road "the greatest distributor of sea shells in the world—and this in Wisconsin, which hasn't known a sea since pre-Cambrian times" (126). Here Steinbeck moves again far back in deep time—to precivilization, to geological ages, "pre-Cambrian times," the earliest geological age, with fossils of flora and fauna preserved in rock millions of years ago.

At the Wisconsin Dells, there is a dizzying move even further back into deep time as he experiences another of this state's surprises: "I had heard of the Wisconsin Dells but was not prepared for the weird country sculptured by the Ice Age, a strange gleaming country of water and carved rock, black and green. To awaken here might make one believe it a dream of some other planet, for it has a non-earthly quality, or else the engraved record of a time when the world was much younger and much different. Clinging to the dreamlike waterways was the litter of our times. . . . I doubt they could dispel the enchantment of the Wisconsin Dells" (98).

Sometime during the Ice Age, eons ago, the Wisconsin Dells—to postmodern eyes "weird" and "nonearthly"—were sculptured. Curiously, Steinbeck's choice of the passive verb "were sculptured" suggests a mind at work behind all this beauty and strangeness. In an understatement, Steinbeck finds these dells perhaps to be "the engraved record of a time when the world was much younger and much different." Just as he has seen, in a transcendent moment, "light penetrating into solid substance," Steinbeck invites readers to see Wisconsin's beauty and the strangeness of its Dells as "an engraved record"—with what Daniel Rivers (2022) calls "deep-time eyes," reading the record of our history and our experiences as humans spatially and temporally—viewing Wisconsin Dells as they were "sculptured" and their record "engraved" in mysterious beauty many ages ago. Such is his experience with beauty and the sublime in Wisconsin.

Dimock maintains that not all human experience are not all determined by temporal and spatial boundaries (2006, 5). Steinbeck's encounter with beauty in Wisconsin is one such experience. He has considered such metaphysical beauty often in his prose—in *Sea of Cortez* and in *Cannery Row* (1945), for example. As in his other works, in *Travels* a Romantic notion of beauty highlights and broadens the depth and variety of human experience. And like his experience with Wisconsin's beauty and the sublime, California redwood trees leave him transfixed, envisioning "another time":

> The redwoods, once seen, leave a mark or create a vision that stays with you always. No one has ever successfully painted or photographed a redwood tree. The feeling they produce is not transferable. From them comes silence and awe. It's not only their unbelievable stature, nor the color which seems to shift and vary under your eyes, no, they are not like any trees we know, they are ambassadors from another time. They have the mystery of ferns that disappeared a million years ago into the coal of the carboniferous era. They carry their own light and shade. The vainest, most slap-happy and irreverent of men, in the presence of redwoods, goes under a spell of wonder and respect. Respect—that's the word. One feels the need to bow to unquestioned sovereigns. (143)

There is something of purity and goodness in Steinbeck's depiction of redwood trees. They leave a mark on a person, creating an everlasting vision of grandeur, majesty, pure glory. In imagination, he tries and fails to trace their origins, comparing them instead to "the mystery of ferns that disappeared a million years ago into the coal of the carboniferous era" (143).

Peering into deep time, Steinbeck surmises that the forebears of the redwoods are these ferns whose demise eons ago gave rise to these mighty giant trees—a transformation of delicacy over time into a gigantic majesty that boggles the mind. In his stay in California, Steinbeck spent two days and nights in the redwood forest, "close to the bodies of the giants." "To me," he writes, "there's a remote and cloistered feeling here. . . . And there's a breathing in the black, for these huge things that control the day and inhabit the night are living things and have presence, and perhaps feeling, and somewhere in deep-down perception, perhaps communication. . . . These are the last remaining members of a race that flourished over four continents as far back in geologic time as the upper Jurassic period" (147). Steinbeck envisions these gigantic trees as a race of beings with presence, perhaps even with feeling, perception, communication. And he intuits "the certainty that a living world will continue its stately way when we no longer inhabit it" (147). And in his mystical vision of the holiness of redwoods, he feels their breath in the blackness of the night. The experience goes beyond appreciation of great beauty, to the sublime, almost to the divine.

Dimock maintains that the human encounter with death is also an experience not entirely predicated along boundaries of time and space (5). And Steinbeck's mood is most somber as he and Charley journey across America: he is recuperating from life-threatening illness; he is aging; he fears for the loss of his creative impetus; he questions his ability to see into the human condition. It is no wonder that he thinks of death when he returns to Monterey—the town is a reminder of friends and acquaintances who are now gone. Here he visits old, familiar places and has "a touching reunion" in Johnny Garcia's bar, where he is greeted with "tears and embraces," and time seems to melt away: "The years rolled away. We danced formally, hands locked behind us. And we sang the southern county anthem, 'There was a jung guy from Jolón—got seek from leeving halone.' . . . I hadn't heard it in years. It was old home week. The years crawled back in their holes" (152). Even though "the years crawled back in their holes" and the present seems subsumed in the past, still, Steinbeck tells Garcia, "There was a great man named Thomas Wolfe and he wrote a book called *You Can't Go Home Again*. And that is true. . . . Let us not fool ourselves. What we know is dead, and maybe the greater part of what we are is dead. What's out there is new and perhaps good, but it's nothing we know" (154). There ensues a dialogue, a kind of call and response—in Greek drama called "stichomythia" for quickly alternating short lines of speech with deep emotion. Thus, Steinbeck and Garcia create a catalogue of "the great ones," dear friends and acquaintances who have now gone on, now dead, beyond time:

> Johnny held his temples between his cupped hands and his eyes were bloodshot.
> "Where are the great ones? Tell me where's Willie Trip?"
> "Dead," Johnny said hollowly.
> "Where is Pilon, Johnny, Pom Pom, Miz Gragg, Stevie Field?"

"Dead, dead, dead," he echoed.
"Ed Ricketts, Whitey's Number One and Two, where's Sonny Boy, Ankle Varney, Jesus Maria Coreoran, Joe Portagee, Shorty Lee, Flora Wood, and that girl who kept spiders in her hat?"
"Dead—all dead," Johnny moaned. (154–55)

Johnny's adverbs and verbs draw death's portrait: hollowness, echoes, moaning. Time has no movement; space has no meaning in this experience. It is an experience of emptiness in which there is no movement, only deep suffering as time stands still. And Steinbeck's use of the Greek stichomythia—rapidly alternating lines of dialogue—brings echoes from across continents, across deep time, memories of self-blinded Oedipus weeping for his self-slain wife and mother, Jocasta.

Before leaving California, Steinbeck drives up to Fremont Peak, looks out over the lovely vista to big oaks, and remembers that his mother once shot a wildcat and his father once burned "his name . . . with the name of the girl he loved on an oak in this place" (157). Imprinting this scene in memory, he hurries "away from the permanent and changeless past where my mother is always shooting a wildcat and my father is always burning his name with love" (158). Past time is lasting, enduring in memory.

Similarly, in the 1937 novel *Of Mice and Men*, in the scene with the death of Curley's wife, Steinbeck captures the essence of death and all its nightmarish horror in the human experience. It is "a moment" in which all sound, movement, and time itself seem to cease to exist. Steinbeck writes, "As happens sometimes, a moment settled and hovered and remained for much more than a moment. And sound stopped and movement stopped for much, much more than a moment. Then time awakened again and moved sluggishly on" (Steinbeck 2002, 88). Death brings cessation not only of life but of moments and time itself—a nightmarish stasis. As anyone who has experienced the passing of a loved one knows, the greatest insult of all when death comes is that the sun keeps rising and setting, life goes on its normal routine, moments and time resume their movement.

Whatever death is, it is not an abstraction. As Steinbeck's catalog shows, it is most personal; here each person lost, gone on before, and dead has a name and lives on in memory. The staccato naming of names in Steinbeck's catalog is like a roll call, for which there will be no resounding, "Here" or "Yo"—only silence, stasis. Such is the nature of death—beyond space and time, beyond movement, just shock, deep sorrow, and horror. Beauty and death are essential considerations in *Travels*, taking readers beyond everyday concerns with society's wastefulness, global threats of nuclear disaster, and lives encased in sanitized plastic. For this emphasis brings both our vulnerability and glory into sharp focus, deepening our sense of identity as human and humane beings.

## Across Time and Space

Dimock has observed that "the concept of a global civil society" invites us to think of the earth as a whole that is integrally joined together across time and space, with the society's membership open not just to contemporaries but to all peoples of all times. Like Dimock, Steinbeck is concerned with the whole—our planet and its people, even those centuries apart, even those who echo from deep time. He has major concerns for America's civil society—especially the abuse of the environment and the Cold War threat of nuclear warfare. He maps out his country across "hundreds of towns and cities," finding them all alike in one particular area—a lack of concern for the earth, our home. And he worries because we have not had "time to develop the means to think" (Steinbeck 1997, 27) about our newfound capacity to destroy ourselves and the world either by nuclear warfare or ecological neglect and abuse of our planet. And everywhere, on outskirts of America's cities, he espies a smothering rubbish.

Sickened by the flotsam and jetsam gathered over time that greets travelers at the outskirts of America's cities, Steinbeck compares them to "badger holes, ringed with trash—all of them—surrounded by piles of wrecked and rusting automobiles, and almost smothered with rubbish. . . . Driving along I thought how in France or Italy every item of these thrown-out things would have been saved and used for something" (22). The "wrecked and rusting automobiles" depict past, present, and future time—first, the wreckage and ruin of the past and then, the "rusting" occurring in present time and continuing into the future. There is no end to such wastefulness, Steinbeck implies, other than following the paradigm set in place by France and Italy, countries in Europe without the vast expanse of land America has at its disposal—land that it is rapidly being contaminated one way or another, whether by lack of foresight in its use or by poisoning.

This destruction is what Steinbeck feared as he worried over "whether there will come a time" when we may not be able to recuperate and recover from our own ravage, rape, and rapine of the land. Of necessity, smaller countries such as France and Italy are more environmentally aware and cautious. Steinbeck fears, however, that Americans may be running out of both precious space and precious time: "I do wonder whether there will come a time when we can no longer afford our wastefulness—chemical wastes in the rivers, metal wastes everywhere, and atomic wastes buried deep in the earth or sunk in the sea. When an Indian village became too deep in its own filth, the inhabitants moved. And we have no place to which to move" (22).

With climate change, that time has come "when we can no longer afford our wastefulness." And, with Steinbeck, we worry that there's nowhere else to go now: this earth is all we have. He has given us a clarion call to reform, to caring, to a sense of the wholeness of a planet and the humans who occupy it, to personal responsibility for survival. Time is of the essence. But he worries we have not had enough time to think about our dilemma, either concerning the environment or the Cold War of his own time—and now the Russian threat in our own.

As he travels, Steinbeck muses over the Cold War, increasing tensions with Russia, and the threat of nuclear warfare. Seeing a sign offering fresh eggs for sale in the White Mountains of New Hampshire, he stops at the farmer's house, buys eggs, asks permission to park Rocinante by a nearby stream for the night, and invites the farmer to come in and to look over his camper and share a cup of coffee. As they sat comfortably situated in Rocinante at a serviceable table-by-day that, covered with cushions, transformed at night into a double bed, their conversation centered around the Russian situation and Khrushchev's presence in New York at the meeting of the United Nations: "You wouldn't believe it," the farmer told Steinbeck, "Mr. K. took off his shoe and pounded the table" in protest over the proceedings. That's about all the news talked about" (25). Of politics, they agree that in past times there had been "pretty peppery arguments," but now there are none, perhaps because nobody knows enough to have an opinion. The sureties are gone now. The farmer opines, "My grandfather knew the number of whiskers in the Almighty's beard. I don't even know what happened yesterday, let alone tomorrow" (26). Steinbeck agrees.

Time seems to have lost all anchorage during the Cold War, as is true today as well. The threat of nuclear warfare looms in the backdrop of human affairs, hovering over, omnipresent. As in Steinbeck's times, all is adrift in the unknown as two of the mightiest nations in the world spar off, so far avoiding the ultimate confrontation of nuclear warfare, but always threatening, teetering on the brink. The New Hampshire farmer intuits the ultimate problem: "We've got nothing to go on—got no way to think about things" (26). Steinbeck opines, "And maybe he had put his finger on it. Humans had perhaps a million years to get used to fire as a thing and as an idea. . . . And now a force was in hand how much more strong, and we hadn't had time to develop the means to think, for man has to have feelings and then words before he can come close to thought and, in the past at least, that has taken a long time" (27).

How do we think about things? How do we figure out things, especially the ecology and the tangle of international affairs? Faced with the annihilation of earth itself—all living things from forests, lakes, trees, and animals to humanity itself—Steinbeck fears we are not even armed with the gift of thought, ratiocination, insight into the nature of things. Now we are running out of time and faced with eradication. If, in our times, Russia's heartless, senseless, power-hungry invasion of Ukraine, our steadily deteriorating ecology brought on by climate change, and our own continuing neglect of the planet we love have taught us anything, it is that time is short. We seem to stand on the brink of World War III and a beloved earth beyond cure. As Steinbeck foresaw in the 1960s, we are running out of time.

Still, in *Travels*, Steinbeck has gathered "small diagnostic truths" that just might bring us back from the brink—among them, time to pause, making way for a calm, quiet spirit and simple neighborliness, kindness, love. He proclaims his love for Montana, for example, as a place where "the calm of the mountains and the rolling grasslands had got into the inhabitants." Recognizing that his attitude toward this state was probably "informed by love," he saw its towns as "places to live in rather than nervous hives," occupied by "people who had time to pause in their occupations to undertake the passing art of neighborliness" (121). Here is another kind of time—time in a pause—when one chooses to pause activities and grasp time as it is passing, in interest of calm, love, caring—seemingly simplistic but nevertheless profound in potential impact. Steinbeck thus proffers a small panacea, "a small diagnostic truth," for a troubled mind, a troubled country, a troubled world.

## The Macrocosm of the Microcosm

Like Dimock, Steinbeck envisions the planet as a whole, embracing all peoples of all times and places. Nearing journey's end, he and Charley spend a night in the Mojave Desert and think of "hermits of the early church piercing to infinity with unlittered minds. The great concepts of oneness and majestic order," he opines, "seem always to be born in the desert" (163). Having viewed America across time and space, as he leaves California and starts on his return journey, he envisions three of these concepts of "oneness and majestic order" in interrelated, overall observations. First, musing over his perceptions—the "barrel of worms" inside his head—he observes that "external reality has a way of not being so external after all" (159). For long ago he had discovered on marine collecting expeditions that whatever he discovered "was closely intermeshed" with his feelings at the time (159).

Second, having gone on this trip in search of America, he has found himself at one, in unity, with his country. And he is jubilant in this discovery: "This monster of a land, this mightiest of nations, this spawn of the future, turns out to be the macrocosm of microcosm me" (159). What he feels at this point is a sense of oneness, a linked identity, between himself and his country, both part of that "global civil society" that Dimock intuits, extending across space and time, into future generations. As Dimock maintains, such a realization is "not entirely predicated on the temporal and spatial boundaries" (2006, 5). Believing in his country and its people, he predicts that it is the "spawn of the future," a designation perhaps carrying with it his hope that America carries the light of a democratic, united people who will overcome and endure.

Third, Americans are a unique breed, their identity "an exact and provable thing" (159–60). Steinbeck finds in America and in himself a wholeness he had not before realized: "If I were to prepare one immaculately inspected generality it would be this: For all our enormous geographic range, for all of our sectionalism, for all our interwoven breeds drawn from every part of the ethnic world, we are a nation, a new breed" (159). Believing in his country and its people, he predicts that it is the "spawn of the future," a designation perhaps carrying within it his hope that America carries within the light of a democratic, united people who will overcome and endure. Having viewed his country across space and time, Steinbeck finds America to be unique, but at the same time truly a part of a "global civil society, . . . a plausible whole," just as Dimock (2006, 5) has suggested we should consider our place in the world.

This realization of oneness involves an inward move, to the inner being. For here is a sense of wholeness. We are all a part of something larger than ourselves, a national and global community of humans—both those in the past and generations to come. Early in his career, in *Sea of Cortez*, Steinbeck was inspired by such a holistic vision: "The whole picture is portrayed by his use of the verb *is*, the deepest word of ultimate reality, not shallow or partial as reasons are, but deeper and participating, possibly encompassing the Oriental concept of being" ([1951] 1955, 125). "Is" and "being"—certainly concepts that both embrace and go beyond time, continuing, existing.

Sadly, these insights, this vision of wholeness, "unfettered minds," "majestic order," and of time extending into infinity will be followed in the *Travels* account by Steinbeck's visit to New Orleans to observe for himself the riotous times of desegregation. In this city he encounters bitter, endemic racism as middle-aged women dubbed "Cheerleaders" fling obscenities and slurs at a tiny Black girl child and a dignified white man in a gray suit, clutching his daughter's hand, who also dares to go up the sidewalk to the school, flanked on either side by US marshals. This appalling image is forever engraved on a nation's conscience, bringing to mind a shameful past of racial conflict.

But Steinbeck knows the other side of the story, believes something was "wrong and distorted and out of drawing" with what he has witnessed, and he remembers the kind people he has known in this place: "I knew New Orleans. I have over the years had many friends there, thoughtful, gentle people, with a tradition of kindness and courtesy. . . . How many days I have spent with Roark Bradford, who took Louisiana sounds and sights and created God and the Green Pastures to which He leadeth us. I looked in the crowd for such faces of such people and they were not there" (196). And now, in the twenty-first century, we are left to peer with trepidation at present day racial conflict and to look with fear into a future of continuing racism. The continuum is there, unless good people, such as the other, fine New Orleanians Steinbeck knew, decide to make a difference so that a global civil society can endure. During the same era of the civil rights unrest of the 1960s, in the midst of racial conflict at its height in Birmingham, Alabama, Martin Luther King Jr. writes "Letter from a Birmingham Jail" (1963). Like Steinbeck, King has a vision of the future, of wholeness, of a national macrocosm at peace and at one: "Let us all hope that the dark clouds of racial prejudice will soon pass away and the deep fog of misunderstanding will be lifted from our fear drenched communities, and in some not too distant tomorrow the radiant stars of love and brotherhood will shine over our great nation with all their scintillating beauty. Yours for the cause of Peace and Brotherhood, Martin Luther King, Jr." Steinbeck numbers himself among King, the good people of New Orleans, and the good people of America. And having considered his beloved country across space and time, he states, "This monster of a land, this mightiest of nations, this spawn of the future, turns out to be the macrocosm of microcosm me" (159). Here, then, is that great civil society of which Dimock writes—the lone individual in unity and harmony with the land, his country, the world. Looking into deep time and thinking of those who follow after us, by implication, Steinbeck further envisions America with its beautiful dream of a democracy with equality and justice for all as enduring, spawning the "the future"—its influence for good extending to peoples yet to come.

True, the visions of Steinbeck and of King have not come to fruition. Climate change, the renewed Russian threat, nuclear warfare, and threat of World War III are all still with us. And Steinbeck's observation that there is still a wholeness among his own people may be about as close to a present-day prophet and prophecy as we are going to get. *Travels with Charley* has taken its place in the literature of a global civil society that reaches across time, deep time, and continents. And in that society Steinbeck and poodle Charley, together with Ma Joad, Tom Joad, and others of their ilk live on. That there is still goodness, there is no doubt. It is all around us. Of such is the macrocosm, the wholeness, of which Steinbeck, American bard, writes. With him, we may look across time, toward the future, always with some hope, however fragile.

# 8

## Of Hurricanes and Hope

### *Travels with Charley* and the Crises of Our Times

Kathleen Hicks

John Steinbeck's *Travels with Charley in Search of America* pointedly begins with a devastating storm. Part 1 of the book is very short and dominated by Steinbeck's description of his battle against Hurricane Donna, the most powerful Atlantic hurricane of the 1960 season. While readers may be tempted to read quickly over Steinbeck's experience of Hurricane Donna in anticipation of his commencing his journey, the storm and his battle against it to save his boat work symbolically in the narrative in important ways. Classically, the storm opens the story by pitting man against nature, a theme found in Steinbeck's narrative in several places as he ponders how well humans are—or are not—living in balance with the landscape. The storm also serves as an apt representation of the gathering multifaceted political and social crises Steinbeck sees America facing, including escalating racial tensions, which Steinbeck finds on stark display in the American South.

Finally, the storm serves as a fitting representation of the tumult Steinbeck was experiencing in his own life at the time as he battled his own illness. Partly due to ill health, Steinbeck was very concerned that his creative capabilities may have reached a permanent decline at this point in his career. He announces at the beginning of *Travels with Charley* that his trip was not just about weathering a storm but also about triumphing and emerging with enhanced creative abilities. Of this prospect he wrote to friends about the trip in 1960, "What I'll get I need badly. . . . I am very excited about doing this. It will be a kind of rebirth" (Steinbeck 1989, 667). In short, the storm metaphor is useful for thinking about the personal, social, and political problems Steinbeck confronts throughout the work. As with the striking similarities between Hurricane Donna in 1960 and Ida in 2021, both of which traveled up from the southern Atlantic to wreak extensive devastation in the Northeast, *Travels with Charley* observes in 1960 the burgeoning, dangerous political and social climate, together with a moral atrophy, that have, in the twenty-first century, grown into full-blown crises. These crises have left America vulnerable to ongoing racial violence, civil unrest, and biological and ecological disasters. Ultimately, Steinbeck triumphs in his battle to save his boat from Hurricane Donna at the outset of the work. This initial triumph cues readers into the possibilities for triumph and hope that Steinbeck points to by the end of the travelogue, a stance that may be as resonant in the twenty-first century as it was in the 1960s.

## The Outer Bands

Before surveying where Steinbeck would go on his journey, it is useful to consider how he was already wrestling with how to live in a world that had experienced fundamental change in a very short period of time. The significant post–World War II political, social, and economic upheavals—the threat of nuclear annihilation foremost among them—were clear indications to Steinbeck that all was not quite right. In particular, the 1959 quiz show scandal that occurred just a year before his departure deeply troubled him and he questioned whether America had become soft, a stance that prompted an open forum, titled "Have We Gone Soft?" in the *New Republic* (February 15, 1960), a few months before he departed on his trip around America. A major thread in *Travels with Charley* is determining how to reconcile massive social and political changes with what he saw as our inability to efficiently conceptualize intellectual and moral paradigms to deal with the consequences of our actions.

In many ways, *Travels with Charley* is a book about thinking. Not only are readers confronted with Steinbeck's thoughts about waste, overcrowding, political apathy, and racism, but Steinbeck also explicitly articulates his motive to determine new methods for thinking at the outset of the trip. And for him, it is first the heretofore unimaginable possibility of nuclear annihilation represented by the atomic bomb that most distinctly demands new systems of thought. Humanity's development of the power to annihilate all life on the planet was a significant turning point in history, as were the complex, burgeoning, geopolitical (and in his mind absurd) machinations that grew up alongside the development of nuclear weapons.

Two key incidents that occur early in part 2 illustrate Steinbeck's perspective on nuclear war and the need for new systems of thought. These include his interchange with a submarine sailor he encounters on the ferry

Figure 7: Steinbeck in Joyous Garde, his hexagonal Sag Harbor writing house, circa 1961. Courtesy of the Martha Heasley Cox Center for Steinbeck Studies at San Jose State University.

crossing the Long Island Sound and then his conversation with a farmer he meets in New Hampshire. Steinbeck incorporates the dark and terrifying forces of mass annihilation through the specter of nuclear submarines that he catches a glimpse of at the outset of the trip. This sighting has the distinct effect of casting a shadow on his journey; as Steinbeck recalls it, "The day lost part of its brightness" (Steinbeck 1997, 18). He tries to reconcile the fear the submarines instill in him with the cheeriness and somewhat mundane ordinariness with which the blue-eyed sailor approaches his commission. While Steinbeck views the subs as instruments of "mass murder, our silly and only way of deterring mass murder," the sailor's practical perspective of his assignment as simply a job for which he earns a decent living dampens their threat somewhat (19). Recalling the dread submarines instilled in him while he was on assignment in World War II, Steinbeck writes, "It's his world, not mine any more. There's no anger in his delphinium eyes and no fear and no hatred either, so maybe it's all right. It's just a job with good pay and a future. I must not put my memories and my fear on him. Maybe it won't be true again, but that's his lookout. It's his world now. Perhaps he understands things I will never learn" (19–20). He then casually waves the young man off with well wishes: "'So long,' I said. 'I hope you have a good—future'" (20). Steinbeck's use of the dash expresses a hesitancy, as he wishes for a good future ahead but is unsure whether the wish will come to fruition.

As casual as the exchange seems, the pause over "future," as though Steinbeck ruminates over the right word to choose, leaves much unsaid hanging in the air. Can there really be a future with such powers of mass destruction within humanity's grasp? If so, what might that future look like? Is it reasonable to think of manning a vessel that has the capability of wiping out large swaths of humanity in a single strike simply as a "job"? The anxiety of what it means to live in a world where one's job includes wielding weapons of mass destruction looms large in *Travels with Charley* and is one of the important facts of the modern American's life that, for Steinbeck, demands new structures of thinking even to contemplate. Early on in the book Steinbeck reflects on how comparatively little time humans have had to come to terms with the enormity of their own "progress"—a word he wields ironically in order to question the worth and rightness of human social, political, economic, and technological advancements. In his reflection, humanity's achievements are pitted against human beings' constrained biological, mental, and ethical capabilities of dealing with them. What happens when human beings' creative ability vastly outstrips the brain's ability to comprehend and manage the consequences of their creations? Reflecting on the relatively little time that has passed between the discovery of fire and the splitting of atoms, Steinbeck observes, "Humans had perhaps a million years to get used to fire as a thing and as an idea. Between the time a man got his fingers burned on a lightening-struck tree until another man carried some inside a cave and found it kept him warn, maybe a hundred thousand years, and from there to the blast furnace of Detroit—how long? And now a force was in hand how much more strong, and we hadn't had time to develop the means to think, for man has to have feelings and then words before he can come close to thought and, in the past at least, that has taken a long time" (27). Grasping new structures for thinking about such unwieldy, almost unfathomable concepts fascinated Steinbeck and informs the methodology for his examination of America in the book.

Steinbeck's thinking about thinking is spurred on by a second significant interchange that occurs near the beginning of his journey when he meets a wise farmer in New Hampshire. Their conversation is short, but poignant. In discussing contemporary politics and people's apparent reluctance to express their opinions about the impending election of 1960, the farmer points to a pervasive lack of certainty and "unknowingness" that seems to plague people. Of his father and grandfather he says:

> "They knew some things they were sure about. They were pretty sure give a little line and then what *might* happen. But now—what might happen?"
> "I don't know."
> "Nobody knows. What good's an opinion if you don't know? My grandfather knew the number of whiskers in the Almighty's beard. I don't even know what happened yesterday, let alone tomorrow. He knew what it was that makes a rock or a table. I don't even understand the formula that says nobody knows. We've got nothing to go on—got no way to think about things." (26)

With "no way to think about things," there is no way to make intelligible the unintelligible forces Steinbeck finds assailing Americans on many fronts on his journey. Hence, the purpose of the trip, and of the book, becomes clear—wrestling to grasp new structures, new truths, to think and articulate about America—"this monster land"—full of beauty, contradictions, folly, and serious threats to humanity's ongoing existence (5). Coming to this realization, Steinbeck is finally able to settle into his journey and drifts off to sleep that first night on the road acknowledging, "And I felt at last that my journey was started. I think I hadn't really believed in it before" (27).

While his encounter with the farmer concretizes the practical truth-seeking and meaning-making mission of the journey in his mind's eye, Steinbeck was predisposed to this approach, at least theoretically, from the outset. He opens the narrative announcing his plan for truth-seeking as a requirement for his art: "Otherwise in writing, I could not tell the small diagnostic truths which are the foundations of the larger truth" (5). He continues, "I had to be peripatetic eyes and ears, a kind of moving gelatin plate" (5). Echoing transcendentalist Ralph Waldo Emerson, he goes on to describe himself as disembodied eyes and ears—deliberately choosing the term "peripatetic," denoting not just a roving traveler but one with a specifically Aristotelian and Wordsworthian bent. Along with an examination of virtue and moral and ethical behavior, Steinbeck applies deductive logic and analysis, as he strives to comprehend natural laws to explain the behavior of his fellow Americans.

In an essay on *Travels with Charley* as American picaresque, Carter Johnson (2021) described Steinbeck as an "aging writer [trying] to discover the metaphysical health of a nation" (154). Steinbeck's ultimate discoveries point to the nation's pathological condition—a type of apathy that affects vital aspects of the political, social, and moral life, ultimately eating away at the fabric of the country and endangering its ability to flourish in the future. Readers are exposed to more and more of the symptoms of this erosive condition as Steinbeck crosses the country. These symptoms, over which Steinbeck is grieved and highly critical, suggest a massive storm front rolling in, which unbeknown to him, will bloom into the major crises facing twenty-first century Americans, including environmental destruction, divisive politics, and violent racism.

## The Eye

Bold claim that it is, one of the most poignant scenes in American literature just may be that of a desolate, depressed John Steinbeck slumped over in a motel bathtub slugging vodka while the admirable French poodle Charley attempts to lift his sprits by playing puppy-like with the plastic bathmat. Steinbeck finds himself in this position after a disturbing encounter with a vacuous woman at an auto court outside of Bangor, Maine—evidence of the nation's apathy. This encounter, which he feels compelled to drink off, is ultimately emblematic of Americans' growing discontent with the status quo; of their vapid addiction to materialism; and of a cheap, tawdry leisure devoid of culture, purpose, and meaning. If the opening of the work suggests that massive disruption—whether by natural disaster or human making—threatens both his own boat and the survival of the world order, the shallow and meaningless status quo Steinbeck finds at the center of the nation definitely serves as a harbinger of more problematic things to come for Americans.

The defining feature of the auto court in which Steinbeck finds himself is that "everything was done in plastics"—the room, the restaurant, and, unfortunately, even the person working there (Steinbeck 1997, 36). The room and restaurant are bad enough, "the floors, the curtain, table tops of stainless burnless plastic, lamp shades of plastic. . . . I went to the small restaurant run in conjunction. It was all plastic too—the table linen, the butter dish. The sugar and crackers were wrapped in cellophane, the jelly in a small plastic coffin sealed with cellophane" (36–37). But what really bothers Steinbeck is the plastic person he finds there—lifeless and soulless. He notes, "She wasn't happy, but then she wasn't unhappy. She wasn't anything. But I don't believe anyone is a nothing. There has to be something inside, if only to keep the skin from collapsing. This vacant eye, listless hand, this damask cheek dusted like a doughnut with plastic powder, had to have a memory or a dream" (37). But she does not—at least he surmises so—and he finds her demeanor unutterably depressing.

In his futile attempt to engage in meaningful conversation with the waitress, Steinbeck quippingly inquires if she is "going to Florida" like so many others he meets on his trip. "Going to Florida" ultimately becomes code in the book for people in quiet desperation looking for any means of escape from the current dissatisfaction with their lives. Not surprisingly, she says she is indeed going to Florida, although, hollow shell of a person that she is, she does not seem to be setting out with an intention to achieve anything different or better. In fact, she does not seem to acknowledge that betterment is a possibility. Perhaps that is what Steinbeck finds so depressing about her—a complacency beyond hope.

In contrast, most of the other people he meets still seem to think there might be something better out there, even if it is only because "there" is not "here." Steinbeck observes, "I saw in their eyes something I was to see over and over in every part of the nation—a burning desire to go, to move, to get under way, anyplace, away from any Here. They spoke quietly of how they wanted to go someday, to move about, free and unanchored, not toward something but away from something" (Steinbeck 1997, 9). He has the conversation over and over again with people envious of his journey and who long to get on the road too:

"Lord! I wish I could go."
"Don't you like it here?"
"Sure. It's all right, but I wish I could go."
"You don't even know where I'm going."
"I don't care. I'd like to go anywhere." (21–22)

This longing to be anywhere but here is a primary symptom of pervasive dissatisfaction with life Steinbeck finds all over the nation—so many people seeking to escape the confines of their lives.

Later, while crossing the great expanse of the Midwest, Steinbeck questions his prior rash, unfair judgment of turkeys. In an earlier reflection Steinbeck had condemned turkeys' stupidity while reflecting on a memory of a trapped flock foolishly stampeding over a cliff. He is greatly disturbed and remembers the turkeys when he comes across a road with signage that reads "Evacuation Route." He reflects, "Of course, it is the planned escape route from the bomb that hasn't been dropped. Here in the middle of the Middle West an escape route, a road designed by fear. In my mind I could see it because I have seen people running away—the roads clogged to a standstill and the stampede over the cliff of our own designing. And suddenly I thought of that valley of the turkeys and wondered how I could have the gall to think turkeys stupid. Indeed, they have an advantage over us. They're good to eat" (Steinbeck 1997, 100). Like the turkeys, Steinbeck's faithful traveling companion Charley has a distinct advantage over humans: "He wasn't involved with a race that could build a thing it had to escape from. He didn't want to go to the moon just to get the hell away from it all. Confronted with our stupidities, Charley accepts them for what they are—stupidities" (100).

The atomic bomb is only one part of the problem here. When the pervasive longing to get away from it all is read alongside both this literal and symbolic escape route and Steinbeck's observations of crowded, polluted, noisy, chaotic, and shallow consumeristic urban life, readers are forced to question the quality of life Americans have built for themselves, resulting in "the assembly-line production of our food, our songs, our language, and eventually our souls" (Steinbeck 1997, 83). What is its meaning and value? Steinbeck observes of the nation's convenience-laden, plastic-wrapped, bland, and undifferentiated existence: "It is life at a peak of some kind of civilization" (71). But what kind? Ironically, it is one that Americans strive to preserve at high ecological and psychological costs, even though the consequences cannot lead to human flourishing, as Steinbeck shows.

When Steinbeck returns to his motel room after his encounter with the plastic lady outside of Bangor, his misery is exacerbated by evidence of a near obsessive attempt to rid the world of both differentiation and disease. He writes, "In the bathroom two water tumblers were sealed in cellophane sacks with the words: 'These glasses are sterilized for your protection.' Across the toilet seat a strip of paper bore the message: 'This seat has been sterilized with ultra-violet light for your protection.' Everyone was protecting me and it was horrible. I tore the glasses from their covers. I violated the toilet-seat with my foot. I poured half a tumbler of vodka and drank it and then another. Then I lay in deep hot water in the tub and I was utterly miserable, and nothing was good anywhere" (38). One can read Steinbeck's reaction as hyperbole designed to produce an entertaining effect; however, when paired with his comments about American's sterile, plastic lives and his own fear of illness and invalidism at the beginning of the narrative, perhaps his misery is serious and genuine. Far worse than his individual emotional response are the larger, cumulative ramifications of these ironic efforts at "protection" on the environment and human health. Artificiality bodes ill for the United States and the natural world at large.

Steinbeck was very much onto something in his lament over plastics. He knew the psychological and environmental costs of all this protection and convenience were high, even in 1960. In addition to an unacceptable, concerning amount of water and air pollution in manufacturing centers, he could not fail to observe that all American cities are "ringed with trash . . . almost smothered with rubbish" (Steinbeck 1997, 22), much of it from excess packaging. In "the mountains of things we throw away," he writes, "we can see the wild and reckless exuberance of our production, and waste seems to be the index" (22). He notes Americans are now living in an "era of planned obsolescence," which both fuels and supplies rampant consumerism, the scope of which has simply exploded since Steinbeck's days (36). This is especially true of plastic production. Steinbeck, noticing across the nation that "everything that can be captured and held down is sealed in clear plastic," observed that Americans seemed perilously wasteful in 1960 (71).

Decades later, the situation has only worsened. As *National Geographic* notes, plastic production has continued to increase exponentially, "from 2.3 million tons in 1950 to 448 million tons by 2015. Production is expected to double by 2050" (Parker 2019). Alarmingly, huge amounts end up in the ocean—about eight million tons every year (Parker 2019). People are only just beginning to understand the devastating toll of plastic pollution on ocean health, which is inexorably linked to human health. Furthermore, scientists now have a clearer picture of the penetrating reach of microplastic pollution into every nook and cranny of the environment, including human bodies; however, we remain woefully ignorant of the biological and ecological impact of this contamination. As A. Dick Vethaak and Juliette Legler (2021) report, "Recent evidence indicates that humans constantly inhale and ingest microplastics; however, whether these contaminants pose a substantial risk to human health is far from understood" (672). Nonetheless, America, along with many other nations, continues to pump out unfathomable amounts of plastic made from chemicals well known to be toxic, with absolutely no feasible plan for recycling it. And for what? No doubt much is ironically used for the protection of human health. In truth, a vast majority is used to supply Americans' insatiable desire for stuff—which even in 1960 Steinbeck characterizes as a sickness, a compulsion, and an imbalanced way of life. Ecologically minded as he was, recognizing the intricate interconnections among all life, no doubt he would understand what we have now learned about how rampant, ongoing pollution of the environment leads to human disease and massive damage to ecosystems with far-reaching, climate-changing ramifications.

The heart of Steinbeck's critique as he crosses the Midwest is that not only is the environment covered in plastic and rubbish but many people's lives are likewise also plastic, superficial, and disposable. The consequences of the march of cleanliness, convenience, and uniformity (now innocuously masquerading as brand consistency) have been enormous, obliterating uniqueness in many facets of American life. Enter the big-box chains and material satisfaction on demand and we are now living with an unimaginable, and clearly unsustainable, pace of resource consumption and waste production. And, as the alarm bells sound all around through surging environmental disasters and a global pandemic, rather than becoming more reflective and developing new systems of thought and ways of being in the world as Steinbeck suggests, many Americans either look the other way or turn to absurd alternative "plan Bs," such as locating another suitable planet to inhabit. The foolishness of this plan is quintessentially the essence of the absurd escape route Steinbeck finds in the Middle West. There was much stupidity to scoff at then, in Steinbeck's view. There is even more so now.

## The Dirty Side

Steinbeck's swing down the West Coast toward the southern part of the United States is punctuated by an interesting, and telling, interchange with his sisters in California. He does not have much to say about visiting his family, other than that the visit degenerated into several screaming matches over politics. After explaining how he came to be a Democrat, Steinbeck writes, "I arrived in Monterey and the fight began. My sisters are still Republicans. Civil war is supposed to be the bitterest of wars, and surely family politics are the most vehement and venomous. I can discuss politics coldly and analytically with strangers. That was not possible with my sisters. We ended each session panting and spent with rage. On no point was there any compromise. No quarter was asked or given. . . . It was awful. A stranger hearing us would have called the police to prevent bloodshed. And I don't think we were the only ones. I believe this was going on all over the country in private. It must have been only publicly we were tongue-tied" (Steinbeck 1997, 151–52).

Steinbeck's hyperbole would be funny if it were not so real to many readers who have experienced similar vitriolic, hurtful arguments about politics among their own family and friends. Evident here is the irrational polarity and inability to listen to another's position that has become the hallmark of highly polarized twenty-first-century politics. Now that everyone has a personal platform, people are no longer tongue-tied, and these polemics take place regularly in homes, on social media, and everywhere on the public stage, including the halls of Congress. The consequences of giving people platforms to spew their divisive rhetoric and, oftentimes, their hatred, was already quite evident in 1960 when Steinbeck arrived in New Orleans. His recollections of what he witnessed there, perhaps more so than any other event in the book, point toward a negative future trajectory for American society. As with the case of the rapid increase in environmental pollution since the 1960s that continues to threaten the health of the planet, an explosion of public displays of irrationalism, bigotry, racism, and hate has emerged as a major threat to the stability of American democracy, in which Steinbeck still held great hope at the end of his career.

Steinbeck has been lauded for his strikingly forward and relevant thinking on any number of contemporary environmental and social issues. That is one of the reasons he continues to appeal widely to readers all over the world. Once again, his keen and prescient observation is apparent when he reaches New Orleans and describes in lurid detail the progenitors of the "Karens"—a popular internet appellation for entitled, white women who leverage their privilege and overblown, misguided self-righteousness to make life hell for pretty much everyone, but particularly Black people. In this case it is a "Nellie" as Steinbeck describes her, though she is quintessentially the same as a Karen. "The name was not Nellie," he writes. "I forget what it was. But she shoved through the dense crowd quite near enough to me that I could see her coat of imitation fleece and her gold earrings. She was not tall, but her body was ample and full-busted. I judge she was about fifty. She was heavily powdered, which made the line of her double chin look very dark" (Steinbeck 1997, 194). Her powdered appearance and demeanor call to mind a bad actor and that is exactly what Steinbeck observes her to be.

Given the national spotlight on the desegregation episode in New Orleans, Steinbeck goes there for the purpose of witnessing a show, and a show is exactly what he gets from the Nellies who come to scream their hate at one tiny Black girl. But their venom is especially directed at the courageous white parent who dares to bring his child to attend the integrated school, holding his daughter's hand, his jaw clenched, as they go up the sidewalk to the building, walking behind the little Black girl. And even though Steinbeck arrives somewhat prepared, having read the papers and watched media reports about the ongoing commotion, he admits he is taken aback by what he observes, which he says is a big deal, considering he has seen quite a bit in his lifetime, including war: "In a long and unprotected life I have seen and heard the vomitings of demoniac humans before. Why then did these screams fill me with a shocked and sickened sorrow?" he asks (Steinbeck 1997, 195). Why indeed? He goes on, "The words written down are dirty, carefully and selectedly filthy. But there was something far worse here than dirt, a kind of frightening witches' Sabbath. . . . Perhaps that is what made me sick with nausea. Here was no principle good or bad, no direction. These blowzy women with their little hats and their clippings hungered for attention. They wanted to be admired. They simpered in happy, almost innocent triumph when they were applauded. Theirs was the demented cruelty of egocentric children, and somehow this made their insensate beastliness much more heartbreaking. These were not mothers, not even women. They were crazy actors playing to a crazy audience" (195). That desire for the crowd's adulation is the crux of the problem. These women, looking for an escape from their purposeless lives, have been given a platform. Rather than attempting a more innocuous escape to Florida, they have channeled their small-mindedness into an egregious display of racism and hate, simply to gain attention from an audience of degenerate onlookers hoping to be entertained at the expense of children.

Steinbeck's fury at this injustice should resonate with contemporary readers who have been continually outraged by the ongoing senseless killings of African Americans, which came to a head with the shocking May 25, 2020, murder of George Floyd displayed on public platforms for the entire world to see. Though his outrage is sincere, Steinbeck has been criticized by some contemporary readers for not going far enough in his condemnation of racism. He has also been accused of promoting American political, economic, and social policies that are historically connected to white, nationalist values, even as he railed against poverty and immigration policies that, in his view, created a permanent underclass. He was unequivocal in his critique of how the existence of poverty and an underclass undermines the viability of democracy and the nation's ongoing economic success. In his 2015 essay on Steinbeck and race, Shane Lynn suggests that "for Steinbeck, the malaise of greed and ignorance takes precedence over racism. Even in the sixties, when he first attempted to grapple with the problem of racial prejudice, the issue was secondary to the creeping rot of the materialistic immorality he saw in American society. For all its present horrors, he confidently presumed that racism would subside with growing prosperity" (150–51). This observation seems true as Steinbeck concludes the episode in New Orleans by admitting his consternation over how things would work out, though he suggests they eventually will, noting, "The end is not in question. It's the means—the dreadful uncertainty of the means" that is so troublesome (Steinbeck 1997, 207).

As suspicious as he was about material wealth, it is interesting that Steinbeck did seem confident that economic prosperity would eventually be the means to bring an end to racism. In *America and Americans* (1966) he states that Black people are now moving toward equality because they are important to the economy. Sadly, this move has not come to full fruition as high numbers of people of color still struggle with poverty while many Americans turn a blind eye to this endemic problem. Steinbeck, however, expressed faith that America would do the right thing by implementing policies that would be to the advantage of all and, in turn, would guarantee the nation's economic, social, and racial stability. In theory, that route seems to make perfect sense. When all people are economically secure, there is no need for strife over real or imagined scarcity. For Steinbeck, however, economic prosperity was a double-edge sword. Americans should be secure, but not too secure, as overabundance, he believed, corrupts both the individual and the polity. Cyrus Ernesto Zirakzadeh (2019) explains this double-edged threat: "In his [Steinbeck's] opinion, private wealth corrupts the human soul by making people more interested in protecting their material possessions than in exercising their imaginations and sharing practical knowledge and novel ideas with others. It is the struggle for physical survival that motivates individuals to question the status quo, to cooperate with both friends and neighbors, and to help those in need. Once a person has become materially secure, curiosity withers, as does the need to exercise self-discipline and to experiment daily. People become lazy, selfish, and morally flabby. Consequently, citizenship wanes" (15).

As in his critique of plastics, Steinbeck was onto something in his observations about the growing material comfort of the middle class he was witnessing in the 1960s and its impact on the American psyche and citizenry. As it turns out, though, he was perhaps a little too optimistic about the eradication of income equality, not foreseeing the massive consolidation of wealth among the top 10 percent of Americans and the actual shrinking of the middle class that has occurred in recent decades (Horowitz, Igielnik, and Kochhar 2020). Nor could he predict at that time the explosion of extreme materialism—which continues to pit the haves against the have-nots in an ongoing battle over resources and is intricately bound up with racism and xenophobia. He was nevertheless apparently right about the power of wealth to corrupt the human soul. Like the unfathomable power of the atomic bomb or a devastating hurricane, Steinbeck would likely, as the average person does, have great difficulty imagining the incomprehensible billions and formidable political power consolidated in the hands of mostly a few white people in the twenty-first century, who act unjustly to protect their enormous wealth out of irrational fear and greed. The net results have been that the poorest of the poor have remained so and that there are still vast, unjust racial and ethnic disparities among those living in poverty in America.

Despite having an overly optimistic view about the end of racism in America, it is clear that the outrage Steinbeck experienced in New Orleans was authentic and had both an immediate and a lasting impact that ultimately affected the trajectory of the remainder of his career. First, it is obvious that what he witnessed in New Orleans killed the trip for him. And it was not just seeing the "Nellies," either. He had other confrontations with both white and Black people that crystalized for him the extent of the bitter and persistent problem of racism in the South. Second, Steinbeck turned up the East Coast from New Orleans and plowed home, only to find himself "lost." There has been some interesting critical debate over what it means that Steinbeck finds himself lost at the end of the book. What is strikingly evident is that he was not lost professionally. The trip, and what he witnessed in New Orleans, galvanized him as a writer, just as he hoped it would. Upon his return, Steinbeck, refusing to go quietly into his twilight years, continued to write until he died in 1968, following up the pieces condemning racism he wrote earlier in 1960—including "The Black Man's Ironic Burden," "Atque Vale," and his novel *The Winter of Our Discontent* (1961)—with *Travels with Charley in Search of America* (1962), *America and Americans* (1966), and his Vietnam dispatches, "Letters to Alicia" (1966–67). Together, *Travels with Charley*, *The Winter of Our Discontent*, and *America and Americans* stand as a trilogy that strongly condemns the shallow consumerism, greed, moral corruption, and social decay Steinbeck observed in American society toward the end of his career. *America and Americans* explicitly picks up on several of the themes in *Travels with Charley*, including moral apathy, environmental destruction, and racism, and articulates them in essay form, leaving no doubt about where Steinbeck stood on the problems America was grappling with in the 1960s and how much he cared about the country, its future, and all Americans' place within it. His genuine concern over how Americans might weather the coming storms is another one of those aspects that continues to endear his work to contemporary Americans and other writers interested in the future of democracy and justice in the United States and the world. As Ariel Andrew (2018) points out, "Steinbeck is a prime example of why artists should neither sequester nor silence themselves, but rather freely indict injustice, expose exploitation, comment on their worlds, and protect the real people affected by their work" (60).

## The Only Way Out Is Through

The similarities between Hurricane Donna, which Steinbeck confronted in September 1960, and ferocious Hurricane Ida, which rolled up a similar path from the South, devastating parts of the Northeast in September 2021, are remarkable. Ida—whose behavior and destruction many scientists agree were greatly exacerbated by climate change—serves as a useful metaphor for thinking about the many social, political, economic, and environmental problems Steinbeck observes in *Travels with Charley* in the year of Hurricane Donna. The problems for which Steinbeck showed great concern then have only been exacerbated by contemporary cultural, social, and political trends. Wearing "the mantle of America's sage," as Susan Shillinglaw (2019) puts it, Steinbeck, in *Travels with Charley*, articulates many thoughtful insights into the developing storms—nuclear threats, unbridled consumption, environmental destruction, divisive politics, and racism among them—that have strengthened into the most critical problems facing America, and the world, today (150). The deep moral fissures Steinbeck notices seem to have widened into gulfs. The deification of materialism, a slavish devotion to political party no matter the costs, the corrosion of public trust brought on by racism, the threat of ecological meltdown, the dearth of leaders with vision or moral integrity all add up to a rather paralyzing list of challenges that do seem to put American democracy and a sustainable future in peril. Appreciators of Steinbeck's work and his fundamental optimism may wonder how he would approach thinking through today's challenges and if his hope might hold up, even in our troubled times.

Steinbeck already recognized America was at a crossroads in the sixties. Nonetheless, in *America and Americans* (1966), he goes on to express faith that Americans will ultimately take the right path and continue making progress toward a more just society. He concludes inspiringly, "We have failed sometimes, taken wrong paths, paused for renewal, filled our bellies and licked our wounds; but we have never slipped back—never" (205). This is a key question worth asking today. Are we slipping back? While Americans have not yet collectively chosen the right path out of the mess Steinbeck foresaw in 1960—and in fact they now seem more divided than ever over what the right path even is—there is still limited time to confront the current circumstances and make just choices for the future. Doing so, however, will require collaborative action on a scale which the world has never seen. Holistically, in Steinbeck's canon, we are provided with several models of selfless Americans, willing to sacrifice their own interests for the good of others in the direst of circumstances, Ma and Tom Joad being foremost among them. The future of the nation urgently requires its citizenry to get its head out of the sand, set aside the rampant self-interest that seriously threatens its future, and adopt similar models. The alternative is to be blown over by the storm that will inevitably come, whether it be war, another devastating pandemic, or climate disaster. When reading the headlines these days and all seems lost, it can help to think of Steinbeck's hope. He saw humanity at its worst—in the Great Depression, in World War II, in the Vietnam War—yet he managed to retain firm hope in the human spirit. Even if it is nigh impossible to believe Americans, much less the world, can come together to confront the challenges of our times successfully, at least there is comfort in knowing it is possible for humans to still find hope after the storm.

# 9

## Travels with John Steinbeck in Search of "True Things"

BRIAN RAILSBACK

In the twenty-first century, at least in the United States of America, we live in an era of post-truth. The term "post-truth" may have been introduced by Serbian American playwright Steve Tesich in a 1992 article criticizing the policies of President George H. W. Bush; it gained ground in Ralph Keyes's 2004 book, *The Post-Truth Era*, and was named the Oxford Dictionaries' "Word of the Year" in 2016 (Brahms 2020). The Oxford English Dictionary (2016) defines the adjective "post-truth" as "relating to or denoting circumstances in which objective facts are less influential in shaping public opinion than appeals to emotion and personal belief." The popular mutation of post-truth concerns insurmountable divisions between people who hunker down in self-imposed echo chambers, fortified by addictive propagandist news sources and social media sites. By 2023 post-truth has become a dominating force in US political and popular culture: any collective agreement regarding what is true seems impossible. The 2020 presidential election remains ever-contested in some minds, and the source of and solution to the COVID-19 pandemic was so hotly (even violently) debated that culture lines were drawn over vaccinations and mask-wearing in public. The notion of truth itself, essential to the maintenance of a modern democracy, appears to have been shattered.

Alone among the writers of his stature and era, John Steinbeck saw it coming.

His lifelong fascination with exploring the nature of truth—while recognizing all the pitfalls of that fascination—resulted in a body of work that is uniquely instructive for our times. *Travels with Charley in Search of America* is a tentative search for his country and much less an accurate account of a road trip. Instead, it is the physical manifestation—the book-length metaphor—of his quest for what is true and his realization that one cannot find it. As it emerges from this travelogue, his position is that truth for the individual is a process, never a conclusion. The companion work, *America and Americans*, is an unabashed last lecture in case readers did not understand what he was telling them in *Travels with Charley*.

## STEINBECK'S EXPLORATIONS IN SEARCH OF TRUTH

A survey of Steinbeck's major works reveals his quest for the truth, its meaning, and the ways to seek it. This search is a preoccupation from the beginning of his career to the end. Early in Steinbeck's first novel, *Cup of Gold* (1929), the ostensible hero of the book, the pirate king Henry Morgan, is recognized by his father, Robert, as a young man of vision who "tests his dreams" (Steinbeck 1976, 12). In search of wider horizons, Henry ruthlessly commands men, women, and slaves as he seeks to wrest control of Panama from the Spanish so he can become the ruler who sits on the "Cup of Gold." His monomaniacal pursuit of La Santa Rosa, the woman who would become his queen, collapses in self-delusion when he realizes she is not what he dreamed—the reality will not conform to his vision. The Red Saint, Ysobel, recognizes his inadequacy as a romantic bumbler and challenges him with her own "truthfulness" (145). Morgan realizes his failures, and, musing on the emptiness of his earlier visions, sits alone at the Hall of Audience in Panama while "his eyes, those peering eyes which had looked out over a living horizon, were turned inward" (158). For all of his abilities, Morgan is trapped within his own powerful echo chamber. Similarly, Joseph Wayne, of *To a God Unknown*, so projects his ego into the tiny universe of his California ranch that he creates for himself his own mythology and, in himself, his own god. Wayne's outward expansion from a humble farm in Vermont to new lands far away, a physical expansion of his horizons, implodes when he cannot make nature bend to his powerful will. Since he cannot save his land from a relentless, indifferent drought cycle, he completely misapprehends his place in the universe and, ultimately, the truth of his situation as a human being. Both early heroes are trapped by a limited perception of "truth."

By the mid-1930s, Steinbeck widened his approach, searching beyond the individual's quest for truth toward social, collective truths. Inspired by his discussions and collaborations with his most important friend and intellectual influence, Edward F. Ricketts, Steinbeck brought a scientific approach to his explorations of what might be true. Looking at the brutality of an agricultural strike in California, *In Dubious Battle* is a novel with, as Steinbeck put it, "no author's moral point of view" (Steinbeck 1989, 105). It is, instead, a clinical examination of a conflict from the varying points of view of the workers, the strike organizers, and the owners. Ideologies, whether Marxist or capitalist, are not important, as Steinbeck indicates: "I'm not interested in ranting about justice and oppression, mere outcroppings which indicate the condition" (Steinbeck 1989, 98). What interests him is the underlying cause, for the real condition concerns elemental, even Darwinian, competition and hatred among human beings.

*The Grapes of Wrath* examines the disastrous situation of Dust Bowl migrants to California from a variety of points of view. The Joad chapters provide an on-the-ground picture that demands a reader's emotional and empathetic involvement. The intercalary chapters provide a biblical, god-like perspective, or snippets of dialogue, like a radio show (the voices of the used car lot, for example), or powerful short stories (such as the Depression-hardened truckers, cook, and waitress in a diner who quietly provide for an impoverished migrant family). In a few of these chapters there emerges a voice that could be that of Steinbeck himself, borrowing from his seven 1936 commentaries for the *San Francisco News* (reprinted together in 1988 as *The Harvest Gypsies*) discussing Darwinian examinations of how the oppressed become stronger while the rich owners grow weaker (chapters 19, 21, and 25). In his masterpiece, Steinbeck explores truth through a variety of lenses and narrative techniques, inviting the reader to engage in the difficult work it takes to understand, or attempt to understand, what is true.

By the time he publishes, with Ricketts, *Sea of Cortez: A Leisurely Journal of Travel and Research* in 1941, Steinbeck's scientific explorations of truth reach their culmination. (His narrative portion was issued alone as *The Log from the Sea of Cortez* in 1951.) He understands the value of a holistic approach to reality, the attempt to describe the whole—such as all the parts and interrelations of an ecosystem—while at the same time noting the limitations imposed by individual perceptions, time, and space. He knows that as the crew of the *Western Flyer* enters the Gulf of California to collect and catalogue marine specimens, the true record of the trip will be "warped, as all knowledge patterns are warped, first, by the collective pressure and stream of our time and race, second by the thrust of our individual personalities" (Steinbeck 1995, 2). Those on the expedition will never "observe a completely objective Sea of Cortez anyway" and therefore will not be "betrayed by this myth of permanent objective reality" (3). Understanding these essential limits to truth as an objective reality, they can proceed as best they can by guarding against their own biases.

In *Sea of Cortez* Steinbeck and Ricketts elaborate on the notion of "is" thinking, or what Ricketts called nonteleological thinking: "Non-teleological ideas derive through 'is' thinking. . . . Non-teleological thinking concerns itself primarily not with what should be, or could be, or might be, but rather with what actually 'is'—attempting at most to answer the already sufficiently difficult questions what or how, instead of why" (139). In *Cannery Row*, Steinbeck beautifully portrays this elastic approach to truth by creating a loosely structured novel in which the stories are allowed to "crawl in by themselves" and one is immediately invited to peer into the varying "peepholes" for a variety of perspectives of the same place, the Row, where people may be interpreted as "whores, pimps, gamblers, and sons of bitches" or "Saints and angels and martyrs and holy men," which ironically could mean "the same thing" (Steinbeck 1994, ix, vii). The most significant iteration of Steinbeck's "Doc" characters (a fictitious avatar of Ricketts) appears in this novel, a guide as consistent as the North Star in his pursuit of truth, a man of science and compassion who, as he notes in a personal essay about his friend, "About Ed Ricketts," "loved true things" (Steinbeck 1994, 214). In *Cannery Row*, Doc has one foot in the chaotic world of Mack and the boys and the other in the natural, if not transcendent, world of the tide pool, where he sets himself apart to contemplate the whole. As a seeker of wider horizons and the truth of things, Doc seems an avatar of Steinbeck as well.

Dealt the double blow in 1948 of Ricketts's unexpected death and a bitter divorce from his second wife, Gwendolyn, Steinbeck tends to admit, and even accept, the state of chaos in things in his pursuit of truth. While the sweeping, scientifically influenced observations made in his earlier works *(The Grapes of Wrath* or *Sea of Cortez*, in particular) persist, albeit faintly, in his later works there exists an important shift in emphasis to the presentation of truth, however it might be found, in a more fragmentary and less systematic way. The strong counterpoint to individual warp, that scientific attempt to see the whole, is largely gone as a significant unifying force.

Introducing *A Russian Journal* (1948), his collaborative expedition across the Soviet Union with his war photographer friend, Robert Capa, Steinbeck explains that the two hatched the scheme while drinking at the Bedford Hotel bar in New York City and lamenting the depressing lack of truth in journalism: "News is no longer news.... News has become a matter of punditry" (Steinbeck 1999, 3). Bombarded by advice based on popular mythology about the Russians, Steinbeck concludes, "it seems to us now the most dangerous tendency in the world is the desire to believe a rumor rather than to pin down a fact" (7). Given the static caused by rumor, by miscommunication, and by politics, Steinbeck knows the attempt to honestly portray the Russian people can be best shown in a collection of photographs and observations limited by the individual perceptions of the author: "It is not the Russian story, but simply *a* Russian story" (8). He acknowledges the same limitation as he introduces selections of his World War II dispatches for

*Once There Was a War* (1958). Regarding his war correspondence over twenty years later, Steinbeck writes in an introduction to the collected dispatches, "I realize not only how much I have forgotten but that they are period pieces, the attitudes archaic, the impulses romantic, and, in light of everything that has happened since, perhaps the whole body of work untrue and warped and one-sided" (Steinbeck 1997, vi).

Steinbeck's final play-novelette, *Burning Bright* (1950), reflects the chaos of life, with abrupt changes of scene, confusing universalized language, and a strange plot (out of love for her older husband, a woman gives herself to a younger man to produce a child; then the characters of the play unite to kill the hapless stud so that the survivors may live happily ever after). Old Joe Saul at the end of the play accepts what his young wife, Mordeen, has done for him and understands he must discard the moral truths he once lived by: "I know that what seemed the whole tight pattern is not important." He comes to understand that in the chaotic human existence, people still exhibit "courage," "flickering intelligence," and "beauty" (Steinbeck 1979, 104, 106). Like Saul of Tarsus on the road to Damascus, Old Saul learns that truth is not written in laws but is a thing to be sought after and that seeking it is a part of being a member of the "staggering" human race (105). These works leave little room for the holistic systems of truth examined in the earlier books.

By the time Steinbeck published *East of Eden* in 1952, his search for truth had swung from the wide horizons of such works as *The Grapes of Wrath* or *Cannery Row* to the individual's tortured interior ruminations. Caleb Trask must break the tight patterns of morality imprinted by the Bible and the weight of generations in his family and his personal burden of guilt as an actor in his own Cain and Abel story. He is freed to find his own path to redemption once his father, Adam Trask, gives him a deathbed blessing. As Robert DeMott (2012) notes, "[Adam Trask] becomes the instrument through which emphasis on free will—a conditional situation symbolized by the word *timshel* (meaning "Thou mayest")—permits human beings (his wayward son Caleb first and foremost) to gain the potential to triumph over sin and to return to the wellsprings of their integrity" (80–81). Here and in Steinbeck's final novel, *The Winter of Our Discontent* (1961), the search for what is true amounts to intensely personal explorations: the final triumphant realization of Adam Trask or the terribly disappointing discoveries made by Ethan Hawley.

Hawley has succumbed to the materialistic, hypercapitalist system so meticulously dissected in *The Grapes of Wrath*. To gain money and status, he cheats friends who depend on him (Alfio Marullo and Danny Taylor), with disastrous results. Confronted with the discovery that his son, Allen, has plagiarized most of his award-winning speech and the fact that lying in the United States can mean material reward (financial gain for Hawley and a scholarship for his son), Hawley retreats to his sea cave to commit suicide. Reaching in his pocket for a razor blade to slit his wrists, he finds instead a talisman that his daughter, Mary Ellen, slipped into his pocket. As Charles J. Clancy (1976) points out in his study of light imagery in the novel, the talisman is "the active, reflected light of his daughter" (95). In a statement that underscores the interior focus of Steinbeck's writing at the time, Hawley decides his "light" has gone out and that there is in fact no "community of light"; instead, "everyone carries his own, his lonely own" (Steinbeck 1961, 280). Unlike Tom or Ma Joad, who believe that there is a greater, transcendent truth to which a person can connect for the greater good of the people, a man like Hawley must find it within himself in order to save himself. Clancy interprets the light as love, or even life itself. Given the context of Steinbeck's long search for what is true and the novel's concern for personal integrity, yet another meaning here is that the precious light Hawley seeks at the end is Truth.

## Evanescent Destinations: *Travels with Charley* and *America and Americans*

By June 1960, John Steinbeck—famous writer, world traveler, troubled parent, and restless thinker—was physically and mentally tired. He was just finishing up *Winter* and, just as he had done after finishing *The Grapes of Wrath*, he wished to escape by way of a collecting expedition. Rather than survey marine specimens in the Sea of Cortez, he planned to collect observations, conversations, and ideas from the species that most interested him at the time: his fellow Americans. "Frequently, of late, I have felt that my time is over and that I should bow out," he wrote in a letter to his agent, Elizabeth Otis (Steinbeck 1989, 668). Losing his way in his mammoth quest to rewrite the Arthurian legends in the late 1950s and feeling old, he looked wistfully back on his mighty ventures in writing and ideas. Feeling his confidence ebbing, he wrote to Otis, "Once I was sure I was right in certain directions and that very surety made it more likely to be right. . . . now my malleableness makes it more likely that I am wrong" (668).

Although Otis had suggested he go on a trip across the country for inspiration, Steinbeck was now arguing with her and his third wife, Elaine, because he wanted to go far beyond the original idea. He wanted to circumnavigate the United States, largely alone, taking back roads in a pickup truck rigged with what he called a self-contained "small apartment" (666). In his letter to Otis, one can see how Steinbeck becomes inspired and how the exhausted, uncertain man intended again to be the explorer of twenty years before: "Now I feel that what I have written here is true and right" (Steinbeck 1989, 669). He was answering an issue he had raised in a letter to her six months earlier: "I'll have to learn all over again about true things" (Steinbeck 1989, 657). The daunting trip and its resulting record would result in the last two books completed in his lifetime. *Travels with Charley* and *America and Americans* reflect John Steinbeck's lifelong pursuit of what he understood to be impossible: the attainment of unblemished truth. As such, these two books are as relevant and essential to understanding Post-Truth USA as any he ever wrote.

Steinbeck's road to rediscovering true things begins with *Travels* and ends with *America*. While the travel book is a collection of observations rendered by an array of fiction techniques, *America* is a bold presentation of what he learned. Commenting on John Ditsky's assertion that whereas *Travels* was Steinbeck's attempt to return to the scientific/inductive nonteleological mode in *Sea of Cortez*, *America* is a teleological summation, Geralyn Strecker (1995) writes that one is "an account of a fiction writer's journey" and the other is "a journalistic essay and more objective in its approach" (214). In a way, *Travels* represents Steinbeck's journey across the nation at the Joad view—on the ground—while *America* is a series of intercalary chapters (between photographs rather than narrative) at the ten-thousand-foot level.

Anyone looking for a conventional, mimetic, or objective portrayal of the United States in *Travels with Charley in Search of America* would be very disappointed. The word "Travels" is less important to Steinbeck than the word "Search." The book asserts that in a search for America or any form of truth, it is the quest itself and its effect on the individual that matters. At the end of the trip, to borrow imagery from the end of *Winter*, does the traveler's light remain or does the wick go black? "Indeed, it would be a mistake to take this travelogue too literally, as Steinbeck was at heart a novelist," Steinbeck's biographer Jay Parini writes, adding that the book is "true" as "an authentic vision of America at a certain time" (2012, xii). Examining the various ways Steinbeck rearranged or omitted details in his book, William Groneman III (2012), notes that "Thom Steinbeck remembers his father saying, 'I don't lie, I remember big,'" and therefore "*Travels* is Steinbeck remembering big" (79). Steinbeck himself put up numerous signposts, overtly and technically, to alert readers that at best *Travels* would be the author's attempt to portray his own recollected vision of America at a certain time.

The writer Rick Bass once visited the office of naturalist and author Barry Lopez and was stunned by its order and neatness, writing, "I knew of [Lopez's] rigorous internal attention to order and rightness, but. . . . I had not fully realized this carryover of precision into his physical world" (Bass 2018, 162). The systematic, meticulous attention to order and detail of a writer like

Lopez and his nearly photographic works is another world from the wild, haphazard approach that John Steinbeck took with *Travels*. As described in Steinbeck biographies by Jay Parini, William Souder, and most completely by Jackson Benson, Steinbeck's writing process sabotaged any attempt at objective truth, had Steinbeck been interested in that at all. Recovering from his trip and then greatly distracted by his attendance at John F. Kennedy's inauguration, Steinbeck started writing *Travels* at home in Sag Harbor and while on vacation in Barbados in February. Working from letters and what Parini (2012) describes as "fragmentary notes," Steinbeck wrote on the porch of his room at the Sandy Lane Hotel, contending with guests who annoyed him and the lure of scuba diving in the afternoon (428). He could not finish there, as another (welcome) distraction loomed ahead with a trip to offshore Mexico, to gather firsthand information on the geological drilling venture Project Mohole. Shortly after, he had surgery in New York to remove a hernia and then had to make the deadline on his Mohole article for *Life* magazine. In May, back at Sag Harbor, considerable concerns about his sons, John and Thom, and Elaine and her daughter, Waverly, among others, gave him insomnia—none of these things helping with the completion of *Travels*.

Another setback came with the mixed reviews of *Winter*; serious writing in the summer of 1961 seemed an insurmountable challenge. Benson (1984) observes that the collision of all these ills doomed any chance Steinbeck had of writing another novel: "It seemed so damned hopeless, so damned useless to go on" (897). Feeling deeply depressed in July, he wrote his editor Pascal Covici, describing the *Travels* manuscript as "a formless, shapeless, aimless thing and it is even pointless" (Steinbeck 1989, 702). Worse, in his despair, he concludes that the nation he witnessed had become materialistic, bored, and without vision: "a discontented land" (703). "I've sought for an out on this—saying it is my aging eyes seeing it, my waning energy feeling it, my warped vision that is distorting it, but it is only partly true" (703). Nearly a year after he started his trek, Steinbeck finished the manuscript for *Travels* in September 1961. As often happened with his work, even *The Grapes of Wrath*, he felt the imagined creation was superior to the completed manuscript. Steinbeck finished up proofs at a villa in Capri in February—in the midst of a stressful extended trip with his family—and *Travels* was published by the time he had returned to Sag Harbor on July 27, 1962.

While well-received by reviewers and readers (*Travels* became a *New York Times* number one bestselling book in October 1962), those who knew Steinbeck's work quickly perceived that the book was not a typical travelogue. In his 1962 review, Orville Prescott (1996) recognized that *Travels* was full of "tall tales" and had suspicions about the accuracy of some of the locations (482). Contemporary reviewers found the book to be subjective, impressionistic; Fanny Butcher (1996) declared that readers looking for "a travel guide to the United States" would be disappointed; and George Mills (1996) concluded Steinbeck "is not pretending to provide his readers with a definitive picture of the nation as it is today" (483, 487). One of the more intriguing observations among the contemporary reviewers was Paul Pickrel's 1996 assertion that the book loses focus and interest in its generalizations but comes to life "whenever Steinbeck fastens on the particular," deploying his considerable techniques as a fiction writer (attention to description, dialogue, and character) so that there are "brilliant" anecdotes (488). Even readers unfamiliar with Steinbeck's approach to nonfiction, his lifelong pursuit of ever-elusive true things, could recognize the numerous red flags regarding the nature of truth the author planted in the text.

Throughout *Travels*, Steinbeck alerts his readers that the book is, as much as anything, an impossible expedition into the evanescent nature of true things. Immediately he warns that for all the careful planning, every trip takes control and has its own "personality, temperament, individuality, uniqueness" and "no two are alike" (767). In his search to rediscover the country, he must overcome the distortions of his earlier memories, he must hide his identity or create new ones (he would inhabit several roles in the book), he must travel alone in order not to unnecessarily "disturb the ecologic complex of an area," and he has to work in a way in which he could be set apart (or hide) in his truck, like "a kind of casual turtle carrying his house on his back" (769). The record of the trip will largely reside in his mind; regarding notetaking and research, he observes that he is bringing all the tools he will rarely use: "I suppose our capacity for self-delusion is boundless. I knew very well that I rarely make notes, and if I do I either lose them or can't read them" (772). Very quickly he hints, too, that his quest to find America is quixotic; his truck becomes Rocinante (in his letters the trip had gone from "Operation America" to "Operation Windmills," a change he blamed on his doubters [Steinbeck 1989, 668, 671]). In the book, before the trip has even begun, the paradoxes pile up: distorted memories will be overcome by fictions; to find the truth he must become a character (or several); in recording the trip, it is important for him "to be peripatetic eyes and ears," but to do so without the use of notes, depending on a memory that he describes as "a faulty, warpy reservoir"; and he frames the quest to find what is real about America by the story of Don Quixote (768). Steinbeck, of course, embraced paradoxes—in *America and Americans*, he would devote an entire chapter to them, "Paradox and Dream."

For "the mapifiers," as Steinbeck calls them, he will briefly review maps (which he disdains), but the factual points on a line mean little to him compared to the impressions he remembers, such as a Maine crossroads, or a deer he saw, or a lumber truck he heard (813). In these impressionistic fragments, perhaps, Steinbeck can build what he calls "the foundations of the larger truth" from the "small diagnostic truths" (768). Along the way he recognizes that he does not trust a journalist's attempt to create "a mirror of reality," because he concedes "there are too many realities" (817). He notes we tend to rearrange the world to suit our own perceptions, like the literary critic who reads a work and turns it "into something the size and shape of himself" (817). Objective, collective truth is impossible as we remake what we see in our own minds, as Steinbeck knew he was doing on his trip across the country: "For this reason I cannot commend this account as an America that you will find" (818). He travels the roads, reading historical markers, regarding the peculiar warps of history and how "the myth wipes out the fact" (820). He recalls someone remembering young Steinbeck's looking like a street urchin, although Steinbeck knows the memory could not be true: "Nothing I can do is likely to change it, particularly the truth" (821).

When Steinbeck arrives on the Monterey Peninsula, the old problem with warp makes writing about the place that should be easiest to discuss almost impossible: what he remembers collides with the present, changed reality "until the whole thing blurs" (895). After making this shocking discovery about his old homeland, he realizes his attempt to "find the truth about my country" is impossible: "What I carried in my head and deeper in my perceptions was a barrel of worms" (905). Not surprisingly, the ostensible mission of his journey in tatters, Steinbeck is ready to speed back to Sag Harbor and get the trip behind him. In Virginia, he admits the trip has ended and the mission failed: "I tried to call it back, to catch it up—a foolish and hopeless matter, because it was definitely and permanently over and finished" (949). He has little memory of the flight back home. In a final appropriate and somewhat manufactured paradox (complete with a cop out of central casting), the only time he becomes lost is when he returns to his East Coast home of New York City and needs directions from a policeman. His last expedition to get at the truth of a big thing (the USA) is a trek marked by all of Steinbeck's usual road signs: self-delusion, perceptive warps, confused memories, mythologies, paradox, and fictions springing from nonfictions. For the impossibility of the trip, for all of his exhaustion, at the end Steinbeck can laugh at himself. In his quest, he knew before he left just how he would arrive: "And that's how the traveler came home again" (951).

Like the final scene with the officer in Manhattan, there is no way to know where the line between fiction and nonfiction lives in *Travels with Charley*. Aside from Steinbeck's running discussion about the slippery nature of truth throughout the book, the author creates a series of patterns that strongly suggest manufactured moments. As suggested by Groneman in his assessment of *Travels*, Steinbeck erased some of the realities of his trip (some visits with Elaine or breaks in fine hotels) and may have borrowed from old stories (the young boy's admiration for Rocinante at the beginning of the book is reminiscent of the boy Frankie in *Cannery Row*). Some moments in *Travels* seem embellished for humorous effect, such as a believable little spat between Charley and a wealthy woman's Pomeranian, which escalates into fancy as Steinbeck grabs the Pomeranian by the throat and then later brings the woman a bottle of brandy to soothe her nerves, at which point she gulps "a slug that should have killed her" (793). The process of Steinbeck's imagination, and how real people might become fictitious characters, is demonstrated when the author occupies an unmade Chicago hotel room while waiting for a clean one. In the empty room, Steinbeck looks at the remnants left behind by the previous occupant and takes these fragments and impressions and builds a character in his mind, Lonesome Harry, who soon becomes "as real to me as anyone I ever met, and more real than many" (846). Here, Steinbeck has no qualms about sharing his method of invention. Throughout the book, Steinbeck also makes characters out of himself, playing roles as needed (fisherman, hunter, expert on hairdressers, etc.). To study the infamous Cheerleaders of New Orleans, he hides his New York identity by pretending to be a British sailor from Liverpool, complete with a blue jacket, navy cap, and a faint accent that even Steinbeck acknowledges is a bad fake.

The most effective creative riff on a real story appears with Steinbeck's witnessing of a tragic moment at the end of the segregation era, as the Cheerleaders and others hurl racial epithets at a Black girl going to a white school. This scene is generally lauded as one of the best episodes in *Travels*, and Benson (1984) calls it "the dramatic centerpiece" of the book (889). The moment in front of the school that Steinbeck witnesses reads like a precisely recorded event and, for all of its horror, is brilliantly described. From this nugget of real observation, Steinbeck builds a series of dialogues that seem too carefully ordered to be believed. Indeed, even Steinbeck's arrival in New Orleans has the feel of a horror movie, with the appearance of an excitable racist parking lot attendant and a shriveled anti-Semitic taxicab driver.

After Steinbeck leaves the city, he recovers at a place by the Mississippi River and invites a learned southern gentleman, complete with white hair and clipped mustache, to join him for coffee. In his balanced comments about race, this man seems a relic from a more genteel age, doomed in the presently divided times (he longs to assume his self-proclaimed surname of *Cit Git*, the French phrase for "Here Lies" on the head of a tombstone). He seems the perfect embodiment of the writer Steinbeck discusses just before the meeting: Roark Bradford, a New Orleans reporter, author, and visiting lecturer at Tulane University whose book *Ol' Man Adam an' His Chillun* (1928) was made into the Pulitzer Prize-winning play *The Green Pastures* (1929) by Marc Connelly. Next Steinbeck picks up a Black field hand, too terrified to talk about the Cheerleaders—a picture of distrust between races and the inspiration for a commentary on hatred and war. The next day, Steinbeck encounters a traveling salesman who turns out to be a one-dimensional racist, enabling the author to tell him off and then to leave him on the side of the road. Finally, in a culmination to this series of dialogues about race, Steinbeck picks up "a young Negro student with a sharp face and the look and feel of impatient fierceness" (947). This character, a man who wants justice for his people and understands the whole picture, is an avatar of Tom Joad. Steinbeck ends the dialogues with his tentative ideas about what it all means (perhaps a coming revolution as frightening as the one he feared for the late 1930s California agricultural system). And Steinbeck adds a disclaimer for the reader, namely, that he has not "presented a true picture of the South" (948).

As Steinbeck's body of work indicates, as well as his complex explorations of the nature of truth and various overt and technical signposts in *Travels*, his search for America does not always provide the mimetic descriptions of a writer, say, like Barry Lopez, Peter Matthiessen, or Terry Tempest Williams. Steinbeck blended photographic descriptions, impressionistic musings, and fictional renderings so well that many readers could take *Travels* at face value.

Yet one of them did not, with fascinating result, when a former newspaper reporter, Bill Steigerwald, attempted to retrace Steinbeck's route in 2010. The culmination of this twenty-first-century trek is Steigerwald's book *Dogging Steinbeck: Discovering America and Exposing the Truth about "Travels with Charley"* (2013). William Souder, the author of a 2020 biography of Steinbeck, *Mad at the World: A Life of John Steinbeck*, outlines some of Steigerwald's unsettling claims, including the startling calculation that Elaine was with her husband for forty-five of the seventy-five days of the journey. Souder notes that Steigerwald applied "the rules of journalism to a work that purported to be journalism" and that "facts matter" (2020, 358). Perhaps most damning is Souder's inclusion of a quote from Steinbeck's oldest son, John IV "Catbird" Steinbeck, who said his father, shy as he was, could never interact with people as depicted in *Travels*: "He just sat in his camper and wrote all that shit. . . . So the book is actually a great novel" (359). Reviewing a later, shortened 2020 e-version by Steigerwald (*Chasing Steinbeck's Ghost: The Timeline for John Steinbeck's "Travels with Charley" Road Trip*), DeMott (2021) applauds the author's project idea, his endurance, and his revelations of exact locations for many of Steinbeck's stops. But he adds that the book has also become a source of controversy, its detractors put off by Steigerwald's "bristling ego" and "self-important hectoring tone" (206).

In his quest for the truth, Steigerwald walks right into the same traps of many of Steinbeck's characters. He begins his expedition with a fatal Steinbeckian error: a series of preconceptions. Steigerwald's 2013 introduction provides a paradox that he fails to recognize: working from the perspective of a "libertarian newspaperman," he writes, "my book is subjective as hell. But it's entirely nonfiction" (7). A man of the twenty-first-century United States, he proudly outlines his political agenda as a libertarian, someone who grew up as "a Baby Boomer from another political planet, a red one" and is a fan of William F. Buckley Jr., and Barry Goldwater (18). He is fired up to take down one of the famed elites, John Steinbeck, a New Deal Democrat who knew and admired the likes of FDR, Adlai Stevenson, and LBJ. Desperate for attention, Steigerwald sends out a "self-promotional email" before setting out (24). Then he cruises the country on the interstates at seventy miles per hour, fighting boredom by listening to satellite radio, comfortably contained in his "personal earthbound space capsule" (25). He writes, "Steinbeck would have killed for such high-speed comfort" (25). Here, somehow, Steigerwald missed how Steinbeck wanted to work, moving slowly on the backroads, keen to hear and see what was going on around him. And Steigerwald wants what Steinbeck never did: those chain stores, like Subway, Walmart, and Costco. Whatever possibility that Steigerwald could see Steinbeck outside of his own warp ends before he leaves New England, as he is convinced Steinbeck lied about a stay in New Hampshire: "I was operating under the assumption that everything in *Travels with Charley* was fiction until proved otherwise" (71). As Steigerwald dogs Steinbeck, the "grumpy old rich fart," his picture of the USA becomes a red state/blue state travelogue, where the scary Americans are progressives or worse (liberal elites like the Steinbeck scholars) and the real Americans are Republicans or, even better, libertarians (220). Steigerwald, trapped in his own blinders, cannot understand that Steinbeck was after a much bigger picture, a much bigger form of truth: "Politics is strangely absent from *Travels with Charley*. Being a political creature, I noticed that right away when I re-read the book. It made no sense" (173).

By the end of the trip, John Steinbeck could have predicted the result: Steigerwald was disappointed. He had set out to shock the Steinbeck community by exposing the great man, who "spoiled everyone's fun" (238). Steigerwald expects a hero's reception from Steinbeck scholars: "I thought they'd thank me for my hard work, or maybe give me an honorary degree in something" (245). None came. Even NPR failed him, not plugging his road blog or adequately presenting his credentials (76). New York publishers did not come calling; his book is self-published. Bill Steigerwald chased after Steinbeck's ghost, bound by preconceptions, dogged by the complexity of Steinbeck's vision, and embroiled in the self-delusion that any work of literary discussion would become a bestseller or make its author a celebrity. He could have been a Steinbeck character, a Henry Morgan or Joseph Wayne, lost in a hall of mirrors, with little chance of understanding the true thing he was seeking.

Steinbeck's final, definitive discussion regarding the nature of truth might have ended with *Travels with Charley*. As best described in Benson's biography, by the mid-1960s, Steinbeck suffered from mounting physical ailments; the loss of friends and family (including his beloved sister, Mary, and his editor at Viking, Pascal Covici); fits and starts with a variety of projects; the endless distractions of (unwanted) fame; and a creeping malaise. In August 1964 Viking president Thomas H. Guinzburg brought a collection of photographs to which Steinbeck agreed to write captions; it was to be a quick commercial job. Instead, Steinbeck found he was writing a series of essays about America, a summation of his findings during the *Travels* expedition. His essays address a variety of concerns, including environmental degradation, racism, hypercapitalism, anxiety, dependence on psychotropic drugs, and the USA's general lack of direction. "He wrote and said exactly what he thought about his country," Parini (2012) writes, "and it is still worth reading" (458). Today the United States remains riddled with the problems Steinbeck identified, and readers now might find *America and Americans* to be unsettlingly relevant. In his review of the book, Tetsumaro Hayashi (1996) comments on the "truths of *America and Americans*" that Steinbeck reveals, adding, "This is a book of prophecy written by a man of mission and vision" (502). In 2024, we might wish his book had been less prophetic and the issues raised not so familiar.

As a lifelong student of truth, Steinbeck urges his fellow Americans to pursue the reality of their situations. In the first line of the foreword, Steinbeck states, "In text and pictures, this is a book of opinions, unashamed and individual" (1966, 7). He adds that the book "cannot even pretend to be objective truth" and even the photographs lack objectivity, for the camera "can set down only what its operator sees, and he sees what he wants to see" (7). Always with Steinbeck, anyone attempting to depict the truth must humbly admit the limitations of personal warp and perception. Nevertheless, also in the tradition of Steinbeck, he will discuss the bigger truths, the whole picture—taking in "America—complicated, paradoxical, bullheaded, shy, cruel, boisterous, unspeakably dear, and very beautiful" (7). And along the way, true of so many Steinbeck characters, we must be wary of self-delusion, particularly the powerful mythology of the American Dream. In the chapter

"Paradox and Dream," Steinbeck lists a dizzying array of paradoxical ideas that Americans hold dear, for "Americans seem to live and breathe and function by paradox; but in nothing are we so paradoxical as in our passionate belief in our own myths" (30). How can we, as Steinbeck attempts to do in *America and Americans*, step outside of our illusions and come closer to the reality of our lives and our place in the world? His answer goes back to his work with Ricketts: "Perhaps we will have to inspect mankind as a species, not with our usual awe at how wonderful we are but with the cool and neutral attitude we reserve for all things save ourselves" (137). Indeed, this is much of the narrative stance Steinbeck adopts in *America and Americans*. Being honest, however, Steinbeck admits even this favored approach to truth is impossible: "If I inspect my people and study them and criticize them, I must love them if I have any self-love, since I can never be separate from them and can be no more objective about them than I am about myself" (142). The foundations Steinbeck created in a lifetime of work concerning the nature of truth provide the substructure of his final word in *America and Americans*. Near the close of his life, he asserted once again that the pursuit of true things is never ending and that the moment you think you have found them, you may be at the end of your journey, laughing your head off.

John Steinbeck never gave up his ever-complicated search for the truth. On June 9, 1966, two and half years before his death on December 20, 1968, he wrote a letter to Elizabeth Otis as he was struggling with yet another dead-end novel idea, which he tentatively titled "And a Piece of It Fell on My Tail" (Steinbeck 1989, 832). His plan was to retell an old story he first heard in second grade, of Henny-Penny, who believed the sky was falling due to a piece of cabbage on her tail, and "adolescent" Chicken Little, who believed she was a fool (832). In Steinbeck's retelling, he wanted a novel that would explore the nature of truth. Chicken Little, armed with objective reality, "the clear vision, the iron nerves and the logical precision of youth," convinces everyone that there is no way the sky could be falling—case closed (833). But, Steinbeck wonders, what if there is another way to see it? What if Henny-Penny, ridiculed by most (but not all) second-grade readers, is onto something else, another perception of reality? Maybe one that is bigger or deeper? What if she is speaking to us "in a quiet philosophic tone, as though to impart a piece of interesting information" (833)? Steinbeck notes that entertaining this different view could change the entire direction of the story and could make the oft-ridiculed Henny-Penny "an exact and penetrating observer of external reality" (833). Prefacing this discussion, Steinbeck suggests that there are truths in novels and fictions in newspapers: "Then—what is fiction? Is it a true thing that didn't happen as opposed to a false thing that did?" (832). Considering this conundrum in all honesty, Steinbeck admits, "I don't know" (832). And that is the point. He does not hide his opinions—*America and Americans* is a bold summation of his views—but John Steinbeck is the last man to say he has the last word. His body of work and his life serve as an example, inviting us to leave our post-truth silos, join others around the campfire, and, with humility and openness, speak with each other again about true things.

# 10

## *Travels with Charley* as a Space for Cross-Cultural Relationality

Danica Čerče

As I demonstrated in my 2019 *Steinbeck Review* article, "John Steinbeck on East European Markets," in the postwar communist part of Europe literature was regarded as an important locus for ideological discourse and one of the paths to social progress. Literary works that were in accord with the officially promoted precepts of social realism were manipulated by communist propagandists, whereas those that lacked historical substance of class struggle, scientific inquiry, and philosophical debate or hinted at any ideological doubts were subjected to fierce criticism and consigned to oblivion. John Steinbeck was among few American authors whose writing appealed to and unwittingly served the ruling communist regimes. The credit for the writer's popular acclaim in these countries went to the social necessity and documentary integrity of his Depression-era novels, particularly *The Grapes of Wrath* (1939). Uncompromisingly exposing the ills of American capitalist economic system, the novel not only conformed to but also strengthened the bleak picture of the United States that had been systematically presented by the state-controlled communist media.

On the other hand, Steinbeck's *Travels with Charley in Search of America* (1962), hereafter referred to as *Travels*, failed to meet the criteria of political correctness. Assessed through an ideological lens, this personal account of a road trip—as *Travels* has often been described—could not be of service to the ruling regimes' objectives. Given that a 1964 translation was published in the climate of critical antipathy and even antagonism toward Steinbeck due to the changed thematic orientation in his later works and his anticommunist political stance in the 1950s and 1960s, hardly any critical interest was paid to what an anonymous author in the Slovene literary journal *Knjiga* (1964) considered a "charming portrayal of America" (9). Those few who reviewed the book largely underrated it on the grounds that, lacking communist rhetoric, it was not in line with the prevailing literary fashion.

Slovene reviewer Marija Cvetko (1964) observed that "many would be ashamed of this work" and reprimanded the author for his "lukewarm personal involvement and the lack of intensity of his critical insight" (7), a view that shows a characteristic disinterest in the aesthetic value of literary works and the reductive assimilation of literature to ideology. Still, despite disparaging Steinbeck on ideological grounds, Cvetko presents the book as a "unique piece of travel writing," highlighting the author's "caring and painful engagement with the issues discussed" (7). Around the same time, Slavko Rupel (1964), another Slovene reviewer, praised the book's topical theme and Steinbeck's sincere stance in discussing both American foreign policy and the country's domestic problems with racism, urbanism, and consumerism (15).

The above evaluations of *Travels* reveal that in Slovenia a relatively positive reception of Steinbeck's works continued well into the 1960s, whereas in other East European countries, Steinbeck was repeatedly under critical attacks already by the late 1940s. According to Petr Kopecký (2011), this was due to his ideological deviations and disapproval of radical ideals (210). Kopecký further claims that, in the early 1960s, "a small backlash against the tendency to discredit Steinbeck" was also seen in the former Czechoslovakia (211). For example, reviewing *Travels*, Czech critic Antonín Přidal (1965) argued that the book clearly demonstrates that Steinbeck "was not politically naïve," as he claimed in several ideologically charged reviews, and ironically concluded that the writer would probably have done better "by writing textbooks of political economics instead of novels" (51).

It was not until after the democratic changes in Eastern Europe at the beginning of the 1990s that *Travels*—along with several other literary works that had formerly been received with skepticism, prejudice, and misunderstanding or had been neglected altogether—were assessed from new, insightful, and politically unbiased perspectives of contemporary critical engagement. Once we bring in critical approaches that consider all the potentialities of literary texts, it is not difficult to notice that *Travels* contains the seeds for many new areas of investigation: ecological readings, political analyses, racial theories. However, although Steinbeck is currently enjoying a renewed level of acceptance in the region, my 2017 statistical evaluation of relevant bibliographies in *John Steinbeck in East European Translation: A Bibliographical and Descriptive Overview* showed that, unlike several other works by Steinbeck, *Travels* has not yet attracted many translators or reviewers in European postcommunist countries.

My reading of *Travels* is framed by an interest in how Steinbeck responded to the public dynamics of racial separation in the United States, that is, his response to the assumptions about the fixity of the dividing lines between domination and subordination, or what Sara Suleri (2003) describes as the "master-myth about the static lines of demarcation" between empowered and disempowered cultures (112). I argue that, despite its preoccupation with the local and national, *Travels* addresses themes of wider, universal relatability and provides a space wherein alternative discourses of race can exist.

Mark Twain (1869) wrote that "travel is fatal to prejudice, bigotry, and narrow-mindedness and many people need it sorely on these accounts" (521). Steinbeck did not need traveling on any of these accounts. What prompted him to set out on the months-long road trip around the United States described in *Travels* was his desire to "learn about his own country," as he explained in his May 25, 1960, letter to his friends Frank Loesser and Jo Sullivan (Steinbeck 1989, 666). His idea for the journey had been conceived about six years before he actually loaded his truck, fancifully dubbed Rocinante after Don Quixote's horse, and left New York in the company of his wife's French poodle Charley. As the writer confessed to Elizabeth Otis in as early as June 1954, he realized that he had "lost track of the country," having been "cut off for a very long time" (Benson 1984, 767). Similarly, Steinbeck reveals early on in *Travels* that for twenty-five years, he had been writing about the America he remembered, but "the memory is at best faulty, warpy reservoir" (11).

Drawing on Steinbeck's low spirit and disillusionment evident in his letter to James S. Pope on March 28, 1960, in which he writes about "the mess in Washington" and confesses that "if [he] had any sense, [he]'d go back to Europe and let the things rot" (Steinbeck 1989, 663), Sally E. Parry observes that Steinbeck must have felt that the America he "had known and loved was veering onto a dangerous path" (2007, 148). Indeed, he did not have to travel far to realize that his concerns for the country's future had been fully justified. Even before witnessing the United States at its worst, Steinbeck was bitterly disappointed by what he saw: "American cities are like badger holes, ringed with trash—all of them—surrounded by piles of wrecked and rusting automobiles, and almost smothered with rubbish. . . . I do wonder whether there will come a time when we can no longer afford our wastefulness—chemical wastes in the river, metal wastes everywhere, and atomic wastes buried deep in the earth or sunk in the sea" (1965, 28–29). What worried Steinbeck were not only the destructive implications of abundance and overpopulation but also the apathetic lack of arguments and discussion that he experienced all over the country: "People just won't put out an opinion" (33), he observes in a conversation about the recent election with one of the locals in the White Mountains.

In line with the view that "truth is circumstantial" (Dunn 1994, 332), that is, that it depends on the point of utterance, Steinbeck was hoping to discuss politics and ideas with other Americans. As he observes not long after leaving home, his representation of the country "is true until someone else passes that way and rearranges the world in his own style" (70); here, he recalls how his impressions of Prague were considerably different from those of Joseph Alsop, a famous journalist with whom he conversed during a return flight to America. He also acknowledges the influence of mood as we age, claiming that "our morning eyes describe a different world that do our afternoon eyes, and surely our wearied evening eyes can report only a weary evening world" (71). Any "truth" is, in short, subjective.

Even given these considerations, however, the demonstration of violence and hostility Steinbeck witnessed in New Orleans, following the integration of the city's schools, seems to have shattered the last shred of his hope that the "true" America was different from the one he saw. Compelled by curiosity and apprehension, he wanted to witness the scene of southern mob violence. Remembering the Coopers, a decent and respected Black family from Salinas, Steinbeck was not prepared for the kind of America in which Black was considered "an inferior race" (1965, 212) and—in Toni Morrison's words—African Americans were merely allowed "a shadowless participation in the dominant cultural body" (Morrison 1992, 129). Steinbeck's perception of Black identity based on childhood memories of Mrs. Cooper's "shining kitchen"; Mr Cooper's honest running of his small trucking business; and their three boys' outstanding performance at school did not match the derogatory representations he encountered in the South. His first thought was that "the authority was misinformed" (212).

Shortly after arriving in New Orleans, Steinbeck got involved in a conversation with a white taxi driver whose intolerance, savagery, and crude energy fully revealed his contempt for Black Americans, hidden behind the facade of civilized behavior or manifested in blatant and insidious forms:

> "Why, hell, mister. We know how to take care of this. . . . Ought to take them out."
> "You mean lynch them?"
> "I don't mean nothing else, mister." (219)

When observing the howling crowd protesting integration before the school where a little Black girl was walking up the sidewalk to the front door escorted by armed guards—an image that mirrored a racially polarized society—Steinbeck searched in vain for the faces of kind and gentle people he knew and had spent time with, for those who would not hesitate to protect "the small, scared, black mite" (223) and oppose segregation. To his dismay, all he could see were faces of those thirsty for "watching any pain or any agony" and enjoying it (223).

The "show of Cheerleaders," as Steinbeck refers to the insulting screaming of white women at the small Black girl and the white man who "dared to bring his white child to school" (221) is in several ways reminiscent of the incident in Georgia depicted in James Weldon Johnson's 1912 novel, *The Autobiography of an Ex-Colored Man*. Just as the brutal execution of the mob's Black victim in Johnson's novel robbed the narrator of hope and left him humiliated, bewildered, and embittered by an unbearable shame, so did the incident in New Orleans more than half a century later affect Steinbeck so deeply that he decided to return home to escape the ugliness he had experienced. As he writes, his journey "was over before [he] returned . . . and left [him] stranded far from home" (236).

Witnessing a precarious borderline between the two races and cultures and sensing numerous areas of contestation arising from the politics of polarity, Steinbeck envisioned the consequences of the boiling tension: "Could there be no relief until it burst," he asks himself, bewildered by the most logical answer (231). In this state of mind, Steinbeck bears similarities to the Black American poet and activist Langston Hughes (1951), who in his poem "Dreams Deferred" asks a similar question and predicts the inevitable result: he wonders whether a dream that is always put off, deferred, dries up "like a raisin in the sun" or whether it explodes (52).

Racial polarization in its overt or covert forms is not the only threat and indicator of society in a state of conflict that Steinbeck encountered on his travel across the United States in an attempt to learn about the country's character, but it surely was the one that saddened and worried him most. After observing the "insane rage" of the New Orleans crowd, he writes, "No newspaper had printed the words these women shouted. On television the soundtrack was made to blur or had crowd noises cut in to cover. But now I heard the words, bestial and filthy and degenerate. . . . My body churned with weary nausea, but I could not let an illness blind me after I had come so far to look and hear" (222–23).

Indeed, Steinbeck never let himself be blinded to miseries and social ills. Still, some critics were dissatisfied with his venturing into new topics and forms in the years following the publication of *The Grapes of Wrath* and suggested the opposite, wondering what changed the spirit and opinion of a man who had once "represented the best in America," as prominent Czech writer Arnošt Lustig wrote (1967, 3–4). The journey with Charley did not veil Steinbeck's vision, however; it made him feel "helpless" and "ill with . . . sorrow" (224). He was appalled by the presence of the legal and cultural barriers that supported and nurtured racism—barriers formed and preserved on the grounds of fallacious cultural assumptions.

What seems to have worried Steinbeck even more than white authoritarian rhetoric was the recognition that the dominant European discourses that had relegated Black people to a subordinate status were deeply ingrained not only in white society but also among themselves. The "massive psycho-existential complex" in some Black psyches, as Frantz Fanon (1986) refers to the psychological internalization of the illusion of white superiority (xvi), is particularly well seen in the episode in which Steinbeck tries in vain to establish a conversation with an old Black man to whom he offered a ride. Rather than being involved in conversation and expressing his opinion, the old man requests to be "let down," finding walking safer than riding with a white man (230). "I was foolishly trying to destroy a lifetime of practice" (230), realized Steinbeck, alluding to the deeply rooted ideology underpinning slavery and white supremacy. And he recalls a similar experience years ago, when his Black employee in Manhattan did not help a tipsy white woman cross the street, fearing a false accusation: "If I touched her, she could easy scream rape, and then it's a crowd, and who believes me? . . . I've been practising to be a Negro a long time" (230).

In "A Preface to Transgression," Michel Foucault (1977) points out that limits and transgressions exist and can be identified because of each other. According to Foucault, what constitutes a limit is discovered not by tracing already existing boundaries but by crossing them. In this way, transgression "forces the limit to face its imminent disappearance to find itself in what it excludes" (35). Disappointed by the presence of a rigid system of binarisms, such as centre and margin, the empowered and disempowered, self and "other," Steinbeck conveys a similar idea through the confession of an elderly white man from the South, who admits that it is hard for white and Black people to "change a feeling about things" (226). Nevertheless, the man acknowledges that there are day-to-day interactions that tend to abolish the color line: "I have an old Negro couple. . . . Sometimes in the evening we forget. They forget to envy me and I forget they might, and we are just three pleasant . . . things living together and smelling the flowers" (227).

Clearly, in line with his own view that an artist has to come forward when needed (Lisca 1972, 860), Steinbeck promotes a vision of broader humanity, with no division between "man and beast" and "black and white" (1965, 227). He wanted America to be for "everyone, white and black, . . . all ages, all trades, all classes" (231), facilitating dialogue and interconnectivity between cultures. That Black Americans will demand and reclaim what has been withheld from them is particularly evident in Steinbeck's discussion with a passionate Black student, a potential "conscious antagonist," as Edward Said (1994) refers to a person who, "compelled by the system to play subordinate or imprisoning roles within [society]," reacts by "disrupting it" (335). The student is not satisfied with Martin Luther King Jr.'s "teaching of passive but unrelenting resistance," proclaiming, "I want it faster, I want action—action now" (234).

Although Steinbeck seems somehow reluctant to draw a general conclusion, reminding the reader again that he is not presumptuous enough to consider his portrayal of the South as undeniably correct, he closes his reflection in line with Walter Mignolo's 2005 view that "there are no democratic possibilities without undoing the colonial and imperial differences" (392). And Steinbeck predicts the inevitability of change: "I know it is a troubled place and a people caught in jam. And I know that the solution when it arrives will not get easy or simple. I feel with Monsieur Ci Git that the end is not in question. It's the means—the dreadful uncertainty of the means" (235).

In a speech delivered in 1959, Black American playwright and activist Lorraine Hansberry proclaims, "All art is ultimately social. One cannot live with sighted eyes and feeling heart and not know or react to the miseries which afflict this world" (Hansberry 1965, 588). In line with this assertion, Hansberry used the stage to advocate a political imperative for liberation of Black people from their subordination. In *Travels*, Steinbeck does not explicitly call for change but sees its inevitability: "The breath of fear was everywhere. I wanted to get away—a cowardly attitude, perhaps, but more cowardly to deny" (231). However, this admission makes the book no less important in terms of its social relevance; French critic Pierre Macherey (2006) has even noted that "what is important in the work is what it does not say" (86). Steinbeck may not reach firm conclusions, but nevertheless he compels us to confront the actions that have institutionalized group identity in the United States through the creation of social structures that protect white privileges at the expense of communities of color. As in other Steinbeck works, *Travels* reveals that Steinbeck never ceased to denounce any kind of injustice and tyranny but remained an artist with a refined sense for human rights, rejecting the discourse that prevents the creation of common ground. For, as Barbara Heavilin (2019) has pointed out, Steinbeck had an "indomitable faith in America's democracy of the people, by the people, and for the people" (x).

## Conclusion

American philosopher Martha Nussbaum (2000) contends that good literature is "disturbing" in a more effective ways than history and social science writing usually are (359). The key to a better understanding of the issues embodied in the representative worlds of literature is imaginative sympathy, by which readers respond to the experiences of the characters with more powerful emotions, disconcertion, and perplexity—leading them to alter some "standing judgments" or to reject some experiences of reading as deforming or pernicious (363). Although not as "deeply engaging" and "utterly consuming" as *The Grapes of Wrath* (DeMott 1997, 148), *Travels* is a "disturbing" critical commentary on several aspects of American society, exposing the dissonances between American ideals and reality. The book is particularly effective in dramatizing the cross-racial encounter and serves as a sort of brief on the country's political, institutional, and cultural reproduction of white privilege and entitlement. Steinbeck offers readers a way of experiencing the ongoing dialectic of self and "other" that is too often accepted "as a permanent way of life" by many southerners—but not all, as Steinbeck is careful to point out (231). And he creates bonds of identification and empathy, enabling readers to see and respond empathically, sympathetically. In this sense and in line with Nussbaum's views about political and ethical implications of literary imagination, *Travels* does not give us the whole story about social justice, but it functions as a "bridge both to a vison of justice and to the social enactment of that vision" (Nussbaum 2000, 364).

According to Luchen Li (2017), "many scholars and readers worldwide continue to read Steinbeck's books to better understand America, the world, and themselves" (3). Indeed, despite its preoccupation with local and national realities, *Travels* has universal appeal as it raises ethical questions about societal, political, and cultural violence and abuse that continue to haunt us all in the twenty-first century. Contesting white racial hegemony and foregrounding the need for racial understanding, *Travels* is a challenge and an invitation to all those around the globe who wish to speak of their experience of human disenfranchisement and urge the repudiation of cultural presumptions and ethnocentrism. Hence, the book deserves the widest possible distribution and circulation, including in the countries of the postcommunist Europe.

# Part III

# CONTEMPLATING AMERICA

*Travels with Charley* as Road Text

# 11

## John Steinbeck and R. K. Narayan in Search of America

NICHOLAS P. TAYLOR

Three-quarters of the way through John Steinbeck's 1962 *Travels with Charley in Search of America*, the exasperated author, frustrated with his inability to "find the truth" about his country, postulates that if "an Englishman or a Frenchman or an Italian should travel my route, see what I saw, hear what I heard, their stored pictures would be not only different from mine but equally different from one another" (185). Though Steinbeck likely did not know it, a major international author had in fact traveled a similar route just four years previously—and had published an account of his journey. The author was R. K. Narayan, recognized today as one of the twentieth century's most important authors of Indian fiction in English. Narayan came to America in 1956 on a grant from the Rockefeller Foundation and, over a year's stay, traveled to many of the same locales visited by Steinbeck on his *Travels with Charley* trip. Thanks to *My Dateless Diary: An American Journey*, the 1960 memoir of Narayan's year in America, we can test Steinbeck's hypotheses. Were a foreigner's "stored pictures" of the *Travels with Charley* route different from Steinbeck's? If so, how were they different, and how should we explain the differences?

### PARALLEL CAREERS

Though there is no evidence that Steinbeck and Narayan ever met, their careers paralleled each other to a remarkable degree. Steinbeck (1902–68) was slightly older than Narayan (1906–2001), but the two authors had their first commercial successes in the same year, 1935, when Steinbeck's *Tortilla Flat* and Narayan's *Swami and Friends* were published to critical acclaim and strong sales. Building on these commercial successes, both men would continue to publish at the rate of a book every year or two for the rest of their lives. They would both go on to win the top literary awards of their countries (the Pulitzer Prize for Steinbeck, the Sahitya Akademi Award for Narayan) as well as recognitions from international organizations, such as the Nobel Prize in Literature for Steinbeck and an American Academy of Arts and Letters citation for Narayan.

The parallels reach beyond chronology into the substance of the two authors' work. Both are closely associated with a particular region of their country—Steinbeck with California, Narayan with South India—and both received the critique that they were "regional" writers. Both wrote extensively about life in rural communities and paid special attention to the concerns of citizens living far from the national, or even regional, capitals of their respective countries. In their fiction, both returned again and again to familiar settings, in both cases based on the communities where they had spent their childhood. Most of Narayan's novels are set in a fictional South Indian town called Malgudi, a place whose closest American analogue is probably Faulkner's Yoknapatawpha County. Malgudi also bears resemblance to the Monterey of Steinbeck's *Tortilla Flat*, *Cannery Row*, and *Sweet Thursday* in the way it seems to exist outside of time, uninfluenced by world events, with an ecology of unique characters and situations that have come to be closely associated with their author. Contemporary literary critics (and travel promoters) sometimes call the Monterey/Salinas area "Steinbeck Country." If Indian critics were to refer to a "Narayan Country," it would be understood that they meant the rural villages of Karnataka (the Indian state where Narayan lived and wrote), so closely is he associated with the culture and geography of the region.

In form, too, the two authors worked in parallel. Both are best known for their long-form fiction but also published numerous book-length works of nonfiction, as well as collections of short stories and short works of journalism. By the end of their lives, both had formidable international readerships, with Narayan's work read particularly widely in Britain, thanks to the advocacy of Graham Greene, and Steinbeck's in Eastern Europe and Japan, among other regions. Beginning in 1956, they even shared an American publisher, Viking Press. Though it is documented that they knew many of the same people at Viking, there is no evidence that they ever met. If they had, one may assume they would have had much to discuss, not least their near-parallel journeys "in search of America" during the Eisenhower administration.

## Steinbeck's Intentions

Steinbeck states his motivation for the *Travels with Charley* trip clearly at the beginning of the book: to "rediscover this monster land" (5). Back in the

1930s, this mode of research served him well. At the urging of his first wife, Carol, he bought an old bakery van, put a mattress in the back, and drove five hours from his home outside San José, California, to a migrant labor camp in Arvin, near Bakersfield. He returned to the camp and to towns throughout California's Central Valley several times to collect stories and character sketches that he adapted first into a series of newspaper articles and later into the novel *The Grapes of Wrath*. Twenty-three years later, now famous, rich, and middle-aged, Steinbeck longed for a way to return to the heady, emotionally wrenching but unencumbered days in that bakery van. So he did what worked for him previously: he bought another van. This time it was a customized pickup truck with a camper shell that he christened Rocinante after Don Quixote's swaybacked horse. He was proud of the purchase, showing it off eagerly to his neighbors in Sag Harbor, New York. Though he relished the personal freedom he expected to find on the road, his motivation for the trip, he tells readers, was professional: he felt that his artistic sensibility was in dire need of recalibration. He had to take this trip, he writes, because "otherwise, in writing, I could not tell the small diagnostic truths which are the foundations of the larger truth" (5).

Figure 8: Jack Ramsey and John Steinbeck looking at Rocinante before trip. Brad Bennett collection. Courtesy of the Martha Heasley Cox Center for Steinbeck Studies at San Jose State University.

Later in the book, Steinbeck elaborates on his research process: "I have never passed an unshaded window without looking in, have never closed my ears to a conversation that was none of my business. I can justify or even dignify this by protesting that in my trade I must know about people, but I suspect that I am simply curious" (105). This desire to "know about people" was a consistent motivation in Steinbeck's career. He wrote often about the need for empathy in human relationships. His elder son, Thomas (1944–2016), liked to tell a story in which his father explained—within the context of a discussion about parents and professions—that his job was "to reconnect humans with their own humanity," a calling that for him held sacred importance (T. Steinbeck, 6:22). In a 1938 journal entry, John Steinbeck lays out one of the most affecting justifications for human empathy one is ever likely to encounter: "If you understand each other you will be kind to each other. Knowing a man well never leads to hate and almost always leads to love" (Shillinglaw 1994, iv). With this philosophy underpinning his work, one is inclined to take Steinbeck at his word when he says that his artistic goal with this cross-country research was nothing more nor less than meeting people and depicting them as they are.

To this end, Steinbeck's dog Charley is more than incidental, as the author observes in a scene from a night spent in northern Maine: "In establishing contact with strange people, Charley is my ambassador. I release him, and he drifts toward the objective, or rather to whatever the objective may be preparing for dinner. I retrieve him so that he will not be a nuisance to my neighbors—*et voilà!* A child can do the same thing, but a dog is better" (59). In later travelogues, for example the "Letters to Alicia" published in *Newsday* in the mid-1960s, Steinbeck laments the absence of a dog in warming up his subjects. The fact that Steinbeck feels that he needs help, via a child or dog, in breaking the ice with the people he meets on the road says more about his own social anxiety than the psychology of the average American. As we will see when we examine Narayan's experience, Americans were hardly known, then or now, for being difficult to approach. In fact, Narayan finds Americans' friendliness with strangers off-putting, perhaps false, but at no point does he report having trouble getting Americans to talk.

Several times in *Travels with Charley*, Steinbeck talks about "generalities," by which he means conclusions drawn from anecdotal observations. Steinbeck had a preference for observing things as they are, trying to avoid personal bias. He and his friend the marine biologist Edward F. Ricketts called this "nonteleological thinking." As they wrote in another travelogue, *Sea of Cortez* (1941), "Non-teleological thinking concerns itself primarily not with what should be, or could be, or might be, but rather with what actually 'is'—attempting at most to answer the already sufficiently difficult questions what or how, instead of why" (135). Steinbeck is understandably hesitant to draw conclusions about America or Americans from the people he meets on his trip. From time to time it occurs to him to draw a conclusion about something—mobile homes, for example, or Texas, or the growth patterns of American cities—but he always presents these observations with caution and skepticism, as though he were reluctant to state them but simply could not help himself: "I have always admired those reporters who can descend on an area, talk to key people, ask key questions, take samplings of opinions, and then set down an orderly report very like a road map. I envy this technique and at the same time do not trust it as a mirror of reality. I feel that there are too many realities. What set down here is true until someone else passes that way and rearranges the world in his own style" (69).

Steinbeck believed that his observations were subjective, personal, and therefore unreliable. He believed this about all observers, hence his conjecture about a Frenchman or an Italian having a different view of the same scene. Yet this does not stop him from offering conclusions. Though reluctant to single out one group of people for characterization, he appears to be happy to make pronouncements about humankind in general, particularly when the pronouncement makes a catchy phrase. Steinbeck is an eminently quotable author, particularly in his nonfiction. For example, in the midst of a passage explaining why he did not stop at any of America's national parks on his cross-country trip, he writes, "One goes not so much to see but to tell afterward" (145).

Steinbeck's trip occurred at the end of the Eisenhower years, a time of relative political harmony in which Democrats and Republicans mostly shared a vision for postwar America. To the contemporary reader it seems quaint that the only time he discusses the 1960 presidential election at any length is the section when he visits his sisters in California. His sisters were Republicans; he was a Democrat. They argued emotionally over Nixon and Kennedy. He writes, "We ended each session panting and spent with rage. On no point was there any compromise. No quarter was asked or given" (177). Perhaps he means this discord to be funny, but it is chilling to read in 2022, when virtually all political discourse in America, among family members as well as total strangers, has reached fever pitch.

## Steinbeck on Race

Reading *Travels with Charley* in the twenty-first century, one is struck not by how much America has changed but rather the opposite. Steinbeck's most disturbing observations—to him and to his readers—are the scenes that take place in the South, particularly the chapter set in New Orleans. In 1960 the city of New Orleans came under pressure to integrate its schools, and a six-year-old Black girl named Ruby Bridges was chosen to attend William Frantz Elementary, previously a whites-only school. In protest, white parents pulled their children out of the school, and some of them stood outside the school building shouting insults and epithets at young Ruby as she arrived for school each morning, and again in the afternoon when she left. Supporters of the white hecklers gathered to cheer them on. Steinbeck read about this spectacle in the newspapers as he was driving across the country and decided to arrange his itinerary so he could see it firsthand. His account of the so-called "Cheerleaders" is the emotional climax of *Travels with Charley*. With his typical precision and eye for detail, Steinbeck presents a scene that serves as a synecdoche for America in the 1960s: "The show opened on time. Sound of sirens. Motorcycle cops. Then two big black cars filled with big men in blond felt hats pulled up in front of the school. The crowd seemed to hold its breath. Four big marshals got out of each car and from somewhere in the automobiles they extracted the littlest Negro girl you ever saw, dressed in shining starched white, with new white shoes on feet so little they were almost round. Her face and little legs were black against the white. . . . A shrill, grating voice rang out. The yelling was not in chorus. Each took a turn and at the end of each the crowd broke into howls and roars and whistles of applause. This is what they had come to see and hear" (226–27).

What is chilling for today's reader is how familiar this all feels. This scene of overt, public racism could be drawn from a Trump rally. Moving beyond rabble-rousing and street fighting, white nationalist groups are now (in 2024) urging their members to attend local schoolboard and city-council meetings and even to run for seats on those governing bodies. If Steinbeck had been driving around America in the 2020s instead of 1960, he might have stopped in Washington, DC, and written something very similar about the mob that stormed the Capitol on January 6, 2021, seeking to overturn an election by ruling out votes from minority communities. That mob, which resulted in the death or injury of both police officers and insurrectionists, was as ugly—and certainly as threatening—as anything Steinbeck saw in New Orleans.

## Narayan's Search for America

Four years earlier, R. K. Narayan documented much of the same social tension on his own tour of America. Like Steinbeck, he began and ended his trip in New York, with lengthy intermediate stays in Chicago, the San Francisco Bay Area, and Los Angeles, and shorter stops for lectures in college towns such as East Lansing, Michigan; Madison, Wisconsin; and Sewanee, Tennessee. Though hardly a household name in the United States, Narayan was by 1956 well-known in American and British literary circles, and he came to America on a fellowship from the Rockefeller Foundation in New York. He had been widowed young, in 1939, and had waited until his only child, Hema, was married until he accepted the Rockefeller grant. He arrived in New York in the fall of 1956 with a plan to spend most of his time in Palo Alto (home of Steinbeck's alma mater Stanford University), where he would compose a new novel. His plan changed slightly when he discovered that a friend, the sociologist Dr. M. N. Srinivas, whom Narayan called Chamu, was spending the term at the University of California, Berkeley, across the San Francisco Bay from Palo Alto. Narayan took a room in a Berkeley hotel and over the next several months wrote the first draft of his eighth novel, *The Guide* (1958).

A diary that Narayan kept during his nine months in America became the basis of a travelogue, *My Dateless Diary: An American Journey*, published in 1960.[1] The 1988 Viking/Penguin edition of the memoir includes an introductory essay by Narayan, and this short piece, written more than thirty years after the Rockefeller trip, offers several insights into Narayan's thinking about the project. To begin, Narayan echoes Steinbeck's disavowal of generalization: "I don't know how to classify this book. It is not a book of information on America, nor is it a study of American culture" (7). Like Steinbeck he makes a clear distinction between a study based on scholarly research (which the book is not) and something more personal and lyrical. Instead he describes the book as "a record of first impressions of people and places . . . a sort of subjective minor history of a country that I love" (7). Note that Narayan emphasizes the subjectivity of his observations, echoing Steinbeck's concern about his own reportage. Like Steinbeck, he is careful, throughout the book, to remind readers that he saw only a tiny slice of America, and that readers must not think they are seeing all of America in his anecdotes. That said, Narayan, like Steinbeck, could not resist the urge to generalize. Here is a passage from the first section of the memoir, shortly after Narayan arrives in New York: "Americans like to know how far they are being liked by others. They have a trembling anxiety lest they should be thought of badly. We Indians are more hardened, having been appreciated, understood, misunderstood, represented, misrepresented, rated, and overrated from time immemorial both in factual account and in fiction" (37).

Narayan does not provide us with a mission statement the way Steinbeck does at the beginning of *Travels with Charley*, but it is possible to synthesize one from his observations: he is interested in American personalities, or what contemporary readers might call the psychological profiles that one encounters in America. Comparison or contrast with corresponding Indian types is sometimes given explicitly, as in the above quotation, and at other times it is only implied. Narayan never states explicitly that he intends the book for an Indian audience, but his cultural context is unmistakably foreign. He observes American life as a foreigner, with a foreigner's detachment and critical eye. In this way he is able to see aspects of America that Steinbeck cannot, or which Steinbeck might not have thought important enough to record. Narayan's observations of American life, from food culture to politics, come from a position of otherness. This is perhaps the most important distinction between the two books.

Narayan does not take sides in American politics, but he does note the peculiarity of the American election schedule. On the day of the 1956 presidential election, he attends a lecture on Roman architecture at Michigan State University and is astonished to find both students and faculty in attendance: "This was the day of the big election. Impossible to think that one would lecture on a subject like this and anyone would listen to it, while a National Election was in progress. No one seemed to care for it. No holiday. In our country it'd be unthinkable to have schools and offices working on a day like this. Election day ought to be a day of complete, total, abandonment to political excitement." (47). Narayan, of course, was not alone in this belief. For decades, voting-rights activists have advocated making election day a holiday in America. The usual rationale is that it would allow more people to vote, which also explains the staunch opposition. To this Narayan adds the additional rationale that it would free those who have to work or study from the burden of distraction. It is a light critique—his travelogue is not de Tocqueville's *Democracy in America*—but the tone of the passage suggests that he rejoices in having found an issue on which the Indian system is superior to the American one. In India, then as now, election days are holidays, and people are not expected to carry on as usual. In fact, elections in India are an occasion for celebration, or at least for political parties to distribute food and gifts as they attempt to sway last-minute voters. No wonder that Narayan, whose experience of democracy would have resembled a carnival as much as a duty, would find the American tradition of squeezing in a trip to the ballot box before or after work "unthinkable" and "impossible."

Rather than commenting on the substance of American political debate, Narayan prefers to poke fun at Americans' ignorance, even when their intentions are benign and their ignorance is perhaps understandable. In this way, he can be much more cutting than Steinbeck. For example, in one of his first interactions in New York, an old man in a Bronx restaurant overhears that Narayan is from India and tries to strike up a conversation:

"I like Gandhi, but Nehru is not like Gandhi, am I right?"
"No, you are wrong," I said.
"Nehru is friendly to the Communists, isn't he?"

"No, if you read the Indian papers you would understand his views better."
"Oh, I don't know. Anyway, Gandhi was great . . ." (19)

Another man tries to join the conversation, but Narayan cuts him down, too:

"Gandhi was a sturdy man. What a strong man was he!"
"But he weighed only ninety pounds," I added.

The scene ends with the crowd of New Yorkers learning that Narayan made the trip from Manhattan to the Bronx by himself—a feat far more impressive, to them, than the journey from India to America.

## On Celebrity and Celebrities

Narayan is more interested in American celebrities than American politics, which explains why, after completing his manuscript in Berkeley, he flies down the California coast and spends several weeks in Los Angeles. He has a connection in town, a film critic named Dorothy Jones, who takes him to visit numerous Hollywood studios. The putative purpose of these visits is to assess American studios' interest in setting a film in India (presumably based on Narayan's work), but the section reads more like a catalogue of the personalities he meets along the way. He is alternately scornful and reverential toward Hollywood people. He observes, "Nothing disturbs film folk so much as the thought that they are not loved and admired" (128). Steinbeck also spent time in Hollywood over the course of his career, and even counted some "film folk," such as Burgess Meredith and John Huston, among his closest friends. Curiously, during the *Travels with Charley* trip, he did not link up with any of his Hollywood friends, and in fact deliberately avoided Los Angeles.

In Narayan's book, celebrity encounters are a major concern. Shortly after his arrival in Los Angeles, Narayan meets up with the English novelist Aldous Huxley and his wife. We are never told how the meeting was arranged, and it is clear the two authors had not met previously in person, but they become frequent companions during Narayan's stay in Los Angeles. Huxley introduces Narayan to several academics studying Asian cultures and religions, and they attend lectures together. They discuss Buddhist meditation, Hindu mantras, and Huxley's favorite subject, hallucinogenic drugs. "Mescalin [sic] and the opening of the doors of perception were of course extremely recurring subjects," Narayan reports. He introduces the subject of drugs without judgement, as if it were any other eccentricity. He clearly enjoys Huxley's wide-ranging, chaotic monologues, which rove in the space of a single paragraph from Indian tantra to Balzac and Blake. Under mescaline, Huxley tells Narayan, "a single bar of music lasts a whole eternity" (123).

Upon his return to New York at the end of his trip, Narayan is introduced by a mutual friend to the film star Greta Garbo, who was by 1956 retired from acting and living a secluded life. Garbo is fascinated with Narayan, and vice versa; in fact, Narayan's encounters with Garbo are so important to the author that he chooses to conclude the book with an entry about the final lunch they shared: "After lunch we part, G.G. saying, 'How I wish we could stop time from moving and always taking us on to a moment of parting. Good-bye!'" (187). A fitting ending to a memoir, perhaps, but also a bit like stepping into a Greta Garbo film, which I suspect was the appeal of the anecdote for Narayan.

Steinbeck's relationship with celebrity in *Travels with Charley* is quite different. He was a celebrity himself, and he took care to avoid being recognized on the *Charley* trip, because he didn't want his public reputation to color the conversations he had with "ordinary" Americans. He avoided locations where he was most likely to be recognized and even donned a disguise before going to see the Cheerleaders in New Orleans. It is interesting to imagine what might have happened if Narayan had met Steinbeck during his trip—perhaps in the Viking office, at a New York cocktail party, or even in California, where Narayan spent the majority of his time. It seems likely, given the other encounters he brings to light, that Narayan would have included a meeting with Steinbeck in his book—and equally likely that Steinbeck would have chosen not to do so in his.

In an odd coincidence, Narayan also comments in *My Dateless Diary* about the utility of dogs in human interaction. During his initial stay in New York, he approaches a man he encounters on the street and asks if he loves dogs. "Such questions," Narayan writes, "however banal, have the effect of bringing humanity closer" (25). Anyone who has spent time in India understands that dogs occupy a different place in Indian society than they do in America. Feral dogs are a common sight in urban environments, and spaying/neutering is less common than in the United States. Indians do keep dogs as pets, but a travelogue about an author and his dog does not push the same emotional buttons in India as it does in America. Nevertheless, Narayan appears to acknowledge the utility, for an author, of a dog, predicting Steinbeck's comment that "a child can do the same thing, but a dog is better."

Another observation to which Narayan returns several times is the phenomenon of advertisements for funeral and burial services, which apparently did not exist in India at the time. The idea of marketing these services annoys him: "In times of War all talent is pressed for propaganda. In peace all talent (the television could make the highest bid) is pressed for sales promotion" (106). Steinbeck would hardly have disagreed with Narayan's argument—he had his own ill feelings about misdirected artistic talent—but on the subject of wartime propaganda, he might have quibbled, as Steinbeck produced several pieces of work during World War II (most notably *The Moon Is Down* and *Bombs Away*) that could be considered propaganda. Narayan was familiar with Steinbeck's work—in fact he once told an interviewer that Steinbeck was the most widely read American author in India—but given his ambivalence about artistic talent being "pressed" for various purposes, one wonders how he would have characterized Steinbeck's wartime output.

## Narayan on Race in America

Perhaps the strongest parallel between the two travelogues has to do with race and racism in America—though the two authors, owing to their different skin colors, approach the issue from opposite angles. As mentioned earlier, the emotional climax of *Travels with Charley* comes near the end of the book when Steinbeck witnesses the forced integration of William Frantz Elementary School in New Orleans. Narayan's journey also takes him through the South, as related in a short chapter titled "Gurukula in Tennessee," an account of his stop at the University of the South in Sewanee. He finds the Sewanee students very polite, and he is impressed by their knowledge of Tagore. The word *gurukula* in the chapter title refers to a type of Indian educational institution, usually sited away from major population centers, where students learn directly from wise men, or gurus. Nobel Laureate Rabindranath Tagore (1861–1941) founded one of the most widely known gurukulas and served as resident master there during his lifetime.

As it turns out, Narayan's idealistic view of the American South doesn't last very long. Later the same day, after his visit to Sewanee, he is at the local bus station waiting for an intercity bus to Nashville. He sees signs marking separate areas of the waiting hall "For Colored" and "For Whites." He reports this fact in a detached, neutral tone. When the bus arrives, white passengers are invited to board first: "The convention seems to be that the last seat should be occupied by coloured passengers. White passengers blink unhappily when I get in. Each tries to cover a vacant seat next to him with an overcoat or hat for fear that I may attempt to occupy a prohibited seat and create a 'situation.' I pass on straight to where two negroes are sitting, and they make place for me" (153). As the final passengers board the bus, white people's dedication to segregation surprises Narayan: "There are still four seats vacant in our row, but none comes there. A fat white man and his short wife prefer to stand on their feet for seventy miles rather than sit down next to me. The short wife cannot reach the strap on the roof of the bus, and the fat husband cannot keep on his feet; they suffer hell, yet they prefer to stand and travel rather than sit by my side" (154).

In reading Narayan's account of the awkward white couple, one can't help but recall Steinbeck's descriptions of the lead Cheerleader in New Orleans, whom he nicknamed "Nellie": "She was not tall, but her body was ample and full-busted. . . . She was heavily powdered, which made the line of her double chin look very dark. She wore a ferocious smile and pushed her way through the milling people" (226).

Narayan closes his chapter, and his tour of the American South, in true Steinbeckian fashion, by immersing himself in his work: "At the Nashville bus terminal I see 'Colored' and 'White' notices everywhere, and immediately take a taxi for the air-port, and 'check' my luggage, have coffee, and correct the novel for two hours, in an effort to forget the problems of human complexion" (Narayan, 154). He does not analyze any further the ugliness he has just witnessed, nor does he use the incident to draw conclusions about southerners or Americans in general. Unlike Steinbeck, who dwells for several pages in lament at what he sees in New Orleans, Narayan seems content to move on.

The difference in the two authors' analysis of racism in America may be as simple as the "problems of human complexion" that Narayan so archly references in the final sentence of his chapter. After all, Steinbeck was of European descent, with pale skin, and Narayan was of South Indian descent, with darker pigmentation. In Tennessee in 1956, that fact alone assured that the two authors would have very different experiences. Steinbeck was able to travel inconspicuously throughout the South, inconvenienced only by having to hold his nose and his tongue when he encountered bigotry. Narayan, on the other hand, must have been reminded every moment of his time in Tennessee that he belonged on the "For Colored" side of the waiting-hall, that he was supposed to board the bus last, and that he was not considered a fitting seatmate for any white person. What man, let alone an internationally famous author on a prestigious academic grant, would want to dwell on that experience?

## Conclusion

Though neither Steinbeck nor Narayan intended to document America with scientific precision, both set out to learn something about the essence of the nation from their cross-country trips. Each encountered a cross-section of the population and prevaricated about whether to generalize from these encounters. Though their routes and timelines were roughly congruent, their experiences differed, thanks to a variety of factors, including skin color, modes of transportation, and the company they kept on the road.

It is tempting to attribute some of the differences between the two travelogues to their different audiences. Steinbeck was writing about America for Americans, while Narayan was writing about America for Indians, more specifically Indians with a reading knowledge of English, which is to say the educated. In the text of the memoir, he largely avoided drawing conclusions about America, but his contemporary observations tend to reinforce his sense that Americans live more easily in the world than their Indian counterparts, thanks largely to their focus on material success, or what Narayan calls their "indifference to eternity." He writes in the foreword to the 1988 edition of *My Dateless Diary* that the typical American "works hard and earnestly, acquires wealth and enjoys life. He has no time to worry about the afterlife, only taking care to draw up a proper will and trusting the funeral home to take care of the rest" (8). This conclusion is typical Narayan: wry and cutting, a quip, but also openminded, a demonstration of his willingness to see foreign scenes as they are, rather than as he expected them to be. His final word on the subject of his American journey, the last line of the 1988 foreword, reminds us that America is, above all, "a country that I love" (8).

When Steinbeck suggested that the impressions of a foreigner traveling his route would be different from his own—and different from one another—his point appears to be that the nationalities would account for the differences, that one would provide the "French" perspective, another the "Indian" perspective, and so on. This assumes a uniformity of perspective among writers of a particular nationality, which seems impossible when one considers how another American author working in 1960—Lorraine Hansberry or Allen Ginsburg, for example—would have written about the scenes Steinbeck witnessed on the road. A better question, and one that surely would have interested Steinbeck, who was highly dubious of "objective" fact, would be this: Is it possible for any two authors, even countrymen, to produce the same account of a time and place?

## Note

1. In 1960, the memoir was published in India by Narayan's own imprint, Indian Thought Publications. A second Indian edition was printed in 1969 by Delhi-based Orient Paperbacks, but the book was not published by a British or American press until 1988, when Penguin issued an edition with a short retrospective preface by Narayan.

# 12

## Inspiring *Travels with Charley*
## John Steinbeck and the Millennial Multitiered Quest

Cecilia Donohue

In a 2002 article celebrating John Steinbeck's Irish heritage, Pulitzer Prize–winning writer Jim Dwyer declares: "All the great novels and stories of John Steinbeck slice into the American experience, clear to the bone." *Travels with Charley* (1962) indeed presents a "slice" of mid-twentieth century USA, but as neither a "novel" nor "story" by strict definition, for its genre classification has proven problematic. The labels attached to this work have included "memoir" (Donohue 2017, 65); a "one-man, one-dog account" (Weeks 1962); a "'mongrel' mélange of fact and fiction" (Dewey 1991, 22); "travel literature" (Astro 1975, 35); a "philosophical travelogue" (Hayashi 1990, 95); an "accurate record of a many-layered journey" (Ditsky 1975, 50); and a "10,000-mile odyssey" (Harden 2007). In response to twenty-first-century doubts about the book's accuracy and authenticity, additional identifiers have surfaced, such as "private discourse" in pursuit of self-enlightenment (Heavilin 2020, v) and "picaresque novel" (Johnson 2021, 149). However one chooses to classify *Travels with Charley*, the work most certainly meets Dwyer's standard for Steinbeckian greatness: the writer's canine-accompanied journey opens deep incisions and makes probing inquiries into the economics, politics, geography, and culture of early 1960s America. As a result, Steinbeck's astute observations continue to supply fodder for debate and emotional response in 2020s America.

This chapter suggests yet another descriptor for *Travels with Charley*—"quest," defined by critic Northrup Frye as "a perilous journey" (1957, 187)—and discusses the lasting influence of the book on America's modern-day travel writers and explorers. Interestingly, the objectives, themes, subject matter, execution, and findings of Steinbeck's quest are clearly echoed in Jessica Bruder's 2017 *Nomadland: Surviving America in the Twenty-First Century*. Steinbeck sets out in his camper van Rocinante on a cross-country trek to reacquaint himself with America—his own country, which he regrets he has "not felt . . . for twenty-five years" (1962, 3). He feels that he will be starting with a blank slate—writing of a place he no longer knows about. Similarly, Bruder explains that her journey was born of an assignment to write a magazine article on the topic of "a growing subculture of . . . folks who live on the road" and the subsequent need to enlighten herself on this group of people (2017, 6).

Searching to regain a sense of America and its people, Steinbeck has conversations with diverse Americans across the country and presents us with surprising revelations about geographical, economic, and social changes. Similarly, Bruder visits several states and utilizes "hundreds of interviews" for her study of an emerging twenty-first-century American socioeconomic phenomenon (2017, 28). For the most part, both writers avoid major metropolitan areas on their respective quests, focusing instead on secondary cities and towns. Neither seeks input from either the celebrated or lettered, although Bruder, writing in a more attribution-conscious era than Steinbeck, includes nearly twenty pages of notes/citations. As Steinbeck prefers to eschew the major highways, Bruder avoids side trips to major vacation attractions except when they provide employment for the nomadic subjects of her study.

Steinbeck and Bruder both ventured out on learning expeditions focused on contemporary American values, and neither could remain indifferent to their discoveries. After finding that their journeys led to more questions than answers, both became personally and emotionally involved and, in Bruder's case, physically involved as well. Indeed, Bruder's transition from observer to participant in the nomadic world of her subjects brings the Steinbeckian travelogue into a new, expanded dimension—that of the multitiered quest.

## The Impact of *Charley*'s Quest

The depth and breadth of Steinbeck's mining of Americana has led academics such as John Ditsky (1975, 46) and Barbara A. Heavilin (2020, vi) to describe *Travels with Charley* as a "quest." And indeed, Steinbeck's portrayal of his trip fits well with Northrup Frye's 1957 three-stage division of the heroic quest: a "perilous journey," "crucial struggles" along the way, and an ending of "recognition" and homecoming.

Steinbeck's journey is potentially perilous, beginning with his lament that he has fallen out of touch with America and does not really know his own country any longer. This professed ignorance spurs him on a personal quest to "look again, to try to rediscover this *monster* land" (Steinbeck 1962, 3, emphasis added)—a monster here not only in its very hugeness but also in its unfamiliarity. Steinbeck simply did not know what he may be facing on this questing trip in search of his country's ethos, its identity. Aware of the difficulties and uncertainties in facing the "monster," he weighs the risks of his planned adventure: "There was some genuine worry about my traveling alone, open to attack, robbery, assault" (Steinbeck 1962, 5). Further, he writes, "During the previous winter I had become rather seriously ill . . . difficulties which are the whispers of approaching age" (Steinbeck 1962, 5, 13). In part 2 of *Travels*, however, misgivings give way as Steinbeck casts off his doubts and begins plans for his trip. To ward off desolation that would come from being "alone, nameless, friendless, without any of the safety one gets from family, friends, and accomplices," he chooses Elaine's French poodle, Charles le Chien—"Charley"—to accompany him as his "one companion" (Steinbeck 1962, 5).

Early in his travels, Steinbeck's struggles take the form of private frustrations with such midcentury phenomena as "planned obsolescence" and the proliferation of "plastics" (32); "traffic-choked streets" and "skies nested in smog" (52); scenery-deprived cross-country "thruways" (66); and the erosion of residential "permanence" (75) in favor of house trailers. Another Steinbeck irritant spurs commentary that proves prescient in light of today's throwaway society: "Everything we use comes in boxes, cartons, bins, the so-called packaging we love so much. The mountains of things we throw away are much greater than the things we use. In this, if in no other way, we can see the wild and reckless exuberance of our production, and waste is the index. . . . I do wonder whether there will come a time when we can no longer afford our wastefulness—chemical wastes in the rivers, metal wastes everywhere, and atomic wastes buried deep in the earth or sunk in the sea" (18). Fear of writer's block presents another struggle for Steinbeck as he ponders how to write about America in light of how "huge" the road maps made the nation seem to him—"beyond belief and impossible ever to cross"—no doubt the product of the expanding highway system (16).

Steinbeck's "crucial struggle," to use Frye's terminology, occurs near the book's conclusion and brings him to a state of "weary nausea"—he witnesses overt racism as white, middle-aged women dubbed "Cheerleaders" taunt a little Black girl as she goes up the walkway to enter a formerly segregated elementary school in Louisiana (187). This event, alongside subsequent disheartening dialogues on race with people Steinbeck meets on the road, contributes to Steinbeck's decision to bring his travels to an abrupt end and return home to Sag Harbor. This homecoming—which could be equated to Frye's final stage of the heroic quest—is heralded by Steinbeck's proclamation "the traveler came home again" (1962, 202). With the guarded optimism and hope with which he began his journey negated by the environmental and social travesties he encountered, it could be argued that while Steinbeck's body completed the round trip, his spirit did not. Suggestions for panaceas for America's social, economic, or environmental ills would come later in *America and Americans* (1966). For the time being, the postjourney Steinbeck is left not so much wiser or victorious as numb as he describes the concluding leg of his travels: "The way was a gray, timeless, eventless tunnel" (201). Even Charley is portrayed as catatonic during the final days of the trip: "He carried out his functions like a sleepwalker, ignored whole rows of garbage cans" (201). And in the concluding episode of *Travels with Charley*, Steinbeck needs assistance with directions from a policeman. Yet Steinbeck returns bearing significant findings on the state of his nation, along with two universal takeaways about travel. He begins the book by acknowledging that "we do not take a trip; a trip takes us" (1). Towards the end, he writes that "the life span of journeys . . . seems to be variable and unpredictable" (200).

Despite *Travels with Charley*'s dénouement, which is infused with societal uncertainty, the book continues to be a source of inspiration for the would-be and future traveler. Long a source for lively discussion in reading groups, it has also encouraged and energized countless Americans to learn about their homeland—and themselves—by getting into their automobiles and taking off across country, some accompanied by their pets and many going on to write about their experiences. At the time of Steinbeck's journey, the automobile was fast becoming the chosen mode of personal transportation as superhighways were, much to his chagrin, beginning to branch out across the country.

Among many Steinbeck-inspired travel narratives is Benoit Denizet-Lewis's 2014 *Travels with Casey* relating his cross-country drive across the United States, accompanied by his yellow Lab/golden retriever mix, to research and ultimately gain a better understanding of the canine-human connection. In *Travels with Max*, Gregory Zeigler (2010) and his Maltese fulfilled a bucket list goal to replicate Steinbeck's itinerary. And Bill Steigerwald's 2013 *Dogging Steinbeck* produces a log of dogless travel wherein the initial goal to retrace Steinbeck's steps shifts focus, and he questions the veracity and accuracy of *Travels with Charley*. The fact that Steinbeck's midcentury, canine-accompanied journey inspired millennium travelers on varied missions speaks to the book's lasting influence. As already suggested, its impact on American mobility continues, as *Travels with Charley* served as a handbook of sorts for the inhabitants of Bruder's *Nomadland*.

In addition to the geographic curiosities that would no doubt be satisfied by a Steinbeckian trek, one cannot dismiss the author's existential inquiries for which he sought answers as he stopped at varied locations. There is no substitute for firsthand observation, conversation, and experience, and *Travels with Charley* showed its readers that inquiries both personal and political can be addressed and explored, if not totally resolved, on such journeys. Also, Steinbeck's insistence on being the sole human on the trip speaks to the spirit of American independence and self-sufficiency—a spirit upheld by Denizet-Lewis, Zeigler, Steigerwald, and Bruder.

Of course, one cannot ignore the role of the canine when assessing the continued appeal of *Travels with Charley*. One particular passage from the book illustrates the bond between two-legged driver and quadruped passenger—a bond that could prove beneficial to staying on schedule: "Charley likes to get up early, and he likes me to get up early too. . . . Over the years he has developed a number of innocent-appearing ways to get me up. He can shake himself and his collar loud enough to wake the dead. If that doesn't work he gets a sneezing fit. But perhaps his most irritating method is to sit quietly beside the bed and stare into my face with a sweet and forgiving look on his face; I come out of deep sleep with the feeling of being looked at. . . . He liked traveling so much he wanted to get started early, and early for Charley is the first tempering of darkness with the dawn" (193). Traveling with a four-legged companion has become increasingly popular in America since Steinbeck took to the road with Charley—one need only to check out pet-oriented retail catalogs, contemporary highway rest stops, and selected hotels to see the products, services, and facilities tailored to the road warrior dog.

## *Nomadland*: *Travels with Charley* Meets the New *Harvest Gypsies*

Like Steinbeck, *Nomadland*'s Jessica Bruder has a dog in her life: "Max . . . aka Mutt-Mutt Wagglebutt" (2017, 254). But unlike Steinbeck, Bruder chooses to leave her pet at home and off the road—a wise decision given the challenges she faces as she transforms herself from observing journalist to novice participant in the nomadic way of living. Yet she acknowledges Max's post-trip contributions to her book, expressing her appreciation for the dog who "sighed and snuggled beside [her] through long writing nights" (254). Bruder's personal cross-country exploration may have been absent the canine companionship Steinbeck appreciated on the road, but in her travels she meets more than a handful of dogs—along with cats and other critters—that provide essential companionship for many of the itinerant workers about whom she writes. Unquestionably, vandwellers identify with the pet ownership aspect of Steinbeck's travels, as readers of *Nomadland* learn that many campers choose to travel with a canine. Beginning with "Coco" and "Doodle," the Cavalier King Charles Spaniel and Toy Poodle owned by Linda May (the principal subject of *Nomadland*'s research), Bruder acknowledges several other canine campers by name and notes the diversity of breeds represented at the Rubber Tramp Rendezvous, an annual gathering of nomads for information-sharing and socializing that is held on public desert land in Arizona: "They came in every shape—from Chihuahua to coonhound to mild-mannered half-wolf—and wandered around during the seminars, greeting each other, soliciting treats, sniffing ashes in the fire pit, peeing on creosote bushes (and once on my audio recorder), and breaking out in occasional scuffles" (143).

For many of the nomads, dog/pet ownership provides unopinionated support and companionship, and pet illnesses spur their owners into action as if human and beast were bound by blood. Bruder relates Linda's reaction—and quick thinking—in response to a drastic change in Coco's behavior: "Coco had a sudden seizure. The dog stiffened and shrieked, then fell limp and stopped breathing. Frantic, Linda pressed her mouth to the dog's jaws and exhaled deeply. Soon Coco was conscious again, rigid but breathing. Linda pressed a bag of frozen vegetables to the dog's back—she'd heard using an ice pack that way could alleviate canine seizures—and called her daughter. Audra had studied essential oils and recommended frankincense. Linda dabbed some on Coco's paws. The dog's muscles relaxed. Soon she was snoring. Linda kept watch for hours, monitoring the gentle rise and fall of her chest. The next morning Coco looked normal" (2017, 160–61).

Many of Bruder's study subjects are accompanied by a pet. Perhaps the uncertainties of nomadic living—moving from state to state, campground to campground, temporary job to temporary job—can be assuaged by the presence of a nonjudgmental living being: the companion animal. The phenomenon may also be explained more concisely by the conclusion Denizet-Lewis drew in researching the human-canine connection: "We keep each other company" (2014, 299). In any case, Bruder and her subjects unquestionably embrace the economic, environmental, and social justice values expressed by Steinbeck in his midcentury travels. As Steinbeck traveled across the United States, he interacted with a number of workers on an individual basis—ranging from a farmer, to truckers, to an aspiring hairdresser, and veterinarians when Charley became ill. The only worker group he encounters are the dozen French Canadian migrants who cross the border to Maine for the annual potato harvest. His initial meeting with these workers and their families, whom he describes as a "hardy people" (Steinbeck 1962, 46), takes place at a campsite, with Charley serving as go-between: "I sent out my ambassador and drank a cup of coffee while I gave him time to operate. Then I strolled to the camp to relieve my neighbors of the inconvenience of my miserable cur" (47). Steinbeck invited them to join him in his camper Rocinante for a drink, where they exchanged good conversation, beer, and cognac. Later, Steinbeck wrote, "I felt very good to be surrounded by warm and friendly but cautious people" (49). Despite his impression of the harvesters as being a wary group, Steinbeck states that his "guests for the evening were neither mistreated nor driven" (49).

Readers of both *Travels with Charley* and *Nomadland* will no doubt compare and contrast Steinbeck's and Bruder's respective commentaries on the traits and treatment of migrants then and now. In describing her interactions with the vandwellers, Bruder is likely to echo some of Steinbeck's positive impressions of the potato harvesters. Much as Steinbeck found the harvesters to be "warm and friendly but cautious," Bruder enjoys the hospitality of the workampers, as many of her subjects invited her into their domiciles on wheels. Arguably, Bruder would find the nomads a cautious contingent, but not for the same reasons as Steinbeck labels the potato harvesters thusly—Bruder's subjects must exercise caution in transit, in camping areas, and in anticipation of employment openings. And, as will be discussed later in this essay, Bruder and Steinbeck would part ways in their assessments of how these two worker groups are treated on the job.

Despite Bruder's title, the term "nomad" is just one signifier identifying the subjects of her investigative report. Bruder often uses the terms "vandwellers" or "workampers" to identify this labor demographic. Estranged from the traditional modern American dream of home ownership, steady wages, and a pension, these people are mostly senior citizens who reside in motorized vehicles parked in campgrounds, on public land, and in the parking lots of benevolent retailers. Nomads support themselves by seasonal work—and travel is required. As she seeks to get a better feel for their lifestyle, Bruder's investigative efforts become immersive; she emulates her subjects' travels and search for employment opportunities, adding another layer to her initial quest. Hence, *Nomadland* becomes a two-tiered *Travels with Charley*, as it follows both Bruder's individual quest and, at the same time, that of the vandweller community.

Although she references Steinbeck's work in the course of her narrative, midway through *Nomadland* Bruder confesses her lack of familiarity with *Travels*. Yet, while Steinbeck's poodle-accompanied journey was not well known to her when she first embarked on her investigation of vandweller culture, neither Steinbeck nor his travel book were strangers to her subjects. She refers to a temporary gig at a Salinas Valley ranch where a number of vandwellers sought in-season work in "Steinbeck Country" (Bruder 2017,

155). As a welcoming gesture to a novice camper named Lori, Linda May, the vandweller with whom Bruder spent over a year and a half and whose quest runs parallel to that of *Nomadland*'s author, gave her a copy of *Travels with Charley*. Bruder states, "Steinbeck's tale of road-tripping in a pickup camper with his French poodle was popular among the nomads, and dog-eared copies passed from hand to hand" (160). In addition, Bruder relates the following experience during her visit to the Rubber Tramp Rendezvous: "One guy . . . was horrified to learn I hadn't yet read *Travels with Charley*; the next day he arrived at the van to lend me a paperback" (162). Hence, *Nomadland*'s residents (and ultimately, Bruder) look to Steinbeck and his travel memoir for inspiration, embarking on quests that echo Northrup Frye's depiction of perilous quests in myth.

*Nomadland* encompasses similar perilous journeys. Initially, Bruder sets out to learn, write, and raise public awareness about the vandwellers. She is primarily situated in the western half of America, although she does mention coast-to-coast workamper opportunities—such as picking berries in Vermont and Kentucky and working during seasonal openings to "run the rides at amusement parks from Dollywood in Tennessee to Adventureland in Iowa, Darien Lake in New York, and Story Land in New Hampshire" (Bruder 2017, 49). Concluding that "immersion might help me understand more deeply the lives I've heard so much about" (184–85), Bruder supplements her role of reporter by taking on that of a vandweller, visiting popular campsites and working alongside these nomads in the strenuous work that has become second nature to them.

Occasionally, the routes the vandwellers must take present challenges that would intimidate even the most adventurous traveler, once more bringing to mind Frye's "perilous journey." Ortega Highway, part of California's State Route 74, for example, is infamous for its traffic fatalities. A reporter from the *Los Angeles Times* describes this highway as "a place where urban sprawl, bad driving and obsolete road-building techniques collide head-on" (Bruder 2017, 11). To retrieve her trailer home, nicknamed "The Squeeze Inn"—not unlike Steinbeck's dubbing his truck "Rocinante"—from storage, Linda May must follow this dangerous route. Later in *Nomadland*, Bruder checks out Douglas, Arizona, a location of interest to Linda May. She writes, "I traversed what felt like endless scrubland, much of it uninhabited. . . . A rotting billboard on the roadside said 'Free Trade Policy: Drugs In $$$ Billions Out.' Occasionally low-slung ranch houses rose from the chaparral. Some appeared to have been abandoned for a long time—open sockets gaped where doors and windows had been, and skeletal rafters peeked through gaps in the warping roof boards. On the left side of the road appeared a small white shrine full of silk flowers and then, farther along, a solitary late model RV, way out in the lonesome distance like an establishing shot from *Breaking Bad*" (230).

Much as Steinbeck comments in *Travels* on the mobile homes that first enjoyed popularity in the 1960s, Bruder observes the diverse vehicles driven by the vandwellers: "Cars and trucks . . . towing all kinds of shelters, from shiny aluminum Airstreams to cargo boxes retrofitted with doors and windows, to teardrop-style trailers the size of pup tents" (116). For some vandwellers, however, vehicle shopping can be as rife with peril as vehicle driving. Bruder explains how another vandweller, Silvianne Delmars, took a gamble on four wheels with an active past and flawed present state. Her 1990 Ford E350 Econoline Super Club Wagon "had been a transit van for the elderly and a work vehicle for convict labor crews. . . . She bought it off Craigslist, complete with leaking head gaskets, bad brakes, cracking power steering hoses, worn-out tires, and a starter that made ominous grinding sounds" (15).

Their perilous journeys in preowned vehicles take Bruder and the nomads to their worksites, where they face what myth writer Frye would call "crucial struggles": first, to earn sufficient income and second, to emerge unscathed—or minimally so—from unpleasant, potentially hazardous working conditions. The spring/summer jobs at campgrounds boast fresh air amid a backdrop of beautiful scenery, but Bruder points out the "less picaresque parts" of such jobs, as they found themselves "babysitting drunk, noisy campers, shoveling heaps of ash and broken glass from the campfire pits . . . and the thrice-daily ritual of cleaning outhouses" (6).

When the amusement parks and other outdoor attractions close at the end of the season, many workampers seek warehouse employment with Amazon, whose packaging Steinbeck would no doubt denounce. Amazon's "Camperforce" program serves as a placement agency, but, as Bruder observes, a position within this megacompany can present more strenuous challenges than jobs in the great outdoors. Applicants are advised of the physical requisites: "They should be ready to lift up to fifty pounds at a time, in an environment where the temperature may sometimes exceed 90 degrees" (Bruder 2017, 52).

At one point Linda and Silvianne accept positions at Amazon as "stowers," who "push carts loaded with yellow plastic tubs . . . full of newly arrived items through the aisles of library-style shelving. . . . Each shelf is split with plastic dividers into units" (Bruder 2017, 100). This job proves hazardous to Silvianne with the discovery that the plastic bins can generate an electrical charge causing static shock: "One time she wheeled over to a bank of metal shelves and tried to stow a book on the top level. Her hand glanced over the metal and a jolt coursed up her arm, which recoiled reflexively, sending the book flying into her face. This left her with a fat lip and bleeding gum" (104).

Before accepting her own stint at an Amazon warehouse in Texas, Bruder experiences workamper employment at a North Dakota sugar beet warehouse. Her description of the processing plant, required tasks, and management style adds up to a work setting in which less hardy investigative reporters would never consider participating: "Our job involved constant cleanup: shoveling masses of spilled beets . . . back into the hoppers with pitchforks and agricultural scoops. (Standing around was discouraged: 'If you can lean, you can clean!' was one manager's favorite slogan.) When the repeated lifting got too hard, we'd give up on the shovels and scoop smaller loads with our hands. If we didn't move fast enough, our overseer . . . would blare a WWII-submarine-sounding horn from the elevated control booth . . . and then make frantic shoveling gestures through the window in our direction. Meanwhile the conveyor belts that churned over our heads shot beet bits and clods of dirt at everything in range, spattering our yellow safety vests and green hard hats" (Bruder 2017, 186–87). Both Jessica Bruder and the subjects of her study undoubtedly earned the label of hero, worthy of recognition for missions accomplished.

*Nomadland* focuses on a worker cohort that has willingly, enthusiastically, and successfully taken on a yearly challenge of seeking and securing sustaining employment, traveling in refurbished vehicles over rough roads to accept these job opportunities, and surviving strenuous jobs. In addition, author Bruder, while "walking the walk" in the workamper's shoes, also "talks the talk" in raising awareness of the vandweller culture. In all likelihood, Steinbeck would have valued the fortitude and self-sufficiency of these nomads as well as Bruder's achievement in calling public attention to the challenges they face.

And he would have been impressed with the efforts of Linda May both before and after her adoption of the vandweller lifestyle. Given his disdain for waste and his proud declaration that "I simply like junk" (Steinbeck 1962, 32), Steinbeck would have praised her ingenuity in repurposing disposed materials to redesign the interior of her van, making it more suitable as a nomad's living quarters. Bruder describes this transformation: "The trailer had a small dinette along its rear wall, so Linda removed the table and cut out a cardboard template to fit on top of the benches" (2017, 10). Using her template, Linda is able to reshape a discarded queen mattress to fit the dinette space and fashion her sleeping quarters. In this situation and so many others, Linda learns to overcome the struggles of nomad life: "She became an expert at focusing on whatever challenge lay immediately ahead, parsing large problems into bite-sized chunks until she felt she could manage anything" (2017, 102). Having already faced and tackled challenges ranging from prior work driving a truck to attending AA and achieving two decades of sobriety, to financial setbacks, and more, Linda May focuses on her goals of constructing a residence that merges stability with the vandweller culture, of maintaining a sense of individualism, and, like Steinbeck, of valuing and loving the previously owned/used: "She wanted to construct an Earthship: a passive-solar home built using discarded materials such as cans and bottles, with dirt-filled tires for load-bearing walls. . . . Earthships are designed to sustain their inhabitants entirely off the grid. The tire walls act like batteries, absorbing the sun's heat through a bank of south-facing windows during the daytime and then releasing it at night to regulate indoor temperature. Rain and snowmelt drain from the roof into a cistern, providing water that gets filtered and reused for drinking and washing, feeding indoor fruit and vegetable gardens and flushing toilets. Electricity is supplied by solar panels and, in some cases, windmills" (34).

Like Steinbeck, Linda has a sense of individuality and independence, and she is attracted to the possibility of singular "fanciful touches" that can be added to the basic earthship (Bruder 2017, 35). Bruder describes the earthship colony in Taos, New Mexico, as resembling "a moon colony coproduced by Dr. Seuss, Antoni Gaudí, and the set designers from *Star Wars*" (35). Linda visits sites in New Mexico; Cochise County, Arizona; and Vidal, California, before deciding on a suitable and affordable construction site in the aforementioned Douglas, Arizona. A onetime thriving town nine miles north of the Mexican border, Douglas is a location "without red tape, where experimental architecture could flourish" (221). Despite the struggles of "remoteness . . . dizzying summer heat, armed drug mules, flash floods, and rattlesnakes" (238), Linda and her friend Gary heroically press on to the site preparation that concludes *Nomadland*.

*Nomadland*'s connections to Steinbeck are not limited to the plot and quest parallels with *Travels with Charley*. Readily apparent similarities exist between the aspirations, challenges, and struggles of California's Great Depression–era migrant workers as reported in Steinbeck's 1936 newspaper series, "The Harvest Gypsies," and those of Bruder's twenty-first-century American nomads. In his journalism on labor and housing conditions in California, Steinbeck informs readers that "there are at least 150,000 homeless migrants wandering up and down the state, and that is an army large enough to make it important to every person in the state" (1988, 19). Bruder does not approximate a workamper headcount but suggests an increase rather than decrease in this demographic: "There's no clear count of how many people live nomadically in America. Full-time travelers are a demographer's nightmare. Statistically they blend in with the rest of the population, since the law requires them to maintain fixed—in other words, fake—addresses" (2017, 49). She adds, "Despite a lack of hard numbers, anecdotal evidence suggests the ranks of American itinerants started to boom after the housing collapse and have kept growing" (50).

Consider Steinbeck's description of the temporary workers of *The Harvest Gypsies*: "They are small farmers who have lost their farms, or farm hands who have lived with the family in the old American way. They are men who have worked hard on their own farms and have felt the pride of possessing and living in close touch with the land" (1988, 22). A parallel portrait of economic misfortune despite playing by prevailing societal rules and expectations is echoed by Bruder in her snapshot of *Nomadland*'s inhabitants: "Many of the people I met felt that they'd spent too long losing a rigged game . . . They gave up traditional 'stick-and-brick' homes, breaking the shackles of rent and mortgages" (2017, 7). The jalopy vehicles and the houses constructed of "corrugated paper" described in *The Harvest Gypsies* (Steinbeck 1988, 26), are replaced nearly a century later with the "vans, RVs, and trailers" (Bruder 2017, 7) that double as domiciles.

In *The Harvest Gypsies* Steinbeck describes a typical migrant campsite: "The squatters' camps are located . . . on the banks of a river, near an irrigation ditch or on a side road where a spring of water is available" (1988, 26). Similar priorities are important to Bruder's vandwellers/campers. For example, Linda selects a site for settlement where "there was . . . a numberless tract. . . . It had a few amenities: a paved parking lot, hookups for water and power, and a picnic area" (2017, 14).

Steinbeck's migrants and Bruder's nomads also share the experience of temporary working conditions. "The migrant is always partially unemployed," he writes. "The nature of his occupation makes his work seasonal" (Steinbeck 1988, 45). Similarly, Linda's seasonal job as Camp Host at Hanna Flat in California's San Bernardino National Forest is wide-ranging, giving new meaning to the generic catchall "other duties as assigned." Not only were workers required to do janitorial tasks, but they also "checked in new campers, collected fees, set out site reservation tags, gave hiking advice, settled petty disputes, shoveled out fire pits, and did paperwork" (Bruder 2017, 22). Shifts at Amazon during nontourist/holiday season entailed working "ten hours or longer, during which some walk more than fifteen miles on concrete floors, stooping, squatting, reaching, and climbing stairs as they scan, sort, and box merchandise" (45).

Steinbeck's concluding remarks in *The Harvest Gypsies* offer a prophecy that may not hold true for Bruder's migrants: "The new migrants to California from the dust bowl are here to stay" (1988, 62). Describing them as being "of the best American stock, intelligent, resourceful; and, if given a chance, socially responsible" (62), Steinbeck implies their aspirations to rise above agrarianism and enter the West Coast mainstream, with a return to land/home ownership as part of the package. Referencing Bob Wells, creator of the website Cheap RV Living, however, Bruder sees the ultimate quest of the millennial nomads as quite the opposite, calling attention to another Steinbeck work in her commentary: "This kind of transience may suggest a modern-day version of *The Grapes of Wrath*. But it's worth noting a critical distinction. "For the nomadic Dust Bowl-era refugees self-worth meant keeping alive . . . one precious hope: that someday the status quo would return, moving them back into traditional housing, restoring at least an iota of stability. . . . Bob saw things differently. He envisioned a future where economic and environmental upheavals become the new American normal. . . . he didn't package nomadic living as a quick fix . . . he aspired to create a wandering tribe whose members operate outside of—or even transcend—the fraying social order: a parallel world on wheels" (2017, 78–79). Nomadlanders take pride in their status, shaking off any of the shame and "destruction of dignity" suffered by Steinbeck's harvest gypsies (1988, 39). For example, one vandweller "preferred to call himself 'houseless' . . . rather than 'homeless'" (Bruder 2017, 142).

Steinbeck's assessment of mobile home culture in *Travels with Charley*—that its proponents "do not buy for the generations, but only until a new model they can afford comes out" (1962, 73)—does not match the purchasing strategy of Bruder's contemporary nomads. Yet Steinbeck expresses admiration for such an independent existence in which people assume responsibility for their own self-preservation. One person Steinbeck encounters in *Travels* embraced the wheel-based lifestyle, making a statement that Linda May or any of her vandwelling compatriots might have uttered: "Who's got permanence? Factory closes down, you move on. Good times and things opening up, you move on where it's better. You got roots you sit and starve" (1962, 75). It comes as no surprise that in their quest for liberation from the pressures of their earlier existences, as they face physical, social, and economic struggles and challenges that test their resilience, *Nomadland*'s residents look to Steinbeck's travel memoir for inspiration.

While Steinbeck expresses disgust with the racism he sees in New Orleans in *Travels*, Bruder notes that the inhabitants of *Nomadland* are overwhelmingly white—reminiscent of Steinbeck's observation in *The Harvest Gypsies* that the "names of the new migrants indicate that they are of English, German and Scandinavian descent" (1988, 23). Bruder's research provides her with a forthright explanation for the lack of diversity: "An article about the experience of 'traveling while black' . . . made me think. America makes it hard enough for people to live nomadically, regardless of race. Stealth camping in residential areas, in particular, is way outside the mainstream. Often it involves breaking local ordinances against sleeping in cars. Avoiding trouble . . . can be challenging, even with the Get Out of Jail Free card of white privilege" (180). Bruder relates the experience of one camper where race played a role in appeasing an officer investigating stealth camping in Southern California: "LaVonne knew she was lucky. Her van looked new and clean. Her dog was adorable. She was white. He didn't write her a citation" (206).

Much as *Travels with Charley* supplied Steinbeck with informative episodes about America, with the racist demonstration in Louisiana often seen as the climactic moment of his travelogue, Bruder experiences a surprising revelation of her own upon returning east to Brooklyn:

> The backstreets are dim and lines with a motley assortment of work vehicles—contractors' vans, delivery fleets, food trucks, utility trailers—providing good cover to mix among for urban campers. Before long I start seeing them: An ancient travel trailer shaped like a tinned ham. A Chevy Astro van with the telltale privacy curtain, its cabin windows blocked with plastic sheeting and American flags. A converted transit shuttle with tinted glass, jaunty red hubcaps, and a propane furnace welded above the rear bumper to provide heat when the engine's off. Plenty of late-model camper vans, their blinds drawn.
>
> The most spectacular dwelling of all is a short yellow school bus. Its windows are covered with sheet metal for zero visibility. Glinting at the edge of the roof, barely noticeable from the ground, are the aluminum frames of four perfectly aligned solar panels. A drape hangs behind the windshield, which has condensation on its inner surface—another tell. (245–46)

Bruder may not have read *Travels with Charley* upon first embarking on her quest-based journey, but her discovery of the geographic proliferation of vandwellers reflects travel-influenced insight that matches Steinbeck's. *Nomadland*'s detailed narrative, attention to the individuals who crossed the author's path, sensitivity to contemporary issues of human welfare and dignity, and appreciation of canine camaraderie all point to the impact and inspiration of John Steinbeck's narrative of an explorer and his dog.

## *Charley*'s Legacy

For several decades, John Steinbeck's *Travels with Charley in Search of America* has inspired a host of writers who have published narratives of their pet-accompanied trips spanning most or parts of the continental United States.

As Steinbeck's journey was focused on a search to reconnect with America, most of his successors undertook quests centered on a monolithic but well-articulated goal, whether it was to replicate Steinbeck's trip with accuracy and precision or to ponder and study a single issue of either personal or public interest. With its combination of travel-related observation and discussion of subject matter essential to the social, economic, and political health of America and beyond, *Travels with Charley* has cemented its status as essential reading for those who want to travel, those who must travel, and those who want to share their impressions of travel and the universal takeaways that ultimately take us along for the ride.

In *Nomadland*, Jessica Bruder adds a new dimension to the Steinbeck travel template. Pursuing a quest in the tradition of Northrup Frye's heroic narrative with its perilous journey, not only does she fulfill her journalistic assignment of reporting on the phenomenon of vandwelling/workamping and its proponents but she takes the added step of walking in their shoes and emulating their life experiences. As in the case of Steinbeck's *Travels*, Bruder's observations lead to reader responses that force reconsideration of long-held assumptions about the American Dream and those from whom it has been withheld or snatched away. Steinbeck, Bruder, and the vandwellers are victorious in their homecoming, as the concept is defined within the pages of these awareness-raising writings.

# 13

## "Takin' on Texas" in *Travels with Charley*

### Mimi R. Gladstein

Steinbeck's biographers have spent little time and given scant attention to that part of *Travels with Charley in Search of America* that deals specifically with his time in Texas. While Jackson Benson (1984) does mention that Steinbeck meets his wife Elaine in Texas, he devotes only one sentence to the description of their celebration of Thanksgiving on a ranch outside Amarillo and subsequent drive to her sister's home in Austin (889). Like Benson, Jay Parini (1994) dedicates only one sentence to Steinbeck's time in Texas, also mentioning the Thanksgiving dinner and visit to Elaine's family in Austin (512). Thomas Kiernan (1979) writes even less, including Texas in a sentence describing the expanse of his trip—from California to Texas and then across the South (312). William Souder's 2020 biography parallels Kiernan, with one sentence listing Texas with Arizona and New Mexico as states through which Steinbeck drives on his way back east (351).

This neglect may explain why Robert Hughes (1987), in his *Steinbeck Quarterly* article "*Travels with Charley* and *America and Americans*" does not even mention Texas, specifically stating that Steinbeck drove through Minneapolis and St. Paul without bothering to stop. In addition, Steinbeck avoided Cleveland, Toledo, and South Bend (79). Hughes does mention that Steinbeck found "a warm spot in his heart for San Francisco" (79). Only Tetsumaro Hayashi (1990) observes that Steinbeck's attitude toward Texas and Texans was one of "affection and enthusiasm" (91). Hayashi assesses the reason for Steinbeck's positive assessment as twofold: one, of course, the presence of Elaine, and the other the care of a "compassionate" veterinarian in Amarillo who took care of Charley's painful bout with prostatitis, tending him for four days until he recuperated from the ailment.

As a Texan myself, I would like to gently correct some of this neglect of Steinbeck's experiences in the Lone Star state. Having lived in the state for decades and having taught at the University of Texas at El Paso for many years, I have a very positive "take" on Texas. Steinbeck begins preparation for his trip with the very Texas-like action of racking a shotgun and two rifles in his truck. Among other provisions, he includes "shotgun shells, rifle cartridges, tool boxes" (11). Those of us who have traversed the wide expanses of desert and open roads in many parts of Texas recognize the need for such provisions. Gun owning is part of the Texas experience. My wallet contains both my driver's license and a concealed handgun license. My husband owned six guns. My brother-in-law has been heard to brag about his latest gun purchase, noting that it would "stop an elephant." My response was to tease him about the slim possibility of getting attacked by elephants in El Paso. But it's a fact that many Texans feel that a gun is an absolute personal necessity.

In another reference to Texas early in his trip, Steinbeck muses about the growing congestion and pollution in America. He comments on "traffic-choked streets, skies nested in smog, choking with the acids of industry" (65). This pollution, he sadly points out, is "as true in Texas as in Maine," comparing Amarillo, Texas, to Stacyville, Maine (65). In recent years, the omnipresence of "Don't Mess with Texas" signs warn drivers, promising heavy consequences if they contribute to the litter.

At one point in his discussion of Texas, Steinbeck (1962) mentions a "booted and blue-jeaned rancher in Neiman Marcus" (205). His recollection reminded me of my husband's adventures as a blue-jean-and-boot-wearing Texan in New York City. For many years, although he was wearing apparel that was normal for his work in the Southwest, his clothing would draw off-putting reactions from New Yorkers. Then came the 1980 film *Urban Cowboy*. Thanks to John Travolta, my husband was suddenly the height of fashion. To this day, jeans, a shirt, and a sports coat are appropriate dress for most any occasion in Texas. For women, the jeans can be topped with a fancy blouse and appropriate jewelry.

One of the great ironies of Steinbeck's "takin' on Texas" is the fact that before he gets there, he asserts that he "dreaded" it (201). It is hard to understand why he felt this way as he has many positive things to say about the state. The Texans he knows are "gracious, friendly, generous and quiet" (202). Praising their history, he writes of the "glorious defense" of the Alamo (202). Besides Elaine's family, one of the most positive experiences he has with individual Texans is with a veterinarian to whom he takes Charley in Amarillo. He has previously described with frustration his experience with a "poor incompetent veterinary in the Northwest" (207) who knows little, cares little, and incites a look of "pained wonder and contempt" (207) from Charley. In contrast, the young doctor from Amarillo has "trained and knowing hands" (207), and Steinbeck describes the instant rapport between dog and man. He has such confidence in this vet that he leaves Charley with him for four days, and when he picks him up, the poodle is cured and content. In addition, the veterinarian anticipates a possible regression and provides medicine to maintain Charley's recovery as Steinbeck and the poodle continue their journey. Gratefully, Steinbeck writes, "There's absolutely nothing to take the place of a good man" (235).

There are a number of puzzling issues in Steinbeck's interaction with Texas and Texans. While almost at the end of his trek across country, Steinbeck writes that he "dreaded" his travels through Texas, earlier in his journey he had written of his love affair with Montana, opining, "Montana seems to me to be what a small boy would think Texas is like from hearing Texans" (158). True, Texans tend to think most highly of themselves, but it is still hard to figure out just what precipitated Steinbeck's "dread." Even after his positive experience with the veterinarian, Steinbeck comments, "I do not intend to dwell long on Texas" (208), explaining that this state has been too much the topic of discussion and attention. He does not tell why this is so.

It is true that Texas has a particular reputation in the country. For example, a 2014 *Houston Press* article noted that Texas has its own identity and that outsiders may "hate" that. The article also notes that Texas as a state has a "really strong personality," to which many people do not respond well. Though this article was published decades after Steinbeck's death, it hints at what Steinbeck may be thinking when he writes early in the Charley book that he wants to "avoid Texas" (201). Still, Steinbeck also notes that even if he wants to "avoid Texas," he cannot, if only because of its huge size—it ranges over an area of 268,597 square miles, or 171,902,080 acres. As he puts it, "Once you are in Texas it seems to take forever to get out, and some people never make it" (201). Explaining this comment, Steinbeck notes that because his wife is a native of the state, psychologically Texas moves through his and Elaine's home in Sag Harbor as well as their house in New York. In addition—probably from personal observation—he calls Texas a "state of mind," a "mystique," and says that it closely resembles a religion (203). In my own experience, Texas does have a kind of mystique, its residents proud to be identified as "Texans." One resident of my acquaintance, originally from China but now a US citizen, even refers to himself as a "Chinese Texan," thus tying himself to this enormous state and its people.

Steinbeck's positive "take" on Texas may have been influenced by his relationship with Lyndon Johnson, the thirty-sixth president of the United States. Johnson invited John and Elaine to spend the night at the White

House at least twice and called on the writer to help with such honors as writing his nomination acceptance speech (Benson 1984, 955). Another connection between the Johnsons and the Steinbecks is that Elaine and Lady Bird had attended the University of Texas at Austin together (Steinbeck 1975, 788). Further, before he left for Vietnam, John IV and his father were invited to the White House by President Johnson. A man I met in Austin recounted the time when Steinbeck visited his son in a Vietnam bunker, made breakfast, and served it to the men. John Steinbeck, like his hosts and the typical Texan, is also noted for being hospitable.

One of the highlights of Steinbeck's Texas visit is a stop at a ranch owned by a friend, who invites him and Elaine for Thanksgiving dinner. Impressed, Steinbeck writes that he presumes the man is rich, although he does not know for sure. My experience is that a person does not have to be rich to own a ranch in Texas. Even my Polish uncles had one not far from El Paso, where they lived. They would travel to their ranch on Saturdays or Sundays. The idea of owning land to a Polish immigrant is tantamount to being part of the nobility. In Europe it had been impossible for them to own land. And it was impossible not only because of their poverty but also because of their lack of social status. Thus, for my uncles, one of the highlights of immigrating to America was becoming landowners.

Steinbeck describes this friend's ranch as beautiful with well-grassed flats. Although the home is not large, having only three bedrooms, it is noteworthy that each bedroom has its own bath with both a tub and a shower. The dinner event, which Steinbeck describes as an "orgy" (209) includes the arrival of neighboring friends who bring food, in this case a large pot of chili con carne, which Steinbeck writes is the best he ever tasted. However, the "orgy" does not await the arrival of these friends. As Steinbeck comments, it begins at once with the Steinbecks' arrival. Their host's welcome includes not only a bath but also scotch and soda. They are then given a tour of the property, which includes dog kennels, a corral, and two dams. The kennels house three pointers and the corral a horse named Specklebottom (209). At the dam they encounter a small herd of cattle. The extensive excursion tires them, and they return to the house for a well-deserved rest.

When they wake up from their nap, the neighbors arrive. Steinbeck points out that these are rich people who conceal their status "in blue jeans and riding boots" (109). Of course, anyone who lives in Texas knows that blue jeans and boots are not a way of concealing wealth. Knowledgeable Texans can ascertain the quality of both. Boots come in a variety of prices and qualities. We used to make regular trips to Tony Lama factory shops to see what—normally out of our price range—might be on the sale rack. After the release of *Urban Cowboy*, visiting friends and relatives from the East and

West Coasts would make regular trips to check out the Tony Lama store. The same can be said of jeans. There are Levis and then there are Wranglers, and then there are many cheap imitations. Also, there is the correct way to wear your Levis. They mustn't look new. Numerous washings precede the first wearing. I suppose the equivalent today is the fashion of wearing torn jeans. And there is no accounting for the ways Texans may wear denim and boots. At a lunch at a local country club to which I was invited in the early 2020s, the young lady at the next table was in a denim miniskirt and cowboy boots. Notably, in his story about the attire of Texans, Steinbeck is reminded of something a hired helper told him some years back in Pacific Grove when they were painting the inside of the family cottage his father had built. When they ran out of paint and Steinbeck suggested that the worker go into town dressed as he was, the man tells him what Steinbeck terms as a "wise and memorable thing": "You got to be awful rich to dress as bad as you do" (211).

Steinbeck comments on the wealth of the company at his friend's ranch repeatedly. He writes, "The smell of money was everywhere" (210). In this case, his illustrative example is a story told by the daughter of the house. She tells them about how Specklebottom, the horse, had jumped the fence and impregnated a neighboring mare. The daughter thinks that should give them rights to the foal, as Specklebottom had a particularly important blood line. For some reason, Steinbeck thinks that particular scene verified what he had heard about "fabulous Texas millionaires" (210). This attitude, coming from Steinbeck, confused me. This is the man who wrote *The Red Pony*. Certainly, he knew how important blood lines are in horses.

Steinbeck's repeated use of the word "orgy" to describe the Thanksgiving dinner provokes questions about his attitude toward this occasion and its celebrants. In one case, he uses the term to explain why the cook rushes him out of the kitchen in the morning, after his third cup of coffee: "She cleared me out because she had to stuff two turkeys for the Thanksgiving orgy" (212). After having showered and shaved and dressed in "white shirts and jackets and ties" because of the holiday, Steinbeck comments, "The orgy came off on schedule at two o'clock" (213). His negative feelings about the event are telegraphed by the next sentence in which he explains that he is not going to give details about the event so as not to "shock" the reader.

I do not want to suggest that there were no positive experiences during the Steinbecks' visit to the ranch. One particularly satisfying event takes place in the morning. When he wakes up and walks out of his door, the writer sees that there are two trout rods positioned just outside their room. These rods are ready to be used, and Steinbeck takes full advantage of the opportunity to go fishing. Almost immediately upon casting his line, he comes up with a "ten-inch rainbow trout," which is soon joined by three more. As Steinbeck puts it, "I cast four times and had four trout" (212). After cleaning them, he delivers them to the cook who, having given him his coffee, dips the fish in cornmeal and fries them in bacon fat. What follows is Steinbeck's detailed description of the culinary pleasure of eating the trout from head to tail, which he dubs as crisp as a potato chip. Accompanying this gastronomically fulfilling meal are three cups of coffee, which he enjoys as having a "special taste" on that particular morning.

Fishing is not the only pleasure of the day. Later, the group goes quail hunting. Steinbeck takes his own gun, which he spends some time describing and deriding, calling it "no great shakes" (212) and commenting that after he bought it secondhand, over a decade ago, it has not improved. He comments, however, that he supposes it is as good as he is. He does look into a glass-doored gun rack at a gun so beautiful that it fills him with "covetousness" (212). He comments that he is sure his host would have loaned him that gun for the hunt but is glad that did not happen, as he worries that he might have tripped and fallen and maybe dropped and damaged the gun. Admiringly, he comments that it would have been like "carrying the crown jewels through a minefield" (212). He is content, knowing that his old beat-up gun will be less worrisome.

Earlier in his career, Steinbeck had written a bit about his attitude toward hunting, an attitude that did not apply in this situation because he was hunting quail or wild turkey. This prey was acceptable, as it might be easily eaten. In *The Log from the Sea of Cortez*, Steinbeck wrote about his negative reaction to having a hunting trip "cluttered up with game." In particular, he is hostile to mounting the heads of animals one has killed. His humorous solution is to mount the animal droppings on a small hardwood plaque, which would communicate this message: "There was an animal, and for all we know there still is and here is the proof of it. He was very healthy when we last heard of him" (Steinbeck 1995, 138).

The hunting experience is not as successful as Steinbeck's solo fishing in *Travels with Charley*. He tells about the dogs "spring-steel pointers" that went ahead of the hunters in the search for quail and notes that they were outworked by a "fat old bitch" named Duchess. Although there is evidence of quail all around and they encounter tracks and quail-feathers, there is nary the sight of an actual quail. While this is disappointing, Steinbeck's assessment is that when it comes to hunting, even if you find no birds, "you'd rather go then *sic* not" (213). His host is concerned, however, that this dearth of birds would be a big disappointment for Steinbeck, and he suggests that they go out in the afternoon and shoot wild turkey. He tells Steinbeck that he thinks there should be about eighty wild turkeys on the place, as he had "planted thirty" a couple of years earlier. This prospect is not appealing to Steinbeck, who responds that he doesn't want turkey and would not know what to do with it in Rocinante. He tells his host to wait a year, hoping that there would be many quail by then. If that happens, he says he will come and hunt with his host, thus establishing a special tie, a special bond as a fellow huntsman. For as in the rest of the country, in Texas hunters and hunt clubs abound—places characterized by a special union and camaraderie among outdoorsmen. Steinbeck clearly wanted to fit into his host's world, and he would understand about the friendly bond among hunters.

Steinbeck does not describe the actual Thanksgiving dinner in too much detail, claiming he does not want to hold the people up to scorn. Drinking precedes the serving of the meal, which is "two brown and glazed turkeys" (214). After the dinner, Steinbeck compares the group to "decadent Romans," claiming that they napped after the post-meal walk. He concludes with "that was my Thanksgiving orgy in Texas" (214). Even with this minimal description, the contradictory message of what Steinbeck says he intends and what he actually accomplishes is glaring. If he does not want to hold these people up to scorn, why compare them to "decadent Romans"? The continuous referrals to the meal as an "orgy" are more telling bits of evidence of Steinbeck's disapproval of this group of Texans. It would be interesting to know what Steinbeck said to his wife during this "orgy" time.

Concluding the Texas chapter, Steinbeck's questionable attitude toward the Texans he meets is clearly delineated. He says that he feels better for having "revealed"—the word he uses is "exposed"—the "decadent practices of the rich Texans" (214). It is hard to know how one should interpret his final comment that he doesn't think rich Texans eat chili con carne and roast turkey every day. Is he trying to indicate that Texan behavior is negatively affected by Thanksgiving and thus they shouldn't be judged by their behavior on that day? Steinbeck's "take" on Texas is complicated. Although Texas is the largest state he travels through, his Texas chapter is one of the shortest in the book. Well, at least, if asked, Charley would have some very positive "takes" as a result of his very good treatment by a Texas veterinarian.

Taking on Texas is quite a daunting task. From the high mountain desert of El Paso to the hill country of Austin, to the humid swamps of Houston, the customs and habits of Texans are as varied as the land on which they live. While a Thanksgiving dinner in El Paso may include chili rellenos and turkey enchiladas, Houston and Galveston feasts may include fish dishes. My own take on Texas would always include a version of such Tex-Mex "orgies"— all gustatory treats, accompanied by warm fellowship.

An important point to note, however, is that Steinbeck's experiences once he leaves Texas are negative by comparison with his pleasant stay there. For as he leaves Texas and moves on to Louisiana, he encounters rampant racism, leaving him disheartened. Dispiritedly, he notes that human beings are a species not clever enough to live at peace with itself. His "take" on Texas has no such discouraging thoughts about the nature of his species: for all his comments on the "orgy," Steinbeck's Texans come across as warm and friendly people.

# 14

## Texas Tales and Beyond

## A Niece Recalls

DONALD V. COERS INTERVIEWING SALLY S. KLEBERG; SUSAN SHILLINGLAW, EDITOR

Figure 9: Elaine and John Steinbeck, 1962, as they arrive at their New York apartment after Nobel Prize announcement. AP photo. Courtesy of the National Steinbeck Center, Salinas.

Donald V. Coers's oral interview with Sally S. Kleberg, Elaine Steinbeck's niece via her first husband, Zachary Scott. Her mother was Zach's sister. San Antonio, Texas, June 16, 2019. [The text is edited for length and style.]

SK: My name is Sally Kleberg, and I am Elaine Steinbeck's niece through the Scott family, Texas pioneers. My grandmother was Sallie Lee Masterson Scott and my mom was Mary Lewis Scott Kleberg, and Zachary Scott Jr., Elaine's first husband, was my mother's brother—and only brother. My mom was the youngest in that family. They had one other sister, named Ann—Ann Scott Hearon. Both Zach and Ann and both of my grandparents predeceased my mom, so she ended up carrying the family goods, all the old silver and the old china and all that other kind of stuff. I have three brothers and we grew up in Kingsville, Texas, on the King Ranch. And the Klebergs are my father's family. They were German immigrants to Texas back in the nineteenth century. Captain King started the King Ranch after making a good business out of riverboating on the Rio Grande River. He started buying land down in South Texas in 1853, during Texas's early statehood [Texas became a state in 1845].

DC: Your relationship with Elaine is an interesting one. Elaine has talked many times about how close she was to the Scott family, and even after they [Zach and Elaine] divorced . . . she stayed very close to the Scott family, and you knew her for a long time, particularly after you moved to New York City in 1990.

SK: I always found it sort of humorous that Uncle Zach married two women, both of them in the theater. It wasn't surprising that they were in the theater because he was too, but one of them lived on East 72nd and the other one lived on West 72nd. . . . And they were great friends.

DC: When did you first meet Steinbeck, and where?

SK: You know, I can't even remember. It must have been in New York. I got married in 1965 and four years before that Uncle Zack had gotten that tumor. He died in '65, and my grandmother was just devastated. And so I remember it vividly . . . I think he was fifty . . . fifty-two, something like that? [He was fifty-one.] He had a brain tumor that I think was from smoking. You know, so many of those actors smoked. In all of his head shots—his publicity photos—he had a cigarette in his hands. And you know, they all smoked in those movies, too. When Uncle Zach got sick, he wanted to go home to Austin and be with his parents because he had lived away from them for so long, and he adored them and he was their only son . . . They had this downstairs guestroom that they put him in, right next to the kitchen so that there was always somebody close by if there wasn't somebody in the room with him . . . Ruth [his second wife] was furious that Zach went to Austin. And she would come down, but she didn't stay there. She would go back and forth. She and my grandparents just did not get along. I mean, it was like an iceberg in the room. Which was very sad. They were very generous and kind, but they just felt like she was a bad influence, because they adored Elaine. They blamed Ruth for breaking up Zach and Elaine because they met in California when Zach and Elaine were out there. But Ruth was in New York, and I don't know if Uncle Zach even knew her at that point.

DC: That's interesting. So your grandparents had their own narrative.

SK: Yes, they did. And I don't think that mother even . . . realized that Elaine and John were having this affair or she forgave her, because she would forgive Elaine anything, she loved her so much. But the good thing about it was that Uncle Zach and Elaine remained friends all their lives.

DC: You told me an interesting story about his calling Elaine when he was in the hospital.

SK: He called Elaine, and I think it was probably when he knew he was going to be leaving New York, and he said, "I want to see you. Will you come to the hospital?" She's the one that told me this story. And she went to see him, and she said, "We had the best visit. We laughed, we cried, we did, you know, did lots of memory talk and all this kind of stuff, and talked about how great our friendship had been in spite of the difficulties of the marriage and all that kind of stuff . . . And then we kind of got off track and started talking about when he played the role of the King in *The King and I*—he followed Yul Brynner on the stage, and he was dancing across the stage with Anna in that big skirt—and apparently that dress weighed like a hundred pounds. And so when he was swinging her around in that waltz, in the 'Shall We Dance' deal, he threw his back out and ended up in the hospital and had to give up the role. His understudy had to come in and take over." And then Zach said to her, "Elaine, I want to have one last dance with you before I go." And he got out of bed—I don't know if he was on IVs or not or if he still had them in his hands and just took the bottle with him and danced around the room—she did not elaborate—but she said, "We had a dance in the hospital room before he left to go to Austin." And I just thought that was such a sweet memory for her to share with me.

DC: Zach had a great role in *Mildred Pierce*.

SK: That was his most famous. But his favorite role, and I think his best role, and mother always thought so, and so did my grandmother, was *The Southerner*, which was a Jean Renoir production, and it was about the South, and Uncle Zach was the lead in it.

DC: He could do a great villain.

SK: Oh! He was the best. He had this eyebrow that would go up.

DC: That's what my wife said. She said he's probably the best Hollywood villain. A suave villain, she said.

SK: Yes, a suave villain for sure. He tried to teach me how to raise my eyebrow, and there's no way I could do it. I just didn't have the right muscles to do it, or something.

DC: What was your lasting impression of John, the first time you saw him?

SK: Well, of course, I was just like bowled over, because I knew he was so famous, and I was sort of in awe of the fact that my aunt had attracted these two very talented, dynamic, famous people. What a life she had, you know? And, he was . . . he was very quiet. He was very gentlemanly. But he didn't say a whole lot, and I don't know . . . even now, I don't think he was that well.

DC: A guy I knew when I was teaching assistant in English at the University of Texas in the mid-sixties, who was also a TA, much older than I was, had met Steinbeck somewhere in the Southwest back in the late thirties or early forties, and I remember asking him what Steinbeck was like, what he said. The guy said, "All I remember about him was that he didn't say anything. He was very quiet, very much in the background." And the folks that I interviewed in Europe when I was doing the research for my book on *The Moon Is Down*, his publishers in the Scandinavian countries and all, said the same thing. That he was very, very quiet. Communicated much better in letters.

SK: Writing was his communication tool.

DC: One of the things I wanted to make sure and zero in on specifically with you was the mention in *Travels with Charley* of the visit to the ranch in Clarendon, Texas.

SK: It may have been on the Masterson side, on my grandmother's side. In the Texas Panhandle, yeah, that's where all the Masterson ranches were. Robert Benjamin Masterson—we called him Big Papa—had two families, and he ended up having eight kids. So we have lots of cousins. LOTS of cousins. And in those days, if you had a house full of kids and the wife died, very often the husband would marry the sister or a cousin or a relative to keep it in the family, so to speak. That's what he did . . . when Eliza died, he married Anna. They weren't twins, but they were very close in age; he had four boys with the first wife, Eliza, and he had four girls with the second one, Anna. My grandmother was the oldest of the four girls. And so, with all those boys there were a lot of Masterson relatives, but then when the four girls got married, they all had different last names, so we've got relatives with all these different names floating around out there. But there's a lot of Annas and there are a lot of Elizas in the family because of the two mothers.

It's very possible that he [Steinbeck] went to one of the Masterson ranches, because when Big Papa died, the eight branches of the family split the ranch up and [each one] got a piece of it. So it's probably one of those. I just don't know which one it would have been. Because the original ranch was in like three counties: Potter, King, Reagan Counties.

DC: And I think this one in *Travels* was not far from Amarillo.

SK: Well, Amarillo is where the home was.

DC: Canyon is in Potter County, I think, so it is not far from there?

SK: My grandmother lived to be in her late nineties. And so I remember her very, very vividly, and going out to the ranch in Amarillo [roughly eighteen miles from Canyon].

SK: I thought everything in [*Travels with Charley* about the ranch] was accurate. Because I remember my mom talking about it, and my grandmother. How charming it was. I remember her saying at least that part of it was accurate. Because my grandmother and mother stayed in very close touch with their Masterson family.

DC: And this is your Masterson grandmother?

SK: Uh huh. That Masterson family—still meet every year. Because what they did, they broke the ranches up, you know, separate ownership, the different branches of the family. They're all basically contiguous, one with the other, and they have a pooling agreement for the oil and gas royalties. It's almost impossible to keep track of who gets what, and so they formed an operating corporation that manages all the minerals under all the ranches, and keeps track of who gets what royalties and all that stuff.

My older brother Tres is kind of our representative on the Masterson Board. He [would always] go up with Mother. As long as Mother was living and able to travel she went to those Amarillo meetings because she loved her Amarillo family so much, and they were very close, and you know, I loved all my grandmother's sisters. They were a hoot. I mean, they were four of the most different human beings I have ever known in my life to have been sisters. Or siblings, whether it was male or female. And they were wonderful women. And real Texas ranching women, you know. But they also had style and grace.

DC: Steinbeck never mentions names, which is interesting to me, looking back at it. He doesn't mention the King Ranch or the Kleberg name, which I suspect he would have thought would have been a little braggadocious.

SK: Yeah, he wasn't that kind of guy.

DC: He just mentions Texas family, ranching.

SK: And I think he came down, at some point, to the ranch.

DC: To King Ranch . . . [the main ranch in South Texas]

SK: To King Ranch. But I just don't remember when that might have been . . . I sort of remember that Elaine went down to visit mother and daddy when she came to Austin. You know, she had family in Texas. Her sister was here in Texas, and her mom and all that, for a long time. And she came fairly regularly. He [Steinbeck] usually didn't come with her. But I think there was one trip that she came down here and he was with her. There has always been a guest book at the King Ranch Main House—they would now be in the King Ranch archives—but he may not have signed it.

SK: So you can't tell from his description [of the ranch] about where exactly he was [in *Travels with Charley*].

DC: Well, the first hint I had that I was wrong in my initial impression when I first read *Travels with Charley* many years ago that Steinbeck's Thanksgiving visit was to the King Ranch in South Texas was when I reread it just a few years ago and caught his reference to catching trout, and I know there are no trout that far south in Texas.

SK: Well, we don't have any rivers down there, either, except the Rio Grande and the Guadalupe, which are like three hundred miles apart.

DC: Well, let's talk more about Elaine and your relationship with her, which, as you say, is where most of what you know about Steinbeck comes from. Talk to me a little bit about your impressions of her managing his reputation, and stories that she may have told you along those lines.

SK: You know, she never said that's what she did. But they were so attached at the hip. It was really a beautiful thing, their relationship. You don't see that very often, the way they were attached to each other. And I think it was very codependent—on his part, for sure. I don't think Elaine needed anything or anybody to feel secure in herself.

Her personality was so big. And she was so vivacious and . . . easy with people. And . . . oh my God, how many times did she tell me, "He was the love of my life." I think she would have gone to the moon and back for this man, and whatever he needed she would have done. She agonized over the trouble in the family. With his boys and stuff, and . . . she called them "my sons." She always considered them her children. She did not consider that Waverly [Elaine's daughter with Zach Scott] was the only child she had.

And she was very saddened by the boys' relationship with their dad, when that relationship with him was not good, and she worked hard to help John in their relationship and to treat them like they were her own in hopes of building bridges back to their dad, you know.

DC: She was at home in the world.

SK: Totally. Absolutely. And I don't think she really needed anybody. I think she just was so in love with this man. In every sense of the word. She revered him; she felt responsible for him, to protect him from the crowds and the noise and the newspapers and all that stuff. She just . . . you know, she was fierce in her protection of him. And that's not managing, in my estimation, but she had the skills to do all those things to protect him because . . . not because, but she was better at it because of what her profession had been, a stage manager.

DC: Are there stories she told you that are vivid to you?

SK: She told me a story of going to see the Kennedys at the White House. And about John and his politics, because she and John were very liberal, and they were fiercely supportive of Kennedy and his policies and . . . I can't remember all the details, but she just said it was such a wonderful experience to be in the White House, to be with him and Jackie, sort of casual . . . it wasn't like for a big steak dinner and everybody in their formal dress and putting on their best face and all that kind of stuff. They were just there as friends. And she absolutely adored John Kennedy, and so did John Steinbeck. They had huge respect for the man, and she talked a little bit about how they both came away from that . . . I think it was a whole weekend they spent there . . . and when they went back to Sag Harbor, she said that John particularly . . . became more fiercely supportive of Kennedy than before that weekend. And he believed even more strongly in him and his leadership and what he was doing and what his dreams for the country were and how to get there. And she said there were moments of great laughter and teasing.

DC: Which Kennedy was really good at. A master at it!

SK: Yes, exactly! You know, she never said that John didn't say very much and I got the impression that he was more conversant on that trip. That it wasn't just Elaine communicating for the two of them. Because he honored Kennedy so deeply and believed in him so greatly. I think that he kind of became unbuckled a little bit, and looser. She said, "We both would laugh," and she wasn't talking about her and Kennedy laughing together; it was she and John laughing with the Kennedys, and so more demonstrative.

DC: Moving from the Kennedy relationship . . . I think that Steinbeck was in Poland, if I'm not mistaken—in any event, he was still on that tour—when they got the news that Kennedy had been shot and of course they came back right away and met Johnson. As you know, Elaine knew Lady Bird from the University of Texas, although Lady Bird was a few years older than Elaine.

SK: Yes.

DC: But anyway, they became close to the Johnsons.

SK: Right.

DC: What stories has she shared with you about that relationship?

SK: She really didn't tell me anything about that, because she knew that our family was close to the Johnsons and that I'd gone to school with the girls and that Johnson had been my grandfather's congressional secretary. That's what got him to Washington in the first place. And so I guess she . . . I don't know. She just never brought it up.

DC: That's interesting. She did talk about it a little bit during the interview my wife and I did with Elaine in 1993, but my impression was, at that time, that she was trying to back off that relationship because of Vietnam, because most of their friends were very liberal and Steinbeck was one of the only major writers in the United States that supported Johnson on Vietnam. But then she said, "Well, you know"—and I thought this was kind of endearingly and uncharacteristically naive of her—she said, "Well, I got the impression later, you know, that Johnson was kind of using Steinbeck to appeal to the liberal side Democratic Party."

SK: That's *totally* possible. He was such a manipulator, that man.

DC: Well, all politicians use people.

SK: Yeah, but he . . .

DC: He raised it to a fine art.

SK: He did. And all you have to do is to read *Master of the Senate* [the third volume of Robert Caro's biography of Johnson] to really see him in action.

DC: That's the volume that won the Pulitzer, right?

SK: It should have. And I have told so many people, I said, if you want to understand the way government works in this country today, Johnson's the one that created the committee system, all that kind of . . . this whole trade-off stuff and getting in people's faces to get what he wanted and all that kind of stuff, you've got to read that. That's the finest political nonfiction I think I've ever read.

In the early '90s I called Caro and I said, "I'm Dick Kleberg, senior's, granddaughter, and I found it curious that, you know, I had these letters that my grandmother [Mamie Kleberg] wrote." They were letters to Johnson that we had in our family archives. I said I found it curious that they didn't show up in *Path to Power* [the first volume of Caro's biography of Johnson] in talking about his early political career. And Caro said, "Well, because they weren't available." Because . . . there were certain boxes that [Johnson] said would not be opened for fifty years after he died.

SK: And he invited me to lunch at the Century Club in New York . . . 'Cause I was trying to find out from him if he knew anything about why my family has this deep animosity for Johnson. And it started out with these loving letters from my grandmother to Johnson. He referred to her as his other mother . . . I was born in 1944, the year that my great grandmother died, Alice Kleberg, who was the one that Johnson adored. You know, when he asked Lady Bird to marry him, he wanted my great grandmother to meet Lady Bird. Because he wanted Lady Bird to meet one of his favorite people.

I mean, he *adored* my great grandmother. He met her because he had worked for my grandfather. And had gone down to the ranch and met my grandfather's family—my grandfather's mother . . . who had two boys and three girls and the family agreed that only one could be the manager of the ranch and the other would be the public relations ambassador for the King Ranch and that would be my grandfather, 'cause he was the one that really had the people skills. And he was a lawyer and he ran for Congress; his district went from like New Braunfels all the way down to the Mexican border. And it was a huge district. It wasn't of course, obviously, as populated as it is now, so it went through San Antonio and all down in there, and my grandfather spoke German and Spanish fluently 'cause he had grown up in a German-speaking household, and so they called him the cowboy congressman. . . . he served for fourteen years in the Congress, and he didn't know any politicians to speak of or young people that could go to Washington and be his secretary, and somebody recommended Lyndon. He was teaching school in Houston at the time and he had been like, president of the student body or something at Southwest Texas State [then Southwest Texas State Teachers College], which is now Texas State University in San Marcos, and he was kind of a natural politician. And so whoever this friend of my grandfather's was, said, "He's up and coming and so you should talk to this young man because I think he would be a great aide for you." My grandfather didn't know Lyndon; he just hired him on that recommendation. He only worked for my grandfather for three years and then . . . my grandfather was a big states' righter even though he was a Democrat. Of course in those days, everybody was a Democrat in Texas. They were conservative Democrats, but they were Democrats. And when Roosevelt was elected, I mean to tell you, my grandfather was not a happy man. And also Lyndon saw which way the world was going and he bailed on my grandfather and took a job with the Texas Youth Administration as the regional head, and that's how he got into the Roosevelt branch of the Democratic Party.

DC: Was that the split between your grandfather and Johnson?

SK: Well, no; that's not what split them. Everybody I've talked to in my family gave me a different reason. Everybody. My grandmother wouldn't talk about him. At all. 'Cause I asked her, you know . . . One story was that Lyndon . . . did not back my grandfather when he was running in 1944. There was a war hero that was fighting in France that Roosevelt was running against my grandfather, and so my grandmother was very concerned because my grandfather wasn't campaigning [back in his Texas Congressional district] since he was in Washington because it was in wartime and they were passing legislation that was critical to the war and he felt like his job was in Washington and not campaigning in South Texas. And so basically it was a campaign that was being run from afar. And the operatives in the Roosevelt administration were managing the campaign in Texas, and nobody really was managing my grandfather's campaign because he wouldn't come home.

DC: But he won anyway?

SK: No, he did not. He lost. He lost because he wouldn't come home in 1944 . . . My grandfather was a big golfer, and he did all of his politicking on the golf course. And Lyndon ran the office. And my grandfather overspent his congressional account and Lyndon would call my uncle, Bob [Kleberg], and say, "You gotta send some money up here. Dick has run out of money," you know. So my grandfather ended up in debt to King Ranch when he died, of a big sum, and my father was so angry about that because he felt that it was our responsibility that my grandfather's family needed to pay the ranch back, for all that money that got sent to support my grandfather's lavish lifestyle . . .

SK: When I interviewed Lady Bird [in 1991], I asked her, "Lady Bird, why did you ultimately allow this interview?" And she said, "Sally, when Lyndon died, I made a promise to myself that I was going to be a bridgebuilder. Because I think in a lot of ways, Lyndon burned a lot of bridges."

DC: That's a role she played while he was alive, too.

SK: Right. And she said, "I feel like that is my principal role from now till the day that I die is to build bridges, and I think you're a bridgebuilder by wanting to tell this story, and it needs to be told. And I'm willing to help you in any way that I can." So I asked her, I said, "Do you know why they fell away from each other so dramatically, because my grandmother . . . she couldn't say Lyndon's name without bile in her mouth. My Aunt Henrietta, who was my grandfather's sister, had the same attitude. And Uncle Bob, who was always the practical one, and always was a manipulator too—and he understood that about Lyndon—he said we gotta keep the connection. We gotta keep the connection, because there are agricultural bills and if you don't have a friendship with this man, you're done. Bob just could look the other way, out of expediency. And so he was the only one that was positive about Lyndon of our entire family."

SK: My grandmother just never forgave him because she had called him her second son, and [during her meeting with South Texas Democratic powerbroker George Parr] he just sat there with his mouth shut saying, "George isn't going to support him, and neither am I." "I'm not going to help him." Lyndon saw which way the wind was blowing. And my grandmother was just devastated over that. And for that to be the only time she ever cried in her daughter's presence? That's how badly it hurt her.

DC: Did Elaine ever talk about her view that Johnson was using Steinbeck?

SK: Oh, yeah!

## Chapter 14

DC: And then she said to me later, "Well, of course he was," as you say, "trying to build bridges to the liberal side of the party. I think he was using him [in Vietnam]." And I remember thinking at that time, Elaine, that's what all politicians do.

DC: The impression I had—was that Elaine was probably trying to put distance between Steinbeck and Johnson. Because, you know, that was a big item, that the author of *The Grapes of Wrath*, who was still widely perceived as a great liberal, was supporting a war that almost no other liberal was supporting at that time.

SK: Right, right. And I guess that it was her only way. I mean, if John was going to support Johnson on Vietnam, she couldn't really tell him not to because that's not the way she worked with John.

DC: But then again she had that relationship with Lady Bird. Did she ever talk about that relationship very much?

SK: No. . . . Lady Bird married Johnson in 1934, which was the year she graduated from college. Yeah, he would have been working for my grandfather then, because he worked for my grandfather from '32 to '35. And that's why he wanted Lady Bird to meet my grandmother, because he was working for my grandfather at the time. And that's how he had met my great grandmother. And thought she was such a wonderful . . . but you know, he had this thing about strong women. And he just really revered them.

DC: Johnson had remarkable perceptions about people. He could size people up, figure out what makes 'em tick.

SK: Yeah.

DC: Just an almost preternatural ability.

SK: Elaine, she was like my mom. My mom would call me or she would call one of the boys or one of her grandkids. She'd say, "I want some company. I'm dying for a hamburger. Let's go get a hamburger. Will you take me to get a hamburger at Cheesy Jane's?" She and Elaine were very much alike. Very, like, sociable and out there and loved to tell stories, and loved . . . if there was a party going on, that's where mom wanted to be. And if there wasn't one, she would make one.

DC: And Elaine apparently loved parties, too.

SK: Well, that's what I'm saying. They were really, really . . . they had lots of things in common, and were very, very close all their lives.

DC: And speaking of parties, the ultimate party, that black-and-white affair that Truman Capote gave.

SK: Oh, that Truman Capote gave? She just told me that she went and that it was just like a . . . I can't remember the term she used. It wasn't zoo, but something to that effect.

DC: Well, I didn't realize that that's the party she was talking about during our 1993 interview with her. She was talking about Steinbeck's shyness, and she said, "But occasionally he would connect," and she said, "Once we were at this party, and there were people everywhere, and I looked over and I saw John looking down and he had a very angry look on his face like he was lecturing somebody."

SK: Was it Truman Capote?

DC: Yes. And then she said, "I walked over there and I realized" . . . Capote was apparently really diminutive.

SK: He was.

DC: " . . . that he was having a friendly discussion with Truman Capote." Well, I didn't realize until later—and I put this in the interview—that that was at Capote's black-and-white party, I guess in '67 or '66 [it was November 28, 1966] maybe that he gave in honor of Katharine Graham, as I recall.

SK: Yes. That's right.

DC: And that was the one people actually flew to London or abroad somewhere if they didn't get an invitation so they could say they were out of the country and couldn't be there for it. Apparently it was *the* social event.

SK: [Laughing] It was. They still talk about it in New York. . . . she did say that she was surprised that John wanted to go.

DC: So she was surprised he allowed her to accept the invitation?

SK: Yes, yeah, yeah, because she said he usually didn't like big to-do's like that.

. . .

DC: Did Elaine talk to you about Steinbeck's writing?

SK: Only that he would get up in the morning and he'd go out to that gazebo and he'd stay out there.

. . .

SK: Oh, I have something to tell you about Waverly. I was reading your question "Tell us something about your cousin Waverly, Elaine's daughter with Zach and any memories she may have shared with you about John Steinbeck." One Christmas . . . 'cause they didn't come down for Christmas very often—for various reasons. Either Uncle Zach was filming in California or he was acting, and of course the height of the season in New York for Broadway shows is in the winter, in the holiday season in particular because that's when the bigger crowds are there to visit and they make their most money on the stage during the holidays. And so he was down—he wasn't working on anything at the time, he and Waverly and mother and daddy and Ann [Zach's and Sally's mother's older sister] and her husband Fanning Heston . . . When was Queen Elizabeth crowned?

DC: '53, June second, '53.

SK: OK, it was that Christmas. The reason I remember that is because my deepest, most passionate desire for my Christmas present was a Queen Elizabeth doll, that was a Madame Alexander Queen Elizabeth doll dressed in her coronation robes with her crown and her ribbons and all that kind of stuff. And I knew I wasn't going to get it because Madame Alexander is . . . this sucker's like this tall. I've got it upstairs. Poor thing; she's turning brown. [Laughing]. I don't want to tell the queen that 'cause she has such pale skin. But my grandparents gave me my Queen Elizabeth doll for Christmas. And I'll never forget it as long as I live. So that was the Christmas that Waverly and Uncle Zach were there [in Austin], and Ann and Fanning.

SK: Sweetbrush Drive [around the Scott grandparents' home in Austin] now has houses all around it because my grandfather developed it before he died, to get it out of his estate. But all those houses that are on Sweetbrush Drive were surrounded by trees. That was all forest . . . it was kind of a red dirt, red gravel, kind of native soil path up to—you know, for the cars to go out, and we would run down the road and get the paper at the front, and there was this smell, this wonderful smell of pine early in the morning when it's moist and the trees smell so good and I still, when I smell that smell, I go back to Sweetbrush. So anyway, we were wandering around in the woods with Waverly, and we went down the hill because their house faced the lake but then you go down the hill and you can come out to the water . . . and down below the hill, there was rabbit tobacco growing. And Waverly was picking it. She had cigarette papers and she was rolling rabbit tobacco cigarettes and smoking down there, and that's when my younger brother, Tio, who was about eight . . .

DC: How old was she?

SK: I think Waverly must have probably been four or five years older than my older brother, Tres, at least. So she was in her mid to late teens. And here we were, these little pipsqueaks that she was corrupting. And that's when Tio started smoking, and . . . he didn't quit, and he was diagnosed with emphysema when he was a freshman in college. So anyway, that's my favorite Waverly story.

DC: Teaching Tio to smoke.

SK: Yeah.

. . .

SK: Elaine's favorite drink, of course, was Stoly [Stolichnaya Russian Vodka]. Oh, and this is what made me think of the meals, her best meals. I've never eaten her cooking but we would always go out . . . she took me to three different places besides Sign of the Dove [then an upscale restaurant on Manhattan's Upper East Side]. We would split . . . I would take her one time, and then she would me, but the only place we ate twice was J. G. Melon. She loved their hamburgers. And it's on the upper East Side, I think in the seventies. I think on Third Avenue or something. Third Avenue and East 74th. And she introduced me to J. G. Melon. Because I always thought that P. J. Clarke's is known for its hamburgers and fries, but J. G. Melon's are better. Then there was a little French café called Heulot—H-e-u-l-o-t, I believe.

DC: I wonder if that's the little bistro she talked about taking Faulkner to [during a visit Faulkner paid to the Steinbeck's in January 1955]?

SK: It may have been, because it was this little tiny French bistro, and it was in the neighborhood. And it was a just delightful little spot, not many tables there.

DC: Well this place they took Faulkner to was close to the East 72nd place.

SK: Yes.

DC: She said, "We just went downstairs, or we just went across the street, or something like that."

SK: And the other place she loved was Shorty's. Shorty's was a restaurant where a lot of famous people had their special tables. And hers was in the window. In the southeast corner. And she took me to Shorty's once with her. Of course, they bowed and scraped all over the place.

DC: I remember at the Sign of the Dove, she ordered a special dish that had several different kinds of oysters. She said that was one of Jackie Kennedy's favorite restaurants.

DC: Did she ever take you to Sardi's, her table there?

SK: No. I remember early on when mother . . . when we would go up there, Uncle Zach's picture was at Sardi's, way back when he was acting on the stage. You know, they have so many drawings in there that they take them down and warehouse them and put new ones up, so he's long been down, but I remember when we were going to Sardi's after going to see Uncle Zach in a play or going to the theater at all during that era and seeing his picture up there. Elaine had her own table there, and she had her own table at Shorty's and she had her own table at J. G. Melon and she had her own table at Heulot. And I'm sure she had one at Sign of the Dove.

. . .

DC: Did she ever talk to you about their time in England in Somerset?

SK: No.

DC: When Steinbeck was dying, they were doing what she did with Zach and talking about good times they had, reminiscing, and she said that he asked her, "What was your favorite time in all of our marriage"? Or maybe she asked him. When she started to tell him, he said, "No, no; write it down, because I know you'll just agree with me if I say it first."

SK: [Laughs]

DC: And so she wrote down "the year in Somerset." And he unfolded his page and it was the same as hers. But she said they loved living there, partly because he was doing research on the *Death of Arthur, Le Morte d'Arthur*. Elaine said that when they were there she would put on her headscarf and go with the local ladies to clean the churches. And she said that there was a kind of village conspiracy when American journalists and British ones as well would find out that Steinbeck was there and they would come looking for him. When they would ask the villagers about Steinbeck, they would say something like, "Oh, yes, yes; we've heard of him, but no, we haven't seen him at all." Elaine said it was wonderful, this village conspiracy. That really appealed to her. And also, I guess, the sense of privacy they enjoyed there. It was one of the few times when they had almost total privacy. Steinbeck absolutely hated that aspect of fame; he did not like to be recognized.

SK: I have to tell you the Eli Wallach story. I learned this at Elaine's funeral, and Eli Wallach was speaking about his friendship with Elaine—and Zach, actually, because they all met at the University of Texas. And he, Wallach, started off with what he was doing at the University of Texas and he said it was because they had a really cheap drama program down there. And he said, "We didn't have two nickels to rub together, and I wanted to go to acting school, and Texas had the reputation of having this really good drama school in those days." And they still do, actually. Their fine arts department is just so amazing, but the dramatic arts department was well known even then and so . . . I think he hitch-hiked all the way to Texas if I remember, 'cause he didn't have a car, and he couldn't afford the bus ticket or the train ticket. He was just like this poor little Jewish mouse there, and he went to a Shakespeare play. He said, "First of all, I couldn't understand what anybody was saying. That Texas accent was just like nothing I'd ever heard before." And he's going like, "How can people down here speak that kind of thing and do Shakespeare? I just can't understand it." And so he goes to this Shakespeare production, a student production at the school, and Elaine and Zach are in it together. And I can't remember which one it was, but anyway they were both in it. And Wallach said, "And here these people were, talking in that . . . however way they talk, and playing Shakespeare, and I just couldn't get over it." And the way he was telling this story, people [at the funeral] were just laughing. And so, Wallach and Elaine and Zach got to be just great friends because they studied together and went to classes together. And then you fast-forward years later and they all lived in New York after they graduated, and they saw each other in New York, and then he [Wallach] went and made movies and Zach made movies, and so they were in and out of New York and in and out of Hollywood and then Wallach said, "We sort of lost touch for a while." Then, he said, "I was at this party. Somebody had a party at their apartment here in New York, and all of a sudden I hear this voice, 'Eli, you know he's my favorite Jew! [SK laughing.] I've got to go speak to my favorite Jew.'" Well, of course, everybody at the funeral just cracked up because they knew Elaine, and it was such an Elaine thing to do. And he said, "she had called me her favorite Jew ever since we met, because they didn't know any others. There weren't any in Austin, Texas. [Or, at least,] I was the only one they knew, so I was always their favorite Jew." Of course, in New York they had many other Jewish friends but Eli Wallach always remained her "favorite Jew." I love that story.

. . .

SK: John had a study in the New York apartment, although that's not where he did all his writing. I think he did a lot of letter writing there, but I don't think he did his book writing. But from what I gathered from Elaine when I went to the apartment, she walked me through the apartment and . . .

DC: The East 72nd?

SK: Yes. And she said, "This is John's study," and all that, but she said, "He did all his writing at Sag Harbor."

DC: They went to Sag Harbor in the summer, spring and summer and fall?

SK: Yes. They were only in New York in the winter.

DC: She told me they were in Sag Harbor during the Cuban Missile Crisis in October of '62, and that they had stayed in there later than they normally did. She said they never ate breakfast there together, but for some reason they did that day, and they turned on the news to hear what was happening with the [Cuban] Missile crisis when they heard the announcement that he had won the Nobel Prize. And the reason that he had not received the notification is that they had sent it to the East 72nd Street address where Elaine and John normally would have been that time of year. So they found out about it . . .

SK: On the news.

DC: Yeah, on the news. And of course, the phone started ringing, and Viking [Viking Press, Steinbeck's longtime publisher] wanted him in their New York office immediately for all the publicity and all and asked them to catch the next plane to New York, and he said, "No, I'd like to ride with Elaine in the car and talk about it." Which I thought was a really cool thing.

SK: [Laughing] Slooow ride back in the car.

DC: Yeah. "Let's do this before we get so taken up in all this and have no privacy to speak of for the next few days and what time we do have together we'll be exhausted."

SK: That sounds perfectly in keeping with his character.

DC: Yeah, savoring the moment privately, rather than in the glare of publicity. Elaine was frying bacon, she said, when they heard the announcement, and she just took frying pan with the bacon and stuck it in the refrigerator and when they got back days later, it was still there in congealed grease.

SK: Did I ever tell you the story about Elizabeth Taylor and Elaine?

DC: No.

SK: Oh, my God. She told me this story. Elizabeth Taylor was performing in *Little Foxes*. It was while I was living in New York. They were doing a remake of *Little Foxes* and Elizabeth Taylor was going to be in it and Elaine called these friends—she was at Sag Harbor, it was in the summer and she was at Sag Harbor—she called these neighbors of hers and she and Jean [Elaine's sister] invited them over for dinner. And one of the neighbors said, "Oh, we have a houseguest. Do you mind if we bring 'em along?" And she said, "Oh, the more the merrier," you know Elaine. And she said, "How many?" And the neighbor friend said one . . . So Elaine gets back to the kitchen and is fiddling around, and she and Jean are setting the table and all that, and so they hear the doorbell ring, and the guest is Elizabeth Taylor. And Elaine is going, "Oh my God." And Elizabeth Taylor had that ring on. The one that Burton gave her the second or third time they got married. And so they're sitting at the dinner table and Elaine said to me, "I can't take my eyes off this ring." She said, "It's the biggest diamond I have ever seen on a human being in my life. Everything else has always been in a museum. But to have it on a human being's hand and having it at my dinner table, it was just too much not to say something." And so she said, "Elizabeth," because she preferred to be called Elizabeth and not Liz, that's kind of what the press hung on her, "That is just the most amazing ring. Do you mind if I try it on?" Only Elaine would have the guts to do that! I wouldn't have. And Elizabeth Taylor said, "Oh, of course, of course." She said, "People think I never take it off, but look at it." She said, "The reason they think that is because, look, it's all gunked up with pancake make-up" and all that kind of stuff. She'd been on the stage and had just come straight out of New York. She said, "Excuse me just a minute." So she goes into the bathroom and she's in there for a while and then she comes back and she hands it to Elaine. And Elaine said, "I just sat there, and I know I looked at this thing on my hand for at least ten minutes." And she said, "Nobody knew whether they should talk or not talk." And she said, "Don't mind me. I'm just relishing the moment." And then she takes it off her finger and gives it back to Elizabeth. And they continue to eat. And then they said their good-nights and all. They had a lovely dinner. And Elaine said, "She [Elizabeth] is such a star that she acts like everybody expects her to act, which is she's got to be the center of attention." And she said, "But, you know, everybody sort of accepts that because that's what she is. She's always been the center of attention all her life, so why not continue to be the center of attention?" Who's going to tell her no? So anyway, they left, and Elaine said they cleaned up the kitchen and put the dishes in the dishwasher and all that, and she said, "I went to get ready for bed and I walked into my bathroom," and she said, "Sally, you would not believe the mess she made in my bathroom." She said, "She had gone in there—I thought she was going to go to the restroom—she had gone in there to clean up the ring. And she used *my* toothbrush. And here my toothbrush was sitting on the sink," she said, "and she obviously had done *this* and so it splattered pancake make-up and soap dots all over my mirror, all over my vanity, all in the sink. It was on the rug and on the floor." She said, "I was so furious." She said, "Imagine! The gall of that woman! Not cleaning up after herself!" I said, "But Elaine, you said, 'She's a star and she acts like one.' What else would you expect?"

DC: [Laughing] But is this coming from a woman who had the nerve to ask her to take off her diamond in the first place.

SK: Exactly! Exactly!

DC: That's a great story.

SK: Anyway, I just hooted. She was so *irritated* that Elizabeth Taylor had trashed her bathroom . . .

DC: The first time Mary Jeanne and I went to New York to see Elaine there on East 72nd . . . just before that visit we had stopped at a little flower shop below her apartment and bought her a dozen yellow roses as would be appropriate for a fellow Texan. She loved those, so much so that every year on her birthday, August 14th, I think, we would wire her a dozen yellow roses. Well, the first year I did that, she called, and when I answered, I heard, "You fool!" And so I said, laughing, "Who is this"? This was before caller ID, which has spoiled a lot of good things. But anyway, she said, "Oh honey, you are so sweet. You couldn't have known this, but John always sent me a dozen yellow roses for my birthday." I hadn't known it, but anyway, I continued to do that every year, and the last call I got from her was in response to yellow roses we had sent the last year she was alive. It was maybe two days after her birthday. I had heard she'd had a stroke, and so I wasn't expecting a call. But the roses were what her call was about. She had remembered, and told her caregiver to please call me. I had written her that we had moved, but she had a little trouble getting our new phone number, and she asked me where we were now living. Well, I had just taken a new job at a university in San Angelo, Texas, which is about fifty miles west of the tiny town of Eden. So I said, Elaine, you might not believe me, but we live west of Eden.

SK: Laughing. I bet she loved that!

DC: She got that immediately, and I thought, the stroke sure hasn't affected her quick mind.

SK: No.

DC: Her voice was a little more halting, but she obviously still had every one of her marbles. Going back, I guess the second time we saw her she was '78 or '79. And she had braces on her teeth, and . . . do you remember that?

SK: I do.

DC: And she said, "Oh, look at these braces!" like they were a necklace or something. She said, "I've just decided I'm going to live forever, and I might as well have straight teeth for all the years I have left." And she did. She lasted years after that. What a remarkable person.

SK: Yeah. I just adored her.

DC: She didn't want to talk about herself, though. I kept trying . . . by the end of the first interview we did, I was really as interested in her as I was in Steinbeck.

SK: Exactly! I know.

DC: But she was having none of talk about her. After I got into trying to pry more details from her about her career in the theater, she said, "Is this interview about me?" I said, "Well, it could be." But no, she wanted to talk just about John.

DC: At one point, we got to talking about Charley, and Elaine turned to me and said, "Don, you know that Charley was *my* dog."

SK: [Laughs]

DC: "It wasn't John's," she said. "I *let* him take Charley."

DC: Did she tell you about her conversations with the Swedish king, during the gala dinner when Steinbeck was getting the Nobel Prize?

She was seated next to him, and—this is testament to her ability to engage people—they discussed the flora and fauna of the Hamptons [close to the Steinbeck's Sag Harbor cottage] and the king ended up saying he was going to send her information on what flowers and plants he thought would grow best at Sag Harbor. Only Elaine could pull something like that off. The crown prince, Bertril, was sitting on the other side of Elaine. He told her he had been watching her have a good time for the past five days, and that he'd never heard anybody talk so much.

[Before John's death, Elaine wrote to Sally]: "All fairly well here. John has his good days and bad. The bad ones are always the result of difficult breathing because of the heart action, and we think God for the big oxygen tank. Our glorious Indian summer goes on but I do hope we'll be moving in by election day as I think John needs a good going-over by the great doctors in town. Speaking of election day, I am saying that I am voting for Muskie. I think he is the most reliable and sane man to appear in our mixed-up politics for a long time. We've known Humphrey for a long time and trust him, so that's the way our votes will go. I think it may be a cliffhanger."

"Don't ever let anyone convince you that you shouldn't discuss politics or religion among family or friends."

SK: Mine was always on the other side of the fence. "People have been telling me that for years and I always say, 'What else is there?'" [SK laughs] Of course that's an exaggeration, but I do think they can be discussed intelligently . . .

[Elaine's letter continues] "I am getting pretty disenchanted with this war anyway. For a while we felt it was our only course and when we were in Viet Nam we got terribly caught up in it all as everyone does on the spot, but the Tet offensive changed my mind. We really don't seem to be getting anywhere near a military victory. Aren't we in a big upheaval politically? For the first time in my life I don't know how I'm going to vote. I know I'll vote for a Democrat, though I vote for a Republican senator, mayor, and governor, but who knows at this point which one? I do think the political scramble is very healthy, though. It gives us a chance for open debate and airing of grievances of which we seem to have a gracious plenty. Our older son Thom leaves for Viet Nam this week and we are so sad about it. He doesn't want to go at all which makes it worse. He has only just gotten married, too. She's such a darling girl and we are thrilled to have her in our family. John and I and her parents tried to talk them into waiting for all the obvious reasons, but you know you can only say so much and no more. And they had to make the ultimate decision. I think it will be harder on her than on him."

SK: This [letter] is from East 72nd. 1967.

> I feel so awful having waited so long to answer your wonderful letter but all my attention has been toward John for the past two months. He went into the hospital on October 8th, had a spinal fusion on the 23rd. The doctors said he was past the age for the fusion, but he demanded one feeling he couldn't come to terms with the restricted life. Anything less in his condition would have been patchwork, so when they found a bone healthy they did the fusion and he has reacted like a man half his age. He is a tough old bird to be sure. He had to learn to walk again, and that was pure hell for him, but he has now been home for two and a half weeks and is doing wonderfully well—so well, in fact, that we are being allowed to go down to Grenada in the Caribbean for the holidays. We go on Saturday. John has a lie-down seat in the plane and will make the trip well. He can do anything except stoop and bend or sit upright for too long at a

time. We can hardly wait for sea and sun, just what the doctor ordered literally."

SK: [reading from another letter]

I'm sure you don't know that John had a heart attack in mid-July, and oh, what a dreadful time it has been. Early in the summer he had several alarming seizures which fetched him up in nearby South Hampton Hospital, but when I realized the gravity of his condition he was taken into New York Hospital by ambulance. Thank God for the move as the heart attack came five days later, and in that great medical center we had everything going for us. It was an awful ordeal for John and a time of desperation for me, but mercifully he's coming out of it beautifully. It seems risky for us to come back out here just now, but John must be here in this beloved oak grove by the water in order to get well. He is being an angel about being absolutely quiet for a while.... We have a tank of oxygen and the village doctor and will stay here as long as the good fall weather holds out. I enjoy every minute of life. We always have, but, oh, there is nothing like a heart attack to promote an enjoyment of every moment of life.... Don't put John on your worry list. We are very optimistic for the future. Love to your family, and a special hug."

# Works Cited

Addison, Richard. [1711] 1858. *Addison's Spectator*. Edited by George Washington Green. New York: Derby and Jackson.
Andrew, Ariel. 2018. "A Personal Note: Contemporary American Power Dynamics and John Steinbeck's Nonfiction." *Steinbeck Review* 15, no. 1 (Spring): 56–61.
Astro, Richard. 1973. *John Steinbeck and Edward F. Ricketts: The Shaping of a Novelist*. Minneapolis: University of Minnesota Press.
———. 1975. "Travels with Steinbeck: The Laws of Thought and the Laws of Things." *Steinbeck Quarterly* 8 (2): 35–44.
Attwood, William. 1955. *Still the Most Exciting Country*. New York: Knopf.
Barthes, Roland. [1967] 1977. "The Death of the Author." In *Image, Music, Text*, 142–48. New York: Hill and Wang.
Bass, Rick. 2018. "Barry Lopez, Carnivore for a Night." In *The Traveling Feast: On the Road and at the Table with My Heroes*, 155–70. New York: Little, Brown.
Bennett, Eric. 2015. *Workshops of Empire: Stegner, Engle, and American Creative Writing during the Cold War*. Iowa City: University of Iowa Press.
Benson, Jackson J. 1977. "John Steinbeck: Novelist as Scientist." *NOVEL: A Forum on Fiction* 10, no. 3 (Spring): 248–64.
———. 1984. *The True Adventures of John Steinbeck, Writer*. New York: Viking.
Bradford, Roark. 1928. *Ol' Man Adam an' His Chillun*. New York: Harper and Brothers.
Brahms, Yael. 2020. "Philosophy of Post-Truth." *Institute for National Security Studies* 24 (February 2020): 1–19. Tel Aviv University.
Braudel, Fernand. [1958] 1980. Translated by Sarah Matthews as "History and the Social Sciences: The Longue Durée." In *On History*. Chicago: University of Chicago Press, 25–54.
Bruder, Jessica. 2017. *Nomadland*. New York: W. W. Norton. Kindle Edition.
Butcher, Fanny. 1996. "Steinbeck Rediscovers His Land and People." In McElrath, Crisler, and Shillinglaw, *John Steinbeck*, 482–84.
Button, John. 2019. *A Dictionary of Green Ideas: Vocabulary for a Sane and Sustainable Future*. New York: Routledge.
Campbell, Joseph. [1949] 1968. *The Hero with a Thousand Faces*. 2nd ed. Princeton: Princeton University Press.
Capa, Robert. 1947. "A Russian Story." In *Modern Man: Slave or Sovereign? Report of the 16th Annual New York Herald Tribune Forum*, proceedings of forum held at Waldorf-Astoria, New York City, October 20, 21 and 22, 1947. New York: New York Herald Tribune. 194–98.

Čerče, Danica. 2017. *John Steinbeck in East European Translation: A Bibliographical and Descriptive Overview*. Newcastle upon Tyne: Cambridge Scholars.

———. 2019. "John Steinbeck on East European Markets." *Steinbeck Review* 16 (2): 183–91.

Cervantes Saavedra, Miguel de. [1605] 1887. *The Ingenious Gentleman Don Quixote of La Mancha*. Vol 1. Translated by John Ormsby. New York: Thomas Crowell.

———. 1949. *Don Quixote*. Translated by Samuel Putnam. New York: Viking.

———. 1950. *Colloquy of the Dogs*. In *Three Exemplary Novels*, translated by Samuel Putnam, 125–219. New York: Viking.

Childers, William P. 2006. *Transnational Cervantes*. Toronto: University of Toronto Press.

———. 2010. "'The Captive's Tale and Circumcision," In "Don Quixote's Racial Other, Part 1," edited by Baltasar Fra Molinero, special issue, *Annals of Scholarship* 19 (2): 51–94.

———. 2023. "'A Mark High and Bright': Cervantes in Steinbeck's Cold War Trajectory." *Steinbeck Review* 20 (1): 1–29.

Clancy, Charles J. 1976. "Light in The Winter of Our Discontent." *Steinbeck Quarterly* 9 (3–4): 83–101.

Connelly, Marc. 1929. *The Green Pastures*. New York: Rinehart.

Cvetko, Marija. 1964. "John Steinbeck: *Potovanjes Charleyjem*." *Tedenska Tribuna*, March 24.

Davidson, Cathy N. 2004. *Revolution and the Word: The Rise of the Novel in America*. Oxford: Oxford University Press.

DeMott, Robert J. 1981. "'Culling All Books': Steinbeck's Reading and *East of Eden*." *Steinbeck Quarterly* 14 (Winter/Spring): 40–51.

———. 1984. *Steinbeck's Reading: A Catalogue of Books Owned and Borrowed*. New York: Garland.

———. 1997. *Steinbeck's Typewriter: Essays on His Art*. Troy, NY: Whitston Publishing.

———. 2012. "Working at the Impossible: The Presence of *Moby-Dick* in *East of Eden*." In *Steinbeck's Typewriter*, 75–106.

———. 2021. Review of *Chasing Steinbeck's Ghost: The Timeline for John Steinbeck's "Travels with Charley" Road Trip*. *Steinbeck Review* 18, no. 2 (Fall): 205–7.

———. 2022. *Steinbeck's Imaginarium: Essays on Writing, Fishing, and Other Critical Matters*. Albuquerque: New Mexico University Press.

Denizet-Lewis, Benoit. 2014. *Travels with Casey: My Journey through Our Dog-Crazy Country*. New York: Simon and Schuster. Kindle Edition.

Dew, Jason. 2007. "Cold War Reflections in *Travels with Charley*: Steinbeck's New Americanist Evaluation of Intra-Imperialist America." *Steinbeck Review* 4, no. 1 (Spring): 49–64.

Dewey, Joseph. 1990. *In a Dark Time: The Apocalyptic Temper in the American Novel of the Nuclear Age*. West Lafayette, IN: Purdue University Press.

———. 1991. "'There Was a Seedy Grandeur about the Man': Rebirth and Recovery in *Travels with Charley*." *Steinbeck Quarterly* 24 (1–2): 22–30.

Dimock, Wai Chee. 2006. *Through Other Continents: American Literature across Deep Time*. Princeton, NJ: Princeton University Press.

Ditsky, John. 1975. "Steinbeck's *Travels with Charley*: The Quest That Failed." *Steinbeck Quarterly* 8 (2): 45–52.

Donohue, Cecilia. 2017. "Logos, Pathos, Ethos, Caninus: Rhetorical Strategies in Steinbeck/Steinbeckian Dog/Travel Memoir." *Steinbeck Review* 14 (1): 65–78.Dunn, Douglas. 1994. "Back and Forth: Auden and Political Poetry." *Critical Survey* 6 (3): 325–35.

Doyle, Arthur Conan. "The Boscombe Valley Mystery." In *The Adventures of Sherlock Holmes*. Page by Page Books. Web.

Dunn, Peter N. 1972. "Two Classic Myths in *Don Quixote*." *Renaissance and Reformation* 9 (1): 2–10.

Dwyer, Jim. 2002. "The Voice of the Dispossessed." *Irish America*, June/July 2002.

Etheridge, Charles. 2009. "*The Grapes of Wrath* and Literary Naturalism." In *The Grapes of Wrath: A Re-Consideration*, edited by Michael J. Meyer, with an introduction by Brian Railsback, 653–86. Amsterdam: Rodopi.

Fanon, Frantz. 1986. *Black Skin, White Masks*. London: Pluto Press.

Fiedler, Leslie. 1960. *Love and Death in the American Novel*. New York: Stein and Day.

Foucault, Michel. 1997. "A Preface to Transgression." In *Language, Counter-Memory, Practice: Selected Essays and Interviews by Michel Foucault*, edited by Donald F. Bouchard, 28–35. Ithaca, NY: Cornell University Press.

Frost, Robert. "The Gidt Outright." Poetry Foundation. Web.

Frye, Northrup. [1957] 1973. *Anatomy of Criticism: Four Essays*. Reprint, Princeton, NJ: Princeton University Press.

George, Stephen K. 2006. "Miguel de Cervantes." In *A John Steinbeck Encyclopedia*, edited by Brian Railsback and Michael J. Meyer, 54–55. Westport, CT: Greenwood Press.

Goffman, Erving. 1956. *The Presentation of Self in Everyday Life*. Edinburgh: University of Edinburgh Press.

Groneman, William, III. 2012. "Travels Unraveled." *Steinbeck Review* 9 (2): 78–88.

Gussago, Luigi. 2016. *Picaresque Fiction Today: The Trickster in Contemporary Anglophone and Italian Literature*. Leiden: Brill Rodopi.

Gunter, John. 1947. *Inside U.S.A*. New York: Harper and Brothers.

Hansberry, Lorraine. 1965. "Scars of the Ghetto." *Monthly Review* 16, no. 10 (February): 588–91.

Haraway, Donna J. 2007. *When Species Meet*. Minneapolis: University of Minnesota Press.

Harden, Mike. 2007. "Stories from the Road: Steinbeck's Journey across Country Captured Soul of America." *Columbus Dispatch*, April 1, 2007.

Hayashi, Tetsumaro. 1990. "Steinbeck's America in *Travels with Charley*." *Steinbeck Quarterly* 23 (3–4): 88–96.

———. 1996. "America and Americans." In McElrath, Crisler, and Shillinglaw, *John Steinbeck*, 501–3.

Heavilin, Barbara. 2019. "'The Beacon Thing': Musings on John Steinbeck, America, and Light." *Steinbeck Review* 16 (2): v–xiv.

———. 2020. "'I Set This Matter Down . . . to Inform Myself': Steinbeck's *Travels with Charley in Search of America* as Private Discourse." *Steinbeck Review* 17 (2): v–xvii.

Hemingway, Ernest. 1999. Epigraph. *True at First Light*. New York: Scribner.

Horowitz, Juliana Menasce, Ruth Igielnik, and Rakesh Kochhar. 2020. "Trends in Income and Wealth Inequality." Pew Research Center. Online. Last modified January 9, 2020.

Hughes, Langston. 1951. *Montage of a Dream Deferred*. New York: Henry Holt and Co.

Hughes, Robert S., Jr. 1987. "*Travels with Charley* and *America and Americans*." *Steinbeck Quarterly* 20, no. 3–4 (Summer–Fall): 76–88.

Jackson, Kenneth T. 1985. *Crabgrass Frontier: The Suburbanization of the United States*. New York: Oxford University Press.

Jacobs, Jane. 1961. *The Death and Life of Great American Cities*. New York: Vintage.

Johnson, Carter. 2021. "Steinbeck Laughing: *Travels with Charley* as American Picaresque." *Steinbeck Review* 18, no. 2 (Fall): 149–61.

Johnson, James Weldon. *The Autobiography of an Ex-Colored Man*. Boston: Sherman, French, 1912.

Jones, Gavin. 2021. *Reclaiming John Steinbeck. Writing for the Future of Humanity*. Cambridge, UK: Cambridge University Press.

Kain, Geoffrey, ed. 1993. *R. K. Narayan: Contemporary Critical Perspectives*. East Lansing: Michigan State University Press.

Kelley, James C. 1997. "John Steinbeck and Ed Ricketts: Understanding Life in the Great Tide Pool." In *Steinbeck and the Environment: Interdisciplinary Approaches*, edited by Susan F. Beegel, Susan Shillinglaw, and Wesley N. Tiffney Jr. 27–42. Tuscaloosa, University of Alabama Press.

Kerouac, Jack. 1957. *On the Road*. New York: Viking.

Keyes, Ralph. 2004. *The Post-Truth Era: Dishonesty and Deception in Contemporary Life*. New York: St. Martin's Press.

Kiernan, Thomas. 1979. *The Intricate Music: A Biography of John Steinbeck*. Boston: Little, Brown.

King, Martin Luther, Jr. 1963. "Letter from a Birmingham Jail." April 16, 1963. Available at "MLK Reflection: Letter from Birmingham Jail," Grace Presbytery, Irving, TX. Web.

Knoeller, Christian. 2005."'A Profession Older than Writing': Echoes of *Huckleberry Finn* in Steinbeck's *Travels with Charley in Search of America*." In *Midwest Miscellany XXXIII*, edited by David D. Anderson, 22–35. East Lansing, MI: Midwestern Press.

Kohrs, Donald, and Richard Astro. 2021. *A Tidal Odyssey: Ed Ricketts and the Making of "Between Pacific Tides."* Corvallis: Oregon State University Press.

Kopecký, Petr. 2011. "The Literary Front of the Cold War: John Steinbeck as an Ideological Object in the Eastern Bloc." *Comparative American Studies* 9 (3): 204–16.

Kubrick, Stanley, dir. 1964. *Dr. Strangelove, or: How I Learned to Stop Worrying and Love the Bomb*. Columbia Pictures.

LeMaster, J. R. 1971. "Mythological Constructs in Steinbeck's *To a God Unknown*." *Forum: A Journal of the Humanities and Fine Arts* 9 (2): 8–11.

Levant, Howard. 1974. *The Novels of John Steinbeck: A Critical Study*. Columbia: University of Missouri Press.

Lévi-Strauss, Claude. 1963. *Structural Anthropology*. Translated by Claire Jacobson. New York: Basic Books.

Li, Luchen. 2017. "Introduction." In *John Steinbeck in East European Translation: A Bibliographical and Descriptive Overview*, by Danica Čerče, 1–3. Newcastle upon Tyne: Cambridge Scholars.

Lieber, Todd M. 1972. "Talismanic Patterns in the Novels of John Steinbeck." *American Literature* 4, no. 2 (May): 262–75.

Lisca, Peter, ed. 1972. *The Grapes of Wrath: Text and Criticism*. New York: Viking Press.

Lisca, Peter. *John Steinbeck: Nature and Myth*. New York: Crowell, 1978.

Lopate, Phillip. 2021. "But What Was He So Cross About?" Review of William Souder, *Mad at the World: A Life of John Steinbeck*. *Times Literary Supplement*, January 1, 2021, 8.

Lustig, Arnošt. 1967. "Našel John Steinbeck pravdu." *Rudé Právo*, January 29, 1967.

Lynn, Shane. 2015. "'A Room of Experience into Which I Cannot Enter': John Steinbeck on Race." *Steinbeck Review* 12 (2): 149–58.

Macherey, Pierre. 2006. *A Theory of Literary Production*. London: Routledge.

Mailer, Norman. 1968. *The Armies of the Night: History as a Novel / The Novel as History*. New York: New American Library.

Malory, Thomas. [1485] 1897. *Le Morte d'Arthur*. London: Dent.

Marín Ruiz, Ricardo. 2015. "Revisiting Rosinante: Reinterpretations of the Cervantine Character in *Rosinante to the Road Again*, *Monsignor Quixote*, and *Travels with Charley*." *Epos* 31:437–52.

McDonough, Richard. 2016. "Organicisim." *Dictionary of the Philosophy of Mind*. Web.

McElrath, Joseph R., Jr., Jesse S. Crisler, and Susan Shillinglaw, eds. *John Steinbeck: The Contemporary Reviews*. Cambridge, UK: Cambridge University Press.

McLuhan, Marshall. 1964. *Understanding Media: The Extensions of Man*. New York: McGraw-Hill.

Mignolo, Walter. 2005. "On Subalterns and Other Agencies." *Postcolonial Studies* 8 (4): 381–407.

Miller, Henry. 1945. *The Air-Conditioned Nightmare*. New York: New Directions.

Mills, C. Wright. 1951. *White Collar: The American Middle Class*. New York: Oxford University Press.

Mills, George. 1996. "Maybe Satchelful of Characters?" in McElrath, Crisler, and Shillinglaw, *John Steinbeck*, 486–87.
Mizener, Arthur. 1962. "Does a Moral Vision from the Thirties Deserve a Nobel Prize?" *New York Times Book Review*, December 9, 1962.
Morrison, Toni. 1992. *Playing in the Dark: Whiteness and the Literary Imagination*. Cambridge, MA: Harvard University Press.
Narayan, R. K. (1960) 1988. *My Dateless Diary, An American Journey*. New York: Penguin. First published by Indian Thought Publications, New Delhi.
Nixon, Richard M. 1960a. "Remarks by the Vice President, Plainfield, NJ, October 04, 1960." American Presidency Project, University of California at Santa Barbara.
———. 1960b. "Speech of Vice President Nixon, Columbian Republican League Luncheon, Commodore Hotel, New York, NY, October 05, 1960." American Presidency Project, University of California at Santa Barbara.
Nussbaum, Martha. 2000. "The Literary Imagination." In *Falling into Theory: Conflicting Views on Reading Literature*, edited by David Richter, 355–65. New York: Bedford.
O'Neill, Sean. 2018. "Myth." *Oxford Bibliography of Anthropology*. Web.
"Ortega Highway, One of California's Bloodiest Drives." Dangerous Roads, June 29, 2017. Web.
Parini, Jay. 1994. *John Steinbeck: A Biography*. London: Heineman.
———. 1995. *John Steinbeck, A Biography*. New York: Holt.
———. 2012. "Introduction." In *Travels with Charley in Search of America*, by John Steinbeck. 50th anniversary edition, ix–xxv. New York: Penguin.
Parker, Laura. 2019. "The World's Plastic Pollution Crisis Explained." *National Geographic*. Online.
Parry, Sally E. 2007. "Into the Heart of Darkness: Travels with Sinclair and John." In *John Steinbeck and His Contemporaries*, edited by Stephen K. George and Barbara A. Heavilin, 145–51. Lanham, MD: Scarecrow Press.
Pickrel, Paul. 1996. "The Changes That Time Brings." In McElrath, Crisler, and Shillinglaw, *John Steinbeck*, 488.
Pirsig, Robert M. 1974. *Zen and the Art of Motorcycle Maintenance: An Inquiry into Values*. New York: William Morrow.
Prescott, Orville. 1996. "Books of the Times." In McElrath, Crisler, and Shillinglaw, *John Steinbeck*, 481–82.
Přidal, Antonín. 1965. "Případ Steinbeck." *Host do Domu* 2:50–51.
Pynchon, Thomas. 1966. "A Journey into the Mind of Watts." *New York Times Magazine*, June 12, 1966.
Ram, Susan, and Narasimhan Ram. 2001. "R. K. Narayan Obituary." *Guardian*, May 14, 2001.
Rankine, Claudia. 2014. *Citizen: An American Lyric*. Minneapolis: Graywolf Press.
Riesman, David, with Nathan Glazer and Reuel Denney. 1950. *The Lonely Crowd: A Study of the Changing American Character*. New Haven: Yale University Press.

Rivers, Daniel Lanza. 2022. "'The Land Doesn't Stretch': Fecundity, Agriculture, and Settler Visions in *To a God Unknown*." *Steinbeck Review* 19, no. 1 (Spring): 1–17.
Rodger, Katharine. 2004. "'Second Try of Opening Preface' by John Steinbeck." *Steinbeck Studies* 15, no. 2 (Fall): 22–30.
Rosenthal, A. M. 1958. "Talk with Rasipuram Krishnaswami Narayan of Malgudi, India." *New York Times*, March 23, 1958.
Rupel. Slavko. 1964. "John Steinbeck: *Potovanje s Charleyjem*." *Primorski Dnevnik*, January 12.
Safire, William. 2009. "The Cold War's Hot Kitchen." *New York Times*, July 23, 2009.
Said, Edward. 1994. *Culture and Imperialism*. New York: Vintage.
Schlesinger, Arthur M. 1949. *The Vital Center: The Politics of Freedom*. New York: Houghton Mifflin.
Schultz, Jeffrey, and Luchen Li. 2005. *Critical Companion to John Steinbeck. A Literary Reference to His Life and Work*. New York: Facts on File.
Shields, David. 2010. *Reality Hunger: A Manifesto*. New York: Alfred A. Knopf.
Shillinglaw, Susan. 1994. "Introduction." In *Of Mice and Men* by John Steinbeck, vii–xxv. New York: Penguin.
———. 2013. *On Reading "The Grapes of Wrath."* New York: Penguin.
———. 2019. "John Steinbeck's Participatory Politics, 1936–1968." *Steinbeck Review* 16 (2): 145–55.
Souder, William. 2020. *Mad at the World: A Life of John Steinbeck*. New York: Norton.
Steigerwald, Bill. 2012. *Dogging Steinbeck: How I Went in Search of John Steinbeck's America, Found My Own America, and Exposed the Truth about "Travels with Charley."* Scotts Valley, CA: Createspace Independent.
———. 2013. *Dogging Steinbeck: Discovering America and Exposing the Truth about "Travels with Charley."* Seattle: Fifty Fifty Books.
———. 2020. *Chasing Steinbeck's Ghost: The Timeline for John Steinbeck's "Travels with Charley" Road Trip*. Steigerwald Media. E-book.
Steinbeck, Elaine. 1983. "Pigasus." Available at the Martha Heasley Cox Center for Steinbeck Studies. Online. Accessed August 24, 2021.
Steinbeck, John. [1929] 1976. *Cup of Gold*. New York: Penguin.
———. [1933] 1987. *To a God Unknown*. New York: Penguin.
———. [1936] 1979. *In Dubious Battle*. New York: Penguin.
———. [1939] 2006. *The Grapes of Wrath*. New York: Penguin.
———. [1945] 1994. *Cannery Row*. New York: Penguin.
———. 1947. *The Wayward Bus*. New York: Viking.
———. [1948] 1999. *A Russian Journal*. New York, Penguin.
———. [1950] 1979. *Burning Bright*. New York: Penguin.
———. [1951] 1995. *The Log from the Sea of Cortez*. Originally published in 1941 as narrative portion of *Sea of Cortez: A Leisurely Journal of Travel and Research*, coauthored by Edward F. Ricketts. New York: Penguin.
———. 1952. *East of Eden*. New York: Viking.

———. 1957. *The Short Reign of Pippin IV: A Fabrication*. New York: Viking.
———. [1958] 1977. *Once There Was a War*. New York: Penguin.
———. 1961a. "Travels with Charley." Manuscript and typescript. Morgan Library.
———. 1961b. "Travels with Charley." Autograph Manuscript. Pierpont Morgan Library, MA2199.
———. 1961c. *The Winter of Our Discontent*. New York: Viking Press.
———. 1962. *Travels with Charley: In Search of America*. New York: Viking.
———. [1962] 1965. *Travels with Charley in Search of America*. London: Pan Books.
———. [1962] 1997. *Travels with Charley in Search of America*. With an introduction by Jay Parini. New York: Penguin.
———. [1962] 2007. *Travels with Charley: In Search of America*. In *Travels with Charley and Later Novels*, edited by Robert DeMott and Brian Railsback, 765–951. New York: Library of America.
———. [1962] 2012. *Travels with Charley: In Search of America*, 50th Anniversary Edition, introduction by Jay Parini. New York: Penguin.
———. [1962] 2012b. *Travels with Charley in Search of America*. Reprint, New York: Penguin Group. Kindle Edition.
———. 1964. *Potovanje s Charleyjem*. Knjiga 1–2: 9.
———. 1966. *America and Americans*. New York: Viking Press.
———. 1969. *Journal of a Novel. The East of Eden Letters*. New York: Viking.
———. [1975] 1989. *Steinbeck: A Life in Letters*, edited by Elaine Steinbeck and Robert Wallsten. New York: Viking Press.
———. 1976. *The Acts of King Arthur and His Noble Knights*. Edited by Chase Horton. New York: Farrar, Straus and Giroux.
———. 1978. *Letters to Elizabeth*. Edited by Florian J. Shasky and Susan F. Riggs, introduction by Carlton A. Sheffield. San Francisco: Book Club of California.
———. 1988. *The Harvest Gypsies: On the Road to the Grapes of Wrath*. Edited by Charles Wollenberg. Berkeley: Heyday Books.
———. 2002. "Americans and the World." In *America and Americans and Selected Nonfiction*, edited by Susan Shillinglaw and Jackson J. Benson. 383–91. New York: Penguin.
Steinbeck, John, and Edward F. Ricketts. [1941] 1962. *Sea of Cortez*. New York: Viking.
———. 2009. *Sea of Cortez: A Leisurely Journal of Travel and Research*. New York: Penguin.
Steinbeck, Thomas. 2012. "Presentation of Steinbeck Award to Rachel Maddow." February 25, 2012. YouTube.
Strecker, Geralyn. 1995. "Reading Steinbeck (Re)-Reading America: *Travels with Charley* and *America and Americans*." In *After The Grapes of Wrath: Essays on John Steinbeck in honor of Tetsumaro Hayashi*, edited by Donald V. Coers, Paul D. Ruffin, and Robert J. DeMott, 214–27. Athens: Ohio University Press.
Suleri, Sara. 2003. "The Rhetoric of English India." In *The Postcolonial Studies Reader*, edited by Bill Ashcroft, Gareth Griffiths, and Helen Tiffin, 111–13. London: Routledge.

Tamm, Eric Enno. 2005. *Beyond the Outer Shores: The Untold Odyssey of Ed Ricketts, the Pioneering Ecologist Who Inspired John Steinbeck and Joseph Campbell*. Boston: Da Capo Press.
Tesich, Steve. 1992. "A Government of Lies." *Internet Archive*, January 1, 1992. Web.
Thompson, Hunter S. 1971. *Fear and Loathing in Las Vegas: A Savage Journey to the Heart of the American Dream*. New York: Random House.
Tocqueville, Alexis de. [1835] 1899. *Democracy in America*. Vol. 2. Translated by Henry Reeve. New York: D. Appleton.
Turner, Victor. [1969] 1977. *The Ritual Process: Structure and Anti-Structure*. Reprinted with a new forward by the author. Ithaca, NY: Cornell University Press.
Turner, Victor, and Edith Turner. 1978. *Image and Pilgrimage in Christian Culture: Anthropological Perspectives*. New York: Columbia University Press.
Twain, Mark. *Innocents Abroad*. [1869] 1984. New York: Literary Classics of the United States.
Tyler, Royall. 1816. *The Algerine Captive: Or, The Life and Adventures of Doctor Updike Underhill, Six Years a Prisoner among the Algerines*. Hartford, CT: Peter B. Gleason.
van Laer, Rebecca. 2018. "How We Read Autofiction." *Ploughshares* (Emerson College), July 1, 2018.
Vethaak, A. Dick, and Juliette Legler. 2021. "Microplastics and Human Health." *Science* 371 (6530): 672–74.
Weeks, Edward. 1962. "*Travels with Charley*, by John Steinbeck." Review of *Travels with Charley* by John Steinbeck. *Atlantic*, August 1962.
Wilde, Oscar. November 17, 1894. "A Few Maxims for the Instruction of the Over-Educated." Originally published in the *Sunday Review*; republished in *The Oscar Wilde Reader*. Ann Arbor, MI: Tally Hall Press, 1997, 675.
Williams, Roy H. 2015. "John Steinbeck's Unfinished Quixote: 'Don Keehan, the Marshal of Manchón.'" *Cervantes* 35, no. 1:111–36.
Wilson, Sloan. 1955. *The Man in the Grey Flannel Suit*. New York: Simon and Schuster.
Wolfe, Tom. 1968. *The Electric Kool-Aid Acid Test*. New York: Farrar, Straus and Giroux.
Wordsworth, William. 1798. "Lines Composed a Few Miles above Tintern Abbey." In *Anthology of Romanticism*, 191–92. 3rd edition. Edited by Ernest Bernbaum. New York: Ronald Press, 1948.
Zeigler, Gregory. 2010. *Travels with Max: In Search of Steinbeck's America Fifty Years Later*. Salt Lake City: Blaine Creek Press. Kindle edition.
Zirakzadeh, Cyrus Ernesto. 2019. "Steinbeck and America's Liberal Political Tradition." *Steinbeck Review* 16 (1): 1–23.

# Contributors

**Danica Čerče** is a full professor of literatures in English and the current head of the English department at the Faculty of Arts, University of Ljubljana. She is the author of three monographs (*Pripovedna proza Johna Steinbecka*, *Reading Steinbeck in Eastern Europe*, and *John Steinbeck in East European Translation*) and has written book chapters on Steinbeck as well as academic articles on a variety of subjects for Slovene and other international journals. Čerče has also contributed accompanying studies for her translations of Steinbeck's works into Slovene: *Of Mice and Men*, *To a God Unknown*, *The Pastures of Heaven*, *The Moon Is Down*, and *The Wayward Bus*. She serves on the editorial board of *Steinbeck Review*, *Coolabah*, and *Acta Neophilologica*.

**William P. Childers** is an associate professor of Spanish at Brooklyn College and CUNY Graduate Center. He is the author of *Transnational Cervantes*, which won the MLA's Katherine Singer Kovacs Prize. With Ignacio Pulido, he coedited *La Inquisición vista desde abajo*.

**Donald V. Coers** enjoyed a forty-three-year career in the Texas State University system as a professor and administrator. He is the author of *John Steinbeck as Propagandist: "The Moon Is Down" Goes to War* and coeditor of *After "The Grapes of Wrath": Essays on John Steinbeck in Honor of Tetsumaro Hayashi*.

**Robert DeMott** is Edwin and Ruth Kennedy Distinguished Professor Emeritus at Ohio University, where he taught from 1969 to 2013. He has published many books on John Steinbeck in the past four decades, most recently *Steinbeck's Imaginarium: Essays on Writing, Fishing, and Other Critical Matters* (2022). He is chief editor of the Library of America's four-volume Steinbeck collection (1994–2007) and a member of the editorial board of *Steinbeck Review*.

**Cecilia Donohue** has authored a book on Robert Penn Warren and edited a full-length collection of essays on Sandra Cisneros's *Woman Hollering Creek*.

Retired from academic life since 2013, she contributes articles to *The Literary Encyclopedia*, reviews essays for *MELUS*, and serves as an associate editor of *Steinbeck Review*. Her most recent research has focused on Steinbeck's *The Long Valley*.

**Charles Etheridge** was first corrupted by Steinbeck during an undergraduate seminar with Mimi Reisel Gladstein back in the 1980s and has never recovered. His work on Steinbeck has appeared in volumes such as *The Steinbeck Question*, *Steinbeck's Americas*, and *A John Steinbeck Encyclopedia*, among others, as well as in the *Steinbeck Review*. He is the author of three novels, including the 2021 comic novel *Chagford Revisited*. He currently serves as a professor of English at Texas A&M University–Corpus Christi and, with Carter Davis Johnson, as the book review coeditor for *Steinbeck Review*.

**Mimi R. Gladstein** is a past president of the John Steinbeck Society of America. She has won a number of awards for her Steinbeck scholarship and teaching. Steinbeck studies is one of the joys of her life.

**Barbara A. Heavilin** is editor in chief of *Steinbeck Review* and Steinbeck bibliographer for Oxford University Press; she has written or edited many books and articles on John Steinbeck. She has given conference presentations at the University of Westminster, London; Oxford Round Table, Oxford University; San Jose State University, California; Edinburgh University, Scotland; Notre Dame University, Indiana; and other venues, on topics ranging from Steinbeck to Harry Potter to the architectonics of Milton's *Paradise Lost* and Christopher Wren's St. Paul's Cathedral, presented at University of London.

**Kathleen Hicks** is a teaching professor and the director of online programs in the department of English at Arizona State University. Since 2013, she has specialized in online teaching and instructional design. She also serves as an associate editor for the *Steinbeck Review*. Her interests in Steinbeck are wide-ranging. She has published work examining Steinbeck's views of environmental ethics, disability, and morality.

**Carter Davis Johnson** is a PhD candidate at the University of Kentucky. His primary focus is American modernist literature, especially the literature of the American West. His dissertation explores the environmental philosophy of John Steinbeck, Jack London, and Robinson Jeffers.

**Gavin Jones** is the Frederick P. Rehmus Family Professor of Humanities at

Stanford University, where he teaches courses on nineteenth- and twentieth-century American literature. He is the author of *Strange Talk: The Politics of Dialect Literature in Gilded Age America*, *American Hungers: The Problem of Poverty in U.S. Literature, 1840–1945*, *Failure and the American Writer: A Literary History*, and *Reclaiming John Steinbeck: Writing for the Future of Humanity*. With Michael J. Collins (Kings College London), he is coeditor of *The Cambridge Companion to the American Short Story*.

**Sally S. Kleberg** is a native of Kingsville, Texas, and currently a resident of Durham, North Carolina, Ms. Kleberg is vice president of Bankers Trust, New York Owner Managed Business Advisory Services. Ms. Kleberg is the author of *The Stewardship of Private Wealth: Managing Personal and Family Financial Assets*, a primer and educational reference book for individuals, families and family offices. She also authored a family oral history, *Kineño Christmas*, in 2003. After thirty years in New York City, she relocated to North Carolina and now devotes herself to work on philanthropic boards in three states and to shepherding her family's office in San Antonio, Texas. She also works for the Duke University Nicholas School of the Environment and is involved in other alumni interests there; and she enjoys expedition travel to endangered landscapes and time spent with the families of her two sons and five grandchildren who are in Texas and Chevy Chase, Maryland.

**Jay Parini** is Axinn Professor of English at Middlebury College. He has written some thirty books, including novels and biographies, poems, and essays. His *John Steinbeck: A Biography* appeared in 1994. His *New and Collected Poems: 1975–2015* appeared in 2016. His most recent book is a memoir, *Borges and Me: Encounter* (2020).

**Brian Railsback** is a professor of English, former department head, founding dean, and faculty chair at Western Carolina University. He has written or edited books and numerous essays on John Steinbeck. In 2023 he was named the Steve Kemp Writer in Residence at the Great Smoky Mountains National Park.

**Susan Shillinglaw** is a professor of English emerita at San José State University, where she taught for thirty-seven years. For eighteen years, she was the director of the Center for Steinbeck Studies and edited *Steinbeck Studies* and the *Steinbeck Newsletter*, and she organized several international conferences on Steinbeck. She has published introductions to several of Steinbeck's works for Penguin Classics; edited a collection of Steinbeck's journalism as well as scholarly essay collections; and written three books on the author, including *Carol and John Steinbeck: Portrait of a Marriage*—and has completed a fourth (now under contract), *Steinbeck's Landscapes*.

**Nicholas P. Taylor** is the author of the novels *The Disagreement* and *Father Junípero's Confessor*. Under the pseudonym T. T. Monday, he also writes a series of thrillers featuring the baseball relief pitcher and detective Johnny Adcock. Taylor is a professor of English and comparative literature at San José State University, where he directed the Martha Heasley Cox Center for Steinbeck Studies from 2012 to 2021.

# Index

*Page numbers in italics refer to illustrations*

Addison, Joseph, xvii, 18, 35, 41, 42, 44, 50, 57–60
*Algerine Captive, The* (Tyler), 65–75
Alsop, Joseph, 45, 157
America, 1960s, 107–61
*America and Americans* (Steinbeck), xvii, 36, 64, 68, 74, 103n2, 134, 137, 139, 143–53, 181, 193
American Dream, the, 7, 151–52, 184, 192
Andrew, Ariel, 136
Attwood, William, 44–45, 86, 87, 88, 93, 96, 97, 102
autofiction, xvi, 3–8, 86

Benchley, Peter, xix
Benson, Jackson J., xv, 51, 59, 60, 145, 148, 151, 193
Berry, Bob, with Steinbeck at the Sag Harbor Whalers Festival, 1964, *20*
Bible, the, 52, 64, 111, 142
Bradford, Roark, 122, 148–49
Braudel, Fernand, 108, 109, 110
bomb, 34, 97, 98, 101, 124, 129–30, 135
Bridges, Ruby, 24, 25–26, 169–70
Bruder, Jessica, xviii, 179–92
*Burning Bright* (Steinbeck), 35, 142

Capa, Robert, 32, 39, 77, 141
Campbell, Joseph, 52
*Cannery Row* (Steinbeck), 7, 14, 43. 60, 115, 141, 142–42, 148, 166
Capote, Truman, 211–12
Čerče, Danica, xviii, 154–61
Cervantes Saavedra, Miguel de, xvi, xvii, 5, 9, 50–64, 76–103, 103nn3–6

Charley (French poodle), 3, 19, 23–24, 30, 31, 32, 39–40, 46, 56, 57, 72, 83, 89, 90–91, 93, 94, 107, 109, 111, 112, 116, 120, 122, 128, 129–30, 148, 156, 159, 168, 180, 181, 182, 183–84, 185, 193, 194–95, 199, 219; drawing of on map, *ii*; in Sag Harbor, *41*; Steinbeck talks to, 45, 46, 86
"Cheerleaders, the," 7, 31, 46, 47–48, 63, 74, 99, 121, 148–49, 158, 170, 174, 180
Chicken Little, 152–53
Childers, William P., xvi, 76–104, 80, 84, 87, 101
civic order, global, xvii
Clancy, Charles J., 143
Coers, Donald V., interview by, 201–21
Cold War, 9–27, 33, 37, 65, 76–104, 109, 110, 111, 118, 119
*Colloquy of the Dogs, The* (Cervantes), 91
Covici, Pascal ("Pat"), xviii–xix, 55, 76, 77, 78, 89–90, 103n4, 110, 111, 145, 151
COVID-19 pandemic, 29, 49n1, 138
*Cup of Gold* (Steinbeck), 139
Cvetko, Marija, 155

Davidson, Cathy, 66–67, 73
deep time, xvii, 24, 33, 107–22. *See also* long duration
Democrats, 38, 94, 132, 150, 169, 208–9, 210, 220
DeMott, Robert, xiii–xix, 35, 76, 80, 88, 142, 149, 161
Denizet-Lewis, Benoit, 181–82, 183

desegregation, racial, 24, 25, 99. 121, 133
de Tocqueville, Alexis, 6, 9, 15–16, 172
Dew, Jason, 33
Dewey, Joseph, 11, 178
Dickens, Charles, 4
Dimock, Wai Chee, 108–10, 113, 115, 116, 118, 120–21, 122
"Don Keehan, the Marshall of Manchon," xvi, 79–81, 90, 94
Donohue, Cecilia, xviii, 45, 178–92
*Don Quixote* (Cervantes), xvi, 5, 50, 52–57, 64, 72, 76–103, 103nn3–6; Don Quixote (character), 9, 53, 55, 57, 64, 65, 77, 78, 79, 81–82, 83, 84, 86, 89, 92, 94–95, 97, 101, 102, 146, 156, 167; Steinbeck as "quixotic," 43, 44, 53, 77, 82, 88, 89, 90, 102, 146
Doyle, Arthur Conan, 4
Dunn, Peter, 51, 157
Dwyer, Jim, 178

*East of Eden* (Steinbeck), 29, 30, 40, 52, 77, 80–81, 86, 100, 142
Ellison, Ralph, 4
Emerson, Ralph Waldo, 127
Etheridge, Charles, xvi-xvii, 50–64

Fanon, Frantz, 159
fiction, xiv–xv, xvi, 4–5, 6, 7, 9, 10, 18, 26, 28, 29, 32, 36, 40, 43–44, 50, 51, 52, 59, 65, 66–68, 70–72, 77, 78, 80, 87, 94, 100, 102, 103n7, 144, 146, 147, 149, 150, 152–53, 165, 166, 171, 178. *See also* autofiction; Johnson, Carter Davis; Jones, Gavin; nonfiction; Parini, Jay
fictive travelogue, xiv
Fitzgerald, F. Scott, 23
Foucault, Michel, 159
Freeman, Don, map for first edition of *Travels with Charley in Search of America*, v
Frost, Robert, 6
Frye, Northup, 178–81, 185–86, 192
future, 9–27

genre, 3–104

George, Stephen, 55, 80
Gielgud, John, 22, 46
Gladstein, Mimi R., xviii, 193–200
Goffman, Erving, 21–22, 24
*Grapes of Wrath, The*, xix, 5, 7, 14, 21, 30, 35, 40–42, 61, 78, 86, 95, 140, 141, 142, 143, 145, 154, 158, 161, 167, 190, 211
Great Depression, xviii, 5, 9, 78, 137, 140, 154, 188
Gunther, John, 87–88, 93
Gussago, Luigi, 66–67, 68

Haraway, Donna, 23
Harrison, Robert Pogue, 108–9
*Harvest Gypsies, The* (Steinbeck) xviii, 140, 182–90
Hayashi, Tetsumaro, 151, 178, 193
Heavilin, Barbara A. xiii-xiv, xvii, 30, 107–22, 160, 178, 179
Henny-Penny, 152–53
hexagonal writing house in Sag Harbor, Steinbeck's (Joyous Garde). *See* Sag Harbor: Steinbeck's hexagonal writing house in (Joyous Garde)
Hicks, Kathleen, xvii, 112, 123–37
history, 7, 18, 30, 33, 41, 46, 58, 65, 96–97, 103, 108–13, 115, 124, 147, 160, 171, 194. *See also* prehistory
Hansberry, Lorraine, 160, 177
*Huckleberry Finn* (Twain), 46, 68
Hughes, Langston, 158
Hughes, Robert, 193
Hurricane Donna, xvi, 5, 6, 9, 34, 55, 82, 123–27, 137
Huxley, Aldous, 173–74

*In Dubious Battle* (Steinbeck), 139–40
interiority, xvii

Jackson, Kenneth T., 15
jeremiad, *Travels with Charley* as, xv, xvii, 107–61
Johnson, Carter Davis, xvi, 65–75, 127–28, 178
Johnson, James Weldon, 158
Johnson, Lyndon, 195–96, 207–11

# Index

Jones, Dorothy, 173
Jones, Gavin, xvi, 9–27, 46, 94, 103, 103n7, 104n10
Joyce, James, 4
Joyous Garde. *See* Sag Harbor: Steinbeck's hexagonal writing house in (Joyous Garde)
Jung, Carl, 50

Kennedy, Jackie, 214
Kennedy, John F., 31, 37, 38, 39, 94, 98, 145, 169, 207
Keyes, Ralph, 138
Khrushchev, Nikita, 11, 12, 13, 119
Kiernan, Thomas, 193
King, Martin Luther, Jr., 63, 122, 160
Kleberg, Sally S., 201–21
Knoeller, Christian, 68–69
Kopecký, Petr, 155

Lévi-Strauss, Claude, 51
Lewis & Clark expedition (Meriwether Lewis and William Clark), 9
Lewis, Sinclair, 20–21, 44
Lieber, Todd M., 51
Li, Luchen, 161
Lisca, Peter, 51, 159
long duration, xvii, 108. *See also* deep time
Lustig, Arnošt, 158–59

Macherey, Pierre, 160
Malory, Thomas, 51, 52, 55, 79, 80–81, 92
Marín Ruiz, Ricardo, 55–56, 103n5
McLuhan, Marshall, 11–12, 14, 61, 62, 100
media, xvii, 10, 11–12, 14, 61–62, 64, 79–80, 85–86, 92, 94–102, 132–33, 138, 154, 176. *See also* nonprint media
Melville, Herman, xvi, 44; *Moby-Dick*, 80
microplastics, 131. *See also* plastic
Mignolo, Walter, 160
Mizener, Arthur, 104n10
Morgan Library, 28, 29, 49n1, 81, 103n1, 104n8
myth, 50–64

Narayan, R. K., xviii, 165–77, 177n1

Nixon, Richard, 13, 37, 38, 94, 98, 99, 104n9, 169
nonfiction, xiv, xv, xvi, 25, 28, 32, 36, 41, 43–44, 50, 51, 65, 66, 67, 68, 70–71, 75, 90, 92, 146, 147, 150, 152–53, 165, 166, 171, 178, 208. *See also* autofiction; fiction
nonprint media, xvii. *See also* media
non-teleological thinking, 140–41, 168–69
Nussbaum, Martha, 160–61

*Once There Was a War* (Steinbeck), 141–42
*Odyssey, The* (Homer), 5, 73, 114
Old Testament, 52. *See also* Bible, the

Parini, Jay, xvi, 3–8, 144, 145, 151, 193
Parry, Sally E., 156
picaresque, xvi, 52, 65–75
Pierpont Morgan Library. *See* Morgan Library
plastic, 13–14, 25, 27, 35, 95, 96, 118, 128, 130–32, 135, 180, 186, 191. *See also* microplastics
Pope, James S., 156
postcard Steinbeck wrote to Jack Ramsey from Chicago, *54*
postmodern, xv, 10, 18, 20, 21, 22, 23, 25–27, 90, 103n7, 112, 114
post-truth, xvii, 138–53
prehistory, 109–13. *See also* history
Přidal, Antonín, 155
Pynchon, Thomas, 25–26

racism, xvii, 7, 27. 64, 87, 121, 122, 124, 128, 132–36, 151, 159, 169–70, 175–76, 180, 190, 200
Railsback, Brian, xvii, 138–53
Ramsey, Jack, *xiii*; postcard Steinbeck wrote to, *54*; and Steinbeck, looking at Rocinante, *167*
realism, xix
relationality, cross-cultural, 154–61
Republicans, 38, 101, 132, 150, 169, 220
Ricketts, Edward F., 10, 18, 33, 35, 39, 59–60, 62, 67, 117, 139, 140–41, 152, 168

Ritter, William Emerson, 59–60
road text, *Travels with Charley* as, xv, xviii, 165–221
Rocinante (Steinbeck's camper van), 5, 9, 13, 28, 33, 36, 52, 53–54, 55, 57, 64, 65, 72, 76, 81–85, 89, 92–94, 100, 102, 103n5, 119, 146, 148, 156, 167, *167*, 179, 184, 185, 199
Rupel, Slavko, 155
*Russian Journal, A* (Steinbeck), 32, 39, 51–52, 77, 80, 87, 100, 141

Saavedra, Miguel de Cervantes. *See* Cervantes Saavedra, Miguel de
Sag Harbor, *xiii*, xvi, 8, *8*, *20*, 40, *41*, 55, 112, *125*, 145, 147, 167, 180, 195, 207, 216, 217, 219; Steinbeck's hexagonal writing house in (Joyous Garde), xvi, *8*, *125*
*Sea of Cortez* (Steinbeck), 12, 18, 23, 32–33, 39, 43–44, 45, 46, 51, 58, 60, 61, 67–68, 108, 114–15, 121, 140, 141, 143–45, 168–69, 198
Sheffield, Carlton, xv
Shields, David, *Reality Hunger: A Manifesto*, xiv
Shillinglaw, Susan, xiii, xv, 28–48, 49n1, 136, 168, 201–21
society, global civil, 109–10, 118, 120–22
Souder, William, 52, 104n10, 145, 149, 193
spatiality, global, xvii
Steigerwald, Bill, 3, 4, 10, 28–29, 65, 67, 69, 99, 149–51, 181, 182
Steinbeck, Elaine, xiv, 3–4, 6, 7, 14, 16, 23, 28–29, 31, 38, 40, 42, 53, 55, 77, 88, 90, 93, 96–97, 143, 145, 148, 149, 180, 193, 194, 195–96, *201*, 202–3, 206–8, 210–20
Steinbeck, John, photos of: with Bob Berry, *20*; and Elaine Steinbeck, *201*; in his hexagonal writing house, *125*; with Jack Ramsey, looking at

Rocinante, *167*; laughing, *66*; in Navy hat, *xiii*
Suleri, Sara, 156
system theory, 59

Taylor, Elizabeth, 217–18
Taylor, Nicholas P., xviii, 165–77
temporality, global, xvii
Tesich, Steve, 138
Texas, xviii, 4, 7, 8, 23, 26, 38, 43, 56, 89, 90, 93, 169, 187, 193–200, 201–21
thinking, xvii, 10, 19, 24, 34, 57, 61, 64, 98, 100, 124–27, 132–33, 136–37, 140–41, 169, 171 183, 195, 211. *See also* non-teleological thinking
Thoreau, Henry David, 6
"Travels with Charley" manuscript (Steinbeck), xiv–xv, 28–48, 49n1, 80–86, 88, 91–92, 95, 97, 98, 101, 102, 104n8, 145, 201
*Travels with Charley in Search of America* (Steinbeck), title for, xixn1
truth, xvii, 138–53. *See also* post-truth
Turner, Edith, 103n6
Turner, Victor, 103n6
Twain, Mark, 6, 44, 46, 68, 156
Tyler, Royall, xvi, 65–75

Underhill, Updike (character in Royall Tyler's *The Algerine Captive*), 66, 69, 71, 73–74

van Laer, Rebecca, 4
Vietnam War, 136–37, 196, 208, 211

Wilde, Oscar, 4
*Winter of Our Discontent, The*, (Steinbeck), 48, 78, 81, 103, 136, 142
World War II, 9, 10, 19, 42, 76, 78, 124–26, 137, 141–42, 175

Zeigler, Gregory, 181–82